SPECIAL FORCES
WEAPONS & EQUIPMENT

SPECIAL FORCES
WEAPONS & EQUIPMENT

James Marchington

Opposite page: The role of special forces is constantly changing – NBC threats and high-speed data communications are part of the modern battlefield. Photo: Racal.

BRASSEY'S

First published in 2004 by Brassey's
The Chrysalis Building
Bramley Road
London
W10 6SP

An imprint of **Chrysalis** Books Group plc

Distributed in the USA by Casemate Publishing
2114 Darby Road
Havertown
PA 19083
USA

Library of Congress Cataloging in Publication Data is available

British Library Cataloguing in Publication Data:
A catalogue record for this book is available from
the British Library

ISBN 1 85753 391 7

Edited and designed by DAG Publications Ltd
Designed by David Gibbons
Layout by Anthony A. Evans

Printed in Spain

CONTENTS

INTRODUCTION

During the storming of the Iranian Embassy in London, two of the SAS team provide cover from the pavement at the front of the building. The assault was carried out in view of live TV cameras. Photo: author's collection.

It was Operation Nimrod – the storming of the Iranian Embassy in London on 5 May 1980 – that thrust the British SAS (Special Air Service) into the limelight, and sparked a fascination with Special Forces that has launched a thousand books, films and TV programmes.

Operation Nimrod was a real-life drama, played out on live Bank Holiday television to an audience of millions. A Hollywood scriptwriter could hardly have planned it better. The drama began on the morning of 30 April, when six Iraqi-sponsored terrorists belonging to the Democratic Revolutionary Front for the Liberation of Arabistan forced their way into the Iranian Embassy at Prince's Gate in London. They took hostage twenty-six of the embassy staff, together with a BBC sound recordist and PC Trevor Lock from Scotland Yard's Diplomatic Protection Group, who was on duty at the door of the embassy that day.

Within hours, the building was surrounded by various specialist police units, including marksmen from D11, the Technical Support Group C7, and anti-terrorist officers of C13. Journalists, photographers and TV news crews swarmed around the area, even erecting scaffolding platforms for their cameras. Behind the scenes the

security services amassed intelligence on the terrorists, hostages and the building itself. In COBRA (the Cabinet Office Briefing Room), Prime Minister Margaret Thatcher listened to the advice of experts from the Ministry of Defence, MI5, MI6 and the SAS.

At the nearby Regent's Park barracks, soldiers of the SAS Counter Revolutionary Warfare wing began preparing their assault plan, working with intelligence gained from surveillance by C7 as well as architects' drawings of the embassy and their own observation of the building.

Several days of negotiations followed. The terrorists had begun by demanding the release of ninety-one Arabs held in Iranian jails, as well as a plane to fly themselves out of the UK. If their demands were not met, they would begin killing hostages and destroy the building. Police negotiators persuaded the terrorists to drop some of their demands, but on 5 May – Bank Holiday Monday – things began to deteriorate. Late in the afternoon a shot was heard, and the dead body of the Iranian press officer, Abbas Lavasani, was pushed out of the embassy door.

Police negotiators continued to talk to the terrorists, but in reality this was just a delaying tactic. At 2000hrs, responsibility for operations at the embassy was formally handed over from the police to Lt-Col Michael Rose, commanding 22 SAS. Minutes later, SAS assault teams were making their way across the embassy roof and along the balconies at the front of the building.

Speed, aggression and surprise are essential to any hostage rescue operation; abseiling gave the assault team access to the entry points with the minimum delay. Photo: author's collection.

The clothing and equipment used today for urban assault-type operations is lighter and more efficient than anything available in the 1980s. Note the lightweight knee protectors worn by these US soldiers for MOUT training. Photo: US DoD.

The plan was relatively simple. Four-man teams would assault the building from various entry points. One would abseil from the roof at the rear of the building, while at the front another team crossed from the balcony of an adjoining building. Once the teams were in position, frame charges would be used to blow out the windows. The troopers would lob in stun grenades, and move quickly through the building to confront the terrorists before they had a chance to kill the hostages.

Each trooper wore black overalls and gloves, black body armour, an S6 respirator and a flame-retardant flash hood. Most of them carried an MP5 sub-machine gun fitted with a powerful torch for target illumination in the darkened, smoke-filled rooms of the embassy. The all-black kit created an 'invaders from space' appearance – a deliberate psychological ploy to strike fear into the hearts of the terrorists and undermine their will to resist.

The black-clad troopers swept through the building, clearing room after room, quickly reaching the telex room where they knew the hostages were being held. The terrorists had already started firing, killing one hostage and wounding two others, when the SAS burst in. Two terrorists were shot where they stood; another, shielded by women hostages, was captured. Two other terrorists were shot dead in the hallway at the rear of the building.

Within seventeen minutes it was all over. The hostages were bundled unceremoniously from the back of the building and pushed roughly face-down on the ground, their hands bound behind their backs with plasticuffs. The SAS team sped away in two vans as fire crews tackled the flames started by the stun and CS grenades used in the assault.

For millions of Britons watching live on TV, Operation Nimrod was more than an unexpected addition to the Bank Holiday entertainment schedule. It was a reason to celebrate, to be proud to be British – like winning the World Cup. The mysterious black-clad figures were the new popular heroes, all the more fascinating because of the secrecy surrounding them. Suddenly the initials SAS were instantly familiar. Asked what they wanted to be when they grew up, little boys would reply, 'A member of the SAS.'

It was just what the SAS didn't need. The very nature of Special Forces operations requires that they are secret. If that secrecy is compromised, the operation is as good as over. This extends beyond the simple 'who, what, when, where' of specific operations. Any Special Forces' modus operandi – Standard Operating Procedures or SOPs – need to be secret too. Otherwise an enemy can predict all too accurately where to find them and how they are likely to be operating.

Special Forces in the spotlight

Operation Nimrod elevated Special Forces in general, and the SAS in particular, to the status of Hollywood heroes. Since then there have been several other Special Forces operations that have caught the public imagination. Examples include:

> SAS and SBS involvement in the Falklands Conflict in 1982 (Op. Corporate).
> The ambush of an IRA bombing team by SAS at Loughall, Northern Ireland, in May 1987.
> The killing of an IRA bombing team on the island of Gibraltar in March 1988 (Op. Flavius).
> The GIGN assault on Islamic terrorists holding Flight 8969 at Marseilles, France, in December 1994.
> The rescue of hostages at the Japanese Ambassador's residence in Lima, Peru, in April 1997.
> The rescue of eleven British soldiers from the West Side Boys militia in Sierra Leone in September 2000 (Op. Barras).
> The assault by Russia's Spetsnaz, using incapaciting gas, on a Moscow theatre where Chechen terrorists were holding more than 800 hostages in October 2002.

These few high-profile operations are just the tip of the iceberg, of course. Every week of every year, there are innumerable Special Forces operations under way around the world, most of them highly secret and known only to a small number of people. Even within the SAS, for instance, one squadron is not told what another is doing.

During the Cold War much Special Forces training focused on the threat of a major land war in Europe between NATO and the Warsaw Pact. The Volunteer SAS Regiments, 21 and 23 SAS, prepared to live in hides for weeks on end, where they

would allow Warsaw Pact forces to roll by and use secure communications to report on enemy troop and vehicle movements. Other Special Forces, like Russia's Spetsnaz, would have covertly entered vital installations such as nuclear power stations and military bases, and placed demolition charges, while others targeted military and political leaders.

With the end of the Cold War, the Soviet threat evaporated. The progress made with the 'Peace Process' in Northern Ireland shifted the focus away from counter-terrorist operations there as well. Special Forces in Britain and elsewhere began to reassess their role, and greater emphasis was placed on fighting organised crime and drugs trafficking.

Towards the end of the twentieth century, peacekeeping operations came to the fore, with considerable Special Forces involvement in attempts to resolve the complicated, messy conflicts in the Balkan states. During

Above: With the end of the Cold War, Special Forces have focused on other areas such as fighting the drugs trade. Here a US Marine trains in jungle operations. Photo: USMC.

Right: Special Forces today play an important role in peacekeeping operations around the world. This Korean ship was boarded and searched for illegal weapons. Photo: US Navy.

NATO's operations against Serb forces in Kosovo in 1999, for instance, it was widely reported that SAS OPs were feeding back intelligence on Serb movements, and using laser target designators to guide precision bombs onto their targets.

After the conflict, SAS 'snatch squads' were tasked with hunting down men such as Ratko Mladic, Milan Milutinovic, Dragoljub Ojdanic and Nikola Sainovic, who were wanted for trial on war crimes charges. It was an SAS team that captured Bosnian Serb General Dusko Sikirica, former commander of the so-called Keraterm concentration camp, for instance – he was captured at his home in Prijedor, north-west Bosnia in June 2000, and taken to the War Crimes Tribunal at The Hague to face charges of genocide, crimes against humanity and breaches of the Geneva Convention.

11 September and beyond

The 11 September 2001 attacks on America – by al-Qaeda terrorists using hijacked civilian airliners – came as a bolt from the blue that has transformed the nature and sheer quantity of Special Forces operations. When the US and UK struck back at al-

The terrorist attack on the World Trade Center in New York, on 11 September 2001, gave a new focus and urgency to Special Forces operations. Photo: US Navy.

New York, 11 September 2001. Photo: US Navy.

Qaeda's heartland in Afghanistan with Operation Enduring Freedom (UK Operation Veritas), the Special Forces of both countries had a significant role to play – for instance hunting down Taliban forces, clearing cave complexes and directing air strikes. And as the threat of war with Iraq grew through the winter of 2002/3, British and US Special Forces were kept busy with reconnaissance, intelligence gathering and planning.

Following the 11 September attacks, the heightened state of alert has also led to many more counter-terrorist operations, both at home and abroad. Special Forces, for example, have boarded vessels suspected of carrying conventional arms or WMD (Weapons of Mass Destruction). Training for counter-terrorist operations has been increased, too, so that specialist units are ready if needed to tackle a hostage situation, suicide bomber or NBC (Nuclear, Biological or Chemical) attack at home. In January 2003, environmental activists broke into a UK nuclear power station, claiming their action highlighted gaps in security that could allow terrorists to stage a spectacular attack.

With all the high-profile media coverage given to the 'war on terrorism', it is important to remember that all the other threats facing governments have not gone away. The intertwined problems of organised crime and drugs gangs still exist, and continue to extend their influence worldwide. With or without a heightened terrorist threat, these problems must be tackled with the full range of resources available, including Special Forces.

Soldiers into authors

During the Gulf War of 1991, the British SAS operated extensively behind Iraqi lines, hunting Scud missile launch sites and destroying fibre-optic cables. They successfully demolished missile launchers and communications links, and caused great inconvenience for the enemy. After the war, the story of one patrol was told in the book *Bravo Two-Zero* by a trooper using the pen-name 'Andy MacNab'. The book became a best-seller, and was quickly followed by a rash of similar books – some about the same patrol, others about other aspects of Special Forces work.

These books, however fanciful some of the stories might be, enable the reader to build up a fairly detailed picture of Special Forces SOPs and capabilities. Many

Above: The guided missile destroyer USS *Cole* was severely damaged by a suicide bomb attack in Yemen on 12 October 2000 which killed 17 US sailors. Photo: US DoD.

Left: Following the 11 September 2001 attacks, the US and its allies took the initiative in what became known as the 'War on Terror'. These US soldiers were fighting Taliban forces in Afghanistan in Operation Anaconda. Photo: US DoD.

people have argued that this is unhelpful, and that Special Forces soldiers should take their secrets with them to the grave. The SAS themselves have clamped down on former troopers writing about their experiences: those who transgress are subject to various sanctions, including being banned from regimental events and excluded from the Regimental Association (cynical observers have commented that these sanctions are applied in inverse proportion to the rank of the former soldier). The lure of huge publishing advances and international acclaim sometimes prove too strong an incentive, and memoirs continue to be published. It is significant, however, that at the time of writing, very little has been published in the way of stories from operations in Afghanistan during 2001/2. The problem is certainly not a shortage of good, dramatic action stories, so the MoD's efforts to suppress publication are clearly working.

The continuing fascination with Special Forces ensures that there is a ready market for books such as the present one, detailing the vehicles, weapons and other equipment used by Special Forces. Indeed, it has long been a standing joke among military writers that sooner or later someone will publish a book entitled *Underpants of the SAS*. It is perhaps worth pointing out that we have gone to some trouble to ensure that this book does not reveal anything that might endanger the safety of Special Forces. All the information contained in these pages is already in the public domain, available either from official sources or from publicly published material.

Special Forces and the media

Modern news-gathering methods make it possible for the public to follow conflicts in real time – and harder for the military to control what the public sees and doesn't see. During the Gulf War of 1991, television reports were beamed back from the war

The Gulf War of 1991 was the first to be televised back home in 'real time'. Commanders and politicians try to control the flow of images such as this, showing the destruction wrought on Iraqi forces retreating from Kuwait. Photo: USMC.

zone and live on to screens across the US and Europe. Viewers back home saw live the fear and uncertainty on the face of a TV reporter crouching in his hotel room in Israel, not knowing whether the incoming Scud missiles carried chemical warheads.

The Gulf War of 1991 became known as the first 'televised war'. Allied forces gave daily briefings, with video clips of guided munitions striking their targets – helping to promote the idea that this war was being fought with clinical precision, keeping 'collateral damage' to a minimum. We also saw the flip side of this, with reporters in Baghdad sending back pictures of damage to non-military targets, and footage of civilians apparently grieving the loss of family members. The media were not just reporting from the battlefield, they were now part of the scene of battle, as both sides tried to gain political and military advantage by manipulating media coverage of the conflict.

This has now become a feature of modern warfare, and much effort goes into controlling television coverage of any conflict. Television broadcasting stations are targeted along with military installations, and camera crews' access to the conflict zone is strictly controlled. Carefully selected video clips are provided to broadcasters eager for exciting footage from the front-line. In the run-up to war on Iraq in 2002/3, the US military allocated individual journalists and cameramen to specific combat

A night vision shot of US Marines at Kandahar airport in Afghanistan in Operation Enduring Freedom. This type of footage may be released to the media in order to boost public confidence. Photo: USMC.

Opposite page:
Special Forces
must be prepared
to operate in any
conditions, in any
part of the world.
This Royal
Netherlands Navy
patrol is using
Diemaco's C7FT
variant of the M16
rifle. Photo:
Diemaco.

units, while strongly discouraging the media from entering the battle zone independently. 'We cannot guarantee the safety of non-combatants' was a regular refrain.

The significance of media coverage in modern warfare means that Special Forces may find themselves involved in the 'media war' – perhaps tasked to take out a broadcasting station, or undertake an operation which is, at least in part, a 'staged' media event. During the second week of America's attacks on Taliban positions in Afghanistan, in October 2001, journalists at a Pentagon briefing were shown footage shot through night vision cameras, showing US Army Rangers parachuting into enemy territory and moving virtually unopposed through a facility described as a Taliban command centre.

The jury is still out on the extent to which this operation was conceived as a media stunt to win public support and boost confidence in the military's ability to strike deep at the heart of enemy territory. Whatever the truth behind that particular operation, the power of television can only increase, and attempts to manipulate media coverage will continue to be a significant part of Special Forces' operations.

This effect is not confined to television; it can be seen across all types of media, particularly the internet. The internet is now an integral part of the command and control system for many insurgent groups, as well as providing them with a means of promoting their message and recruiting support worldwide. The Zapatista movement in the Chiapas region of Mexico, for example, was noted for its use of websites and email, which enabled it to muster sympathy and support from all over the world.

War itself is becoming increasingly high-tech, and SF soldiers frequently find themselves challenged by the sophisticated electronic hardware and software they need to master. Modern battlefield communications and navigation systems are designed to be simple for the individual soldier to operate, but Special Forces' tasks go way beyond what is required of the average infantryman, and consequently they require a deeper understanding of systems that are becoming increasingly complex. Where necessary, a Special Forces team will take a technical specialist with them on a CTR (Close Target Recce) – to emplace a non-standard surveillance device, perhaps, or install 'Trojan' software on a target computer. Whenever possible, however, it is preferable for the Special Forces soldiers themselves to have the necessary skills and avoid the risk of compromise that comes from 'nannying' a techie who does not have the same training and skills in CTR work.

SF weapons and equipment

People are generally surprised to learn that the weapons and kit used by Special Forces are largely the same as those used by regular forces. The British SAS are a good example. OK, they get to play with the latest high-tech toys, and individuals are often tempted to spend their hard-earned cash trying out various items of 'Gucci' kit. But on the whole the Regiment uses the same stuff as the rest of the British army.

There are good reasons for this. Not least, it helps the Regiment to preserve the anonymity that is vital to many of their operations. Where necessary they will use the standard issue SA80 instead of their favoured M16s or MP5s, or even adopt AK47s etc. to blend in with local forces. And, of course, when you are miles behind enemy

lines or deep in the jungle, you have to make do with what is available. If your resupply contains standard issue boots, that's what you wear.

This book details a great deal of kit that is used by regular infantry soldiers as well as Special Forces. Certainly the weapons shown here are, by and large, used by the ordinary rank and file as well as more specialised units. What really distinguishes Special Forces from regular troops is not their weapons and kit, but the individuals themselves. SF soldiers are a rare breed, with unusually high levels of dedication, motivation, experience, skills and training. Simply giving a regular infantryman a fancy rifle and kit does not make him Special Forces.

Every Special Forces unit in the world has a selection process designed to filter out the rabble and pick those soldiers who are capable of being genuinely 'special'. The selection procedure of the British SAS is notoriously harsh, demanding a high level of fitness and motivation as well as basic skills such as navigation. Continuation training ensures that individuals develop new skills, and learn from the experience of others. Those who fail selection may deride the process, but the result is a unit that is widely recognised as one of the finest in the world, capable of operating successfully in any conditions, and striking an enemy hard where and when he least expects it.

Murphy's Laws of Combat

Special Forces soldiers are fond of quoting 'Murphy's Laws'. There are many different versions of these 'Laws' in circulation, one of which is reproduced below. Although written as a joke, they summarise what years of military experience have shown – that if something can go wrong it probably will, and at the most inconvenient moment. They highlight the importance of keeping things simple, whether you are designing a weapon or preparing an assault plan:

1. Friendly fire – isn't.
2. Recoilless rifles – aren't.
3. Suppressive fire – won't.
4. You are not Superman. Marines and fighter pilots take note.
5. A sucking chest wound is nature's way of telling you to slow down.
6. If it's stupid but it works, it ain't stupid.
7. Try to look unimportant; the enemy may be low on ammo and not want to waste a bullet on you.
8. If you are forward of your position, your artillery will fall short.
9. Never forget that your weapon was made by the lowest bidder.
10. If your attack is going really well, it's an ambush.
11. The enemy invariably attacks when they're ready and you're not.
12. No OPLAN ever survives initial contact.
13. Five-second fuses always burn for three seconds.
14. A retreating enemy is just falling back and regrouping.
15. The easy way is always mined.
16. Teamwork is essential; it gives the enemy other people to shoot at.
17. Don't look conspicuous; it draws fire and irritates everyone around you.
18. If you are short of everything but the enemy, you are in the combat zone.
19. When you have secured the area, make sure the enemy knows it too.
20. Incoming fire has right of way.
21. No combat-ready unit has ever passed inspection.
22. No inspection-ready unit has ever passed combat.
23. If the enemy is within range, so are you.
24. The only thing more accurate than incoming enemy fire is incoming friendly fire.

25. Things that must be shipped together as a set aren't.
26. Things that must work together can't be carried to the field that way.
27. Radios will fail as soon as you need fire support.
28. Radar tends to fail at night and in bad weather, and especially during both.
29. Anything you do can get you killed, including doing nothing.
30. If you make it too tough for the enemy to get in, you won't be able to get out.
31. Tracers work both ways.
32. Professional soldiers are predictable; the world is full of dangerous amateurs.
33. Weather ain't neutral.
34. The one item you need is always in short supply.
35. Interchangeable parts aren't.
36. When in doubt, empty your magazine.
37. The side with the simplest uniforms wins.
38. Combat will occur on the ground between two adjoining maps.
39. Never stand when you can sit, never sit when you can lie down, never stay awake when you can sleep.
40. The most dangerous thing in the world is a Second Lieutenant with a map and a compass.
41. The more a weapon costs, the farther you will have to send it away to be repaired.
42. Combat experience is something you don't get until just after you need it.
43. The more stupid the leader is, the more important the missions he is ordered to carry out.
44. Success occurs when no one is looking, failure occurs when the General is watching.
45. The enemy never monitors your radio frequency until you broadcast on an unsecured channel.
46. If at first you don't succeed, call in an air strike.

1 BEHIND ENEMY LINES

Much of Special Forces' work is carried out deep in enemy-held territory, where their special combination of skills can be put to good use – disrupting enemy communications, gaining intelligence on the enemy's matériel and movements, and directing air strikes against strategic targets such as communications facilities, bunkers and missile launch sites.

Working 'behind enemy lines' has long been a feature of Special Forces soldiering. The SAS was born out of David Stirling's vision of small raiding forces attacking airfields and logistics bases deep in enemy territory during World War Two. More recent examples include the now-famous Scud-hunting patrols in Iraq during the 1991 Gulf War, and operations against Taliban forces in Afghanistan following the 11 September 2001 attacks on the USA.

Operating behind enemy lines enables Special Forces to inflict damage on the enemy out of all proportion to their numbers, and the cost of the operation in terms of support and matériel. It also presents a whole set of problems to be overcome. The Special Forces patrol operating in enemy territory must be self-sufficient, and not dependent on conventional logistics support and resupply. They must carry their own food, water, fuel and ammunition. And they must have the necessary skills to maintain radio contact, carry out any repairs necessary to vehicles and equipment, and provide medical treatment to any of their number who is injured or falls ill.

US soldiers training in the use of military explosives. Special Forces operating behind enemy lines can use demolition charges to inflict damage out of all proportion to their numbers. Photo: US DoD.

All this requires Special Forces soldiers to be highly motivated, well trained and practised in a wide range of skills, and to have the right equipment for the job. Sometimes it is necessary to use very sophisticated, high-tech equipment to carry out a specific task – such as a Laser Target Designator to 'mark' a target for the latest generation of guided munitions or 'smart bombs'. The most sophisticated equipment is not always the most suitable for military operations, however; often the reverse is true. Following the principles encapsulated in 'Murphy's Laws of Combat' (see page 18), more complicated equipment is more prone to failing when it is most needed, and is less readily repaired in the field. The equipment favoured by Special Forces behind enemy lines is kit that is simple, robust, and has proved to be reliable in a wide range of harsh conditions. Enemy territory is no place to discover that your latest piece of whizz-bang kit is prone to jamming up with sand, or short-circuits in damp weather.

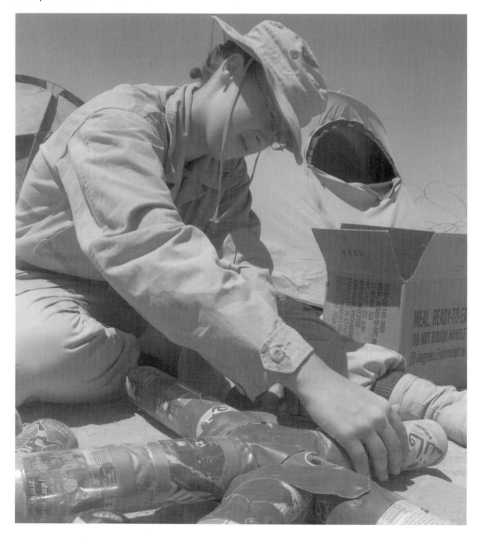

Special Forces soldiers quickly learn to improvise and use what's available to get the job done. Here a US radio operator constructs a field-expedient satellite antenna from empty drinks cans. Photo: USMC.

Special Forces must be able to operate effectively in extreme conditions, such as the severe cold of the Arctic. Simple, robust and well-proven kit is essential. Photo: US DoD.

History is littered with stories of military operations that failed for stupid reasons. Not because the enemy outmanoeuvred them, or had better guns or more inspired leaders. But because their buttons fell off, their boats were in one place and their oars another, or they went down with diarrhoea.

Special Forces soldiers learn to check and recheck their equipment so that they can depend on it when it really matters. The equipment carried on a patrol is carefully planned, and pared down to the bare minimum – even to the extent of cutting down the handle of a toothbrush so that it takes up less space and weight. Carrying capacity is always limited, whether it is the amount that can be stowed on a Land-Rover or carried by a soldier on foot. Any weight saved allows the soldier to carry more of the essential bulk items like food, water, fuel and ammunition.

The same principles are followed when kitting out a Land-Rover for a vehicle patrol, or packing a belt kit: non-essential equipment is left behind, everything else is cut down to the bare minimum – except for ammunition, which you can never have too much of!

PERSONAL KIT

Under the direction of the patrol leader, each soldier in a patrol is responsible for his own kit, which is divided between his 'belt kit' (worn as PLCE-type webbing and pouches, and/or assault vest) and his bergen (rucksack). The soldier requires his own rations, water, brew kit (metal mug or cooking pot, plus blocks of 'hexy'' fuel), wash kit, first aid kit, survival kit, sleeping bag and waterproofs.

Many Special Forces soliders also carry a combat knife, such as a Ka-Bar, although this is primarily a tool, not a fighting weapon. Often a Leatherman Tool or

Lower left: Special Forces soldiers carry a knife as a field tool rather than a weapon. This UK survival knife can be used for a wide range of tasks such as building shelters and clearing vegetation. Photo: author's collection.

Below: The soldier's kit is carried in webbing pouches and in his bergen or rucksack. Essential kit such as ammunition, survival equipment and water is worn on the body so it is not left behind if he has to abandon his bergen. Photo: Diemaco.

Swiss Army-type knife will be carried for its sheer practical value, despite it being useless as a weapon. Peter Ratcliffe, DCM, explodes the fighting knife myth in his excellent book *Eye of the Storm*, a highly readable account of SAS operations in the 1991 Gulf War:

> One of these myths concerns the so-called 'fighting knife'. In actual fact, there is no such weapon issued in the British Army, despite what other accounts may say, although individuals within the SAS may choose to carry a knife they have acquired themselves. Nor is there much use for them: wielding a knife in combat, rather than a firearm, is likely to get you killed sooner rather than later, and for clandestine operations, or those requiring a high degree of stealth, members of the Regiment are issued with silenced weapons. Where a knife could be useful, though, is in situations where a soldier is forced to live by his wits in a hostile environment, and without the usual support in the way of weapons, rations, transport, and so on.

In other words, a combat-type knife is useful as a field tool, for jobs such as building a shelter, making traps to catch animals for food, building fires and so on. It is of little or no value as a weapon.

In addition to the kit already mentioned, the individual soldier carries his personal weapon and ammunition, plus any additional equipment being carried on behalf of the patrol – this depends on the mission, and also on the individual soldier's special skills, but could be a manpack radio, spare batteries, medical pack, or further weapons and ammunition such as an anti-tank launcher, part of an 81mm mortar, mortar rounds, demolition charges, etc. Packing is always done so that if the soldier has to abandon his bergen in a contact, he still retains his belt kit, with a bare minimum of equipment necessary for survival. The belt kit will always contain, for example, a compass, knife, survival tin, water, ammunition for his personal weapon and basic medical items.

The amount of equipment to be carried can easily get out of hand, especially when planning an extended operation in hostile territory. Peter Ratcliffe describes in his book how he tried to persuade 'Andy McNab' to cut down on the amount of equipment he was taking on the ill-fated Bravo Two-Zero patrol.

> I knew to a certainty they were taking far too much … when they pulled out the next night 'McNab' estimated that each of Bravo Two-Zero's men was carrying 150lbs. That's the same as hefting a 10½ stone man around with you. I gave them a dozen paces – maximum … An SAS unit, to mis-quote Muhammad Ali, should be capable of floating like a butterfly and stinging like a swarm of killer bees.

Indeed, before long the members of the Bravo Two-Zero patrol had been forced to abandon their bergens and were having to make do with the contents of their belt kits. It would be interesting to compare the kit carried by Bravo Two-Zero with that

taken by T. E. Lawrence, better known as 'Lawrence of Arabia', on his highly successful raids in similar terrain during World War One.

CamelBak hydration systems

Traditionally, soldiers would carry water in a canteen, mounted in a pouch on the belt.
Recently, however, Special Forces as well as regular units are turning to the Camel-
Bak water-carrying system made by CamelBak Products Inc., of Petaluma, California.
The CamelBak system features a 2–3-litre insulated flexible plastic pouch that can be
strapped on a soldier's back. There is a flexible plastic tube that reaches over the
soldier's shoulder, with a mouthpiece so that he can drink while on the move.

The story goes that the idea was invented by Michael Edison, a paramedic who
was also a cycling enthusiast. Wanting to drink water without stopping or taking his
hands off the handlebars, he put together a pouch system using medical tubing and
an IV pouch in a sock sewn onto the back of his T-shirt. The system has been developed over the intervening ten years or so, and there is now a range of products that
are compatible with standard military load-bearing equipment. Chuck Hunter, vice
president of the firm's military-industrial division, explains that the system has significant advantages for the soldier: 'Unlike a canteen, the CamelBak system doesn't
require a soldier to put down his weapon,' he says. 'You don't have to pull the

Explosives and
ammunition
usually make up
the bulk of a
Special Forces
patrol's load – as
a rule of thumb,
you can never
have too much!
Photo: US Navy.

canteen off your belt and unscrew the cap before relieving your thirst. It takes two hands to do that.'

The CamelBak holds up to 3 litres – three times as much as a standard canteen. This can be important in a combat situation, particularly in a hot climate such as Iraq, where the human body can lose more than a litre of water per hour. If it is not replaced, the soldier may suffer heat stress, with headaches, nausea, fatigue and loss of performance. Medical advice to soldiers fighting Taliban and al-Qaeda forces in Afghanistan was to drink around 6 litres of water a day.

Operating in a hot climate demands large quantities of water. These US soldiers in Afghanistan are using the Camel-Bak system, which holds 3 litres in a flexible pouch. Photo: US DoD.

Today, CamelBak systems are used by every branch of the US Military, the US Border Patrol, tactical law enforcement, the US government, and the armed forces of many foreign countries. The CamelBak Storm is the standard-issue hydration system with the US Armed Forces' new MOLLE system pack.

CamelBak ThermoBak 3-Liter

The ThermoBak 3-Liter is one of CamelBak's upgraded hydration systems, and is replacing the 2-litre model as the standard hydration system among many US Armed Forces. The ThermoBak 3-Liter has been redesigned to feature multiple D-ring attachment points, allowing it to be attached to load-bearing vests and other load-bearing equipment. It also features a new Velcro strap management system that keeps straps from getting caught or tangled in other gear.

The system's insulated reservoir holds up to 100 ounces (3 litres) of water and keeps the water cool (or warm) for hours. Even completely filled, the ThermoBak 3-Liter is comfortable to wear, thanks to its ergonomic design, making it ideal for virtually any type of environment or use.

The ThermoBak 3-Liter also features quick-release straps, which stow away inside a built-in pocket for easy integration with load-bearing equipment or web harness platforms. These stowable quick-release straps make it easy to slip a ThermoBak 3-Liter inside a larger system. And, in the case of NBC (Nuclear-Biological-Chemical) field conditions, the built-in pocket easily accommodates CamelBak's Chemical Resistant Reservoir. The ThermoBak 3-Liter is available in desert or woodland camo, black, or olive drab.

Like most of CamelBak's current military hydration systems, the ThermoBak 3-Liter includes the company's unique HydroLock tap, which provides positive water

This US Navy SEAL, operating against Taliban forces in Afghanistan, is carrying a Camel-Bak hydration system. The water is quickly accessible via a flexible tube topped with a bite valve. Photo: US Navy.

shut-off, and controls the flow of water with a positive lever action. The patented Big Bite valve, made from medical-grade silicone, has no moving parts and is easy to use – you simply bite down and sip. The one-piece design makes it easy to clean as well. Closed cell foam insulation on the reservoir and a neoprene tube cover keep liquid cooler (or warmer) for longer. The innovative Omega Reservoir has a wide-mouth opening for easy filling and cleaning. It provides a quiet, slosh-free environment that drains liquid smoothly and maintains a balanced load. The reservoir itself is made of polyurethane that is strong, flexible and easy to clean and maintain.

CamelBak Mule

CamelBak has recently redesigned the Mule Hydration System. This is basically a daysack with a 3-litre CamelBak hydration system built in. It is suitable for training, recon missions or other environments where users need to carry several hours' worth of water and essential gear, such as radios, first aid kits and MREs.

Among the new features is a ventilated back panel designed to keep the user cooler and more comfortable. An Independent Suspension Harness helps to keep the system's load stable as the user moves through fast-paced missions or over tough terrain. The Harness also makes it easy to fit the Mule. to most body sizes and types.

The redesigned Mule has CamelBak's patented, wide-mouthed Omega Reservoir. Improved zipper access makes it easy to load the reservoir. Other recent additions to the Mule include D-rings for attaching to load-bearing equipment, an integrated MOLLE system attachment, a Velcro strap management system and a stowable and adjustable weight belt. The Mule is available in black, woodland and desert camo.

NAVIGATION

Navigation is vital in any military operation, but especially so for Special Forces who may be operating in small units in hostile territory away from the main force for days or weeks on end. During this time they may have to navigate to a target and back, find their way to an agreed rendezvous, call in an air strike or artillery fire, and report back on the locations of enemy forces. At all times they must know their own position with reasonable accuracy, and identify and agree ERV (Emergency Rendezvous) points to which each individual can return if the patrol becomes split up in a contact. All this requires precise navigation to a standard far higher than that demanded of a regular infantryman.

Not surprisingly, then, Special Forces make full use of the most advanced navigation equipment, including sophisticated GPS (Global Positioning System) receivers, electronic compasses and laser rangefinding equipment. High-tech equipment can fail, however, at the most inconvenient moment. Many of the problems faced by the ill-fated Bravo Two-Zero SAS patrol during the 1991 Gulf War came about because of the failure of various items of comms equipment.

Although modern satellite navigation systems are used extensively, Special Forces soldiers also learn to use traditional magnetic compasses such as this Silva model. Photo: Silva.

So as well as using the latest high-tech navigation kit, Special Forces also train in basic navigational principles, and practise with techniques and equipment that are antiquated by today's standards – such as using stick-and-shadow methods to take bearings from the sun, and calculating speed and distance covered by pace-counting.

This might seem pointless when everything is working properly – and indeed there is no need to waste time on complicated calculations if you can check your position simply by glancing at the screen of your GPS unit. But when you are miles behind enemy lines, have been 'bumped' and forced to abandon your bergen, and are trying to evade the enemy and find your way home, the ability to navigate by the stars can make the difference between life and death. This is not a matter of theory – the story of Chris Ryan's escape from Iraq, told in his book *The One That Got Away*, shows that these skills really can be life-savers even in modern warfare.

Global Positioning System (GPS)

The Global Positioning System (GPS) has revolutionised navigation, not just for military users but for civilians too. In recent years, it has become commonplace for yachts and motor vehicles to be fitted with GPS navigation systems. Hikers, taxi-drivers and motorcycle couriers rely on GPS to find their way around. GPS technology will increasingly be built into mobile electronic equipment such as mobile phones – enabling them to broadcast their location, with obvious benefits when, for example, calling the emergency services.

All this has been possible because of the United States' development of GPS technology for military purposes; GPS is key to much of modern, precision warfare such as 'smart' bombs, cruise missiles, and all the paraphernalia of the 'electronic battlefield'.

The Navstar Global Positioning System consists of a constellation of orbiting satellites operated and controlled by the 50th Space Wing, located at Schriever Air Force Base, Colorado. A number of GPS satellites orbit the earth every twelve hours, emitting continuous navigation signals. With suitable equipment, any user can receive these signals to calculate time, location and velocity. The signals are so accurate that time can be measured to within a millionth of a second, velocity within a fraction of a mile per hour and location to within less than 10 feet. Receivers have been developed for use in aircraft, ships and land vehicles, as well as for hand-carrying.

The GPS Master Control Station at Schriever is responsible for monitoring and controlling the GPS satellite constellation. The ground system consists of five monitor stations and four ground antennas located around the world. The monitor stations use GPS receivers to passively track the navigation

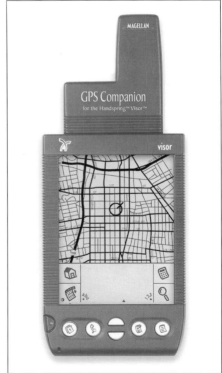

Developed for military use, the Global Positioning System (GPS) is now used extensively by civilians for leisure and business, often combined with sophisticated digital mapping technology as in this Magellan unit fitted to a Visor palmtop. Photo: Magellan.

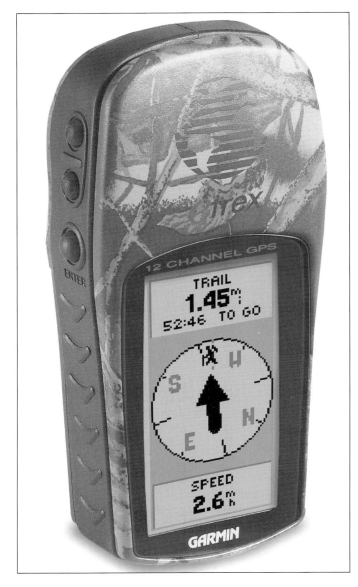

Soldiers sometimes purchase their own civilian GPS receivers, such as this Garmin eTrex, to supplement issued equipment. Photo: Garmin.

signals of the satellites. Information from the monitor stations is then processed at the master control station and used to update the satellites' navigation messages. The master control station sends updated information to the satellites through ground antennas using an S-band signal. The ground antennas are also used to transmit commands to satellites and to receive 'state-of-health' data from the satellites.

The system received its first real military test in operations Desert Shield and Desert Storm. Allied troops relied heavily on GPS to navigate the featureless Saudi Arabian desert. Forward air controllers, pilots, tank drivers and even cooks used the system successfully.

The primary contractors for the GPS satellites are Rockwell, Boeing and Lockheed Martin. The satellites are powered by solar panels generating 800 Watts, and weigh between 3,670 lbs (1,816 kg) and 4,480 lbs (2,217 kg). They have a wingspan of between 208.6 ins (5.3m) and 449 ins (11.4 m) and are launched into orbit by the Delta II rocket. The constellation became fully operational in July 1995.

In the early days of GPS, the signals deliberately included an unpredictable degree of error. Accuracy was typically around 100–200m, and the system's full potential could only be achieved with a special military GPS receiver that could decode the encrypted data and correct the error. This error, known as 'selective availability', could be turned on or off at will by the US military. During the Gulf War of 1991, it was largely turned off as Allied units were making widespread use of civilian receivers. On 2 May 2000, selective availability was permanently turned off, allowing civilian receivers to be accurate to 10–20m. Modern receivers can be even more accurate, with accuracies of 3m or less being achievable.

Inevitably, the GPS system is targeted by Electronic Warfare (EW) specialists in any modern conflict: modern armies are highly dependent on accurate GPS information, and there is significant military advantage to be gained by denying its use to an enemy. Modern military GPS receivers operate on signals separate from the civilian GPS system, and are designed to be highly resistant to attempts to jam or interfere with ('spoofing') the signal.

Magellan NAV 1000M

In the Gulf War, SAS and other Special Forces units used the Magellan NAV 1000M hand-held GPS receiver. This is a robust unit encased in rubberised plastic, which weighs 0.85kg and measures 210 x 90 x 50mm. It was developed for military use, and is fast, powerful and accurate, yet reasonably easy to use. It is powered by six AA batteries and can store up to 500 waypoints. It has a display that shows three screens giving present position, elevation, time and date, satellite status, and a figure of merit or 'FOM'. This is the estimated error of a position fix: the lower the number the more accurate the position.

Rockwell Collins PLGR ('Plugger')

As GPS navigation was rapidly taken up by armed forces around the world, the Rockwell Collins PLGR (Precision Lightweight GPS Receiver) – referred to as 'Plugger' – became widely adopted by regular forces as well as Special Forces units

The Rockwell Collins PLGR (Precision Lightweight GPS Receiver) issued to British forces is referred to as 'Plugger' and receives encrypted data from GPS satellites to resist jamming. Photo: © James Marchington.

of the US, UK and their allies. There are still many of these units in service, despite the introduction of modern replacements such as the PLGR II.

The AN/PSN-11 PLGR is a small, hand-held, GPS receiver featuring selective availability/antispoofing (SA/A-S) and antijam capability. It provides precise positioning and timing based upon signals received from the GPS satellite constellation. It is a five-channel receiver, capable of Precision Code (P Code) and Y Code (encrypted P Code) reception. Positioning information can be displayed in latitude, longitude, military grid reference system, Universal Transverse Mercator, British National Grid and Irish Transverse Mercator Grid coordinates. It contains forty-nine map datums, and can be programmed to support navigation. The PLGR has a built-in-test feature, and is compatible with NVGs (Night Vision Goggles).

The current version, PLGR+96, is upgraded with the latest secure GPS capabilities, and is flexible enough to meet the needs of a wide variety of military users. In addition to hand-held operation, the units can be installed into vehicles and airborne platforms with a vehicle mount.

Specifications – PLGR+96	
Length:	9.45ins
Width:	4.23ins
Weight:	2.75lbs
Unit replacement cost:	$1,200
Power:	External: 9 to 32 v DC, 5W.
Battery:	Lithium, Nickel Cadmium, or Alkaline AA.
Temperature range:	Operation –20°C to 70°C.
	Storage –57°C to 85°C.
Humidity:	0 to 100% (no precipitation).
Time accuracy:	100 nanoseconds.
Position accuracy	SDGPS: < 1m.
	CEPWAGE: < 4 m.
	CEPPPS: <16m.
	SEPSPS: <100m SEP (Spherical Error Probable).
Acquisition time:	Time-to-first-fix < 90 sec.
	Time-to-subsequent-fix < 60 sec.
Velocity accuracy:	0.03m/sec RMS steady rate.
Storage capacity:	999 usable waypoints; 15 user-definable reversible routes of up to 25 legs each.
MTBF:	>15,000 hours.
Battery life:	BA5800 1.5 V DC Lithium, 27 hours.
	8 AA Alkaline, 10 hours.
	NiCad, 4 hours.
Coordinate systems:	8 pre-defined, 3 user-defined.
Datums:	50 pre-defined, 2 user-defined.

Rockwell Collins PLGR II

The Rockwell Collins PLGR II is the second generation of portable military global positioning system receivers. This unit is smaller, faster and more accurate than its predecessors, and offers more features. It has fast acquisition, dual-frequency, all-in-view navigation, backlit keypad and display, and extended jamming protection. A fast direct Y-code acquisition option provides the ability to quickly acquire Y-code, even from off mode.

The basic hand-held PLGR II is green in colour, and has an integral antenna. There is also a Vehicular PLGR II (VPLGR II), which has a large display and fonts for easy viewing in difficult terrain. For ease of installation, several kits have been developed with a receiver mount, remote antenna and cables. For underwater use, the PLGR II receiver is capable of both surface and underwater operation, making it ideal for Special Forces' use.

All hardware versions of the PLGR II can be loaded with the Rockwell Collins GLS (Gun Laying System) software, and integrate with laser rangefinder and direction

PLGR II is the second generation of military GPS receivers. It can integrate with laser rangefinding and direction indicating equipment. The vehicle version, VPLGR II, is shown here fitted to a Special Forces Land Rover. Photo: © James Marchington.

indicating equipment such as Viper (see next chapter). This combination allows a soldier to call down and correct direct and indirect fire with extreme precision.

Rockwell Collins list the features of the PLGR II family as follows:

- Outstanding GPS performance and history
- Mature GPS technology
- Backlit display and keypad which provides illumination without causing night vision goggle blooming
- Excellent user interface in low-light situations
- Ergonomically designed keyboard interface
- Programmable function keys
- 24-hour battery life, continuous usage (typical)
- Removable battery packs
- 8 AA cells for extended mission life
- 6 AA cells with external power connection (N/A for VPLGR II)
- External power per QSTAG 307 (VPLGR II)
- Leading edge receiver performance
- Cold start without time, position or almanac in less than 120 seconds from turn on
- Rapid signal acquisition
- Dual frequency tracking
- Continuous 9-channel All-In-View navigation
- Integrity monitoring (RAIM)
- Extended jamming protection performance
- 41 dB J/S while tracking
- 27 dB J/S in acquisition
- Waterproof remote antenna connector
- Immersion options
- Standard green unit – 1 metre

The PLGR II family uses the most advanced receiver performance available in a hand-held military GPS receiver. The highly integrated NightHawk signal processor incorporates the latest features in GPS signal processing. It uses over seventy acquisition correlators to provide three times the acquisition speed available in previous-generation hand-held receivers.

Designed for vehicular applications, the VPLGR II provides enhanced display readability with its large display. The display area is approximately 2.2 times larger than PLGR II's display and characters are approximately 1.5 times larger. This enhanced display visibility is especially important in vehicular applications. VPLGR II's 128 x 64 pixel Liquid Crystal Display (LCD) is designed to provide superior contrast, brightness, and viewing angle for maximum visibility under a full range of operating conditions. The display is fully compatible with Gen III Night Vision Goggles (NVG), in accordance with MIL-L-85762A. Backlighting for the display is carefully colour adjusted to match the requirements of NVGs – the backlight colour is optimised towards the blue-green spectrum, to provide good contrast and low infra-red. Backlighting on the display is adjustable from 0% (off) to 100% (full backlight).

The removable battery pack makes battery replacement quick and easy, without the need for tools. This is a major consideration on the battlefield. Rockwell Collins offers battery packs in two configurations: an eight-cell version provides maximum battery life between changes, and a six-cell version that also contains an external power interface.

Operations kits have been developed specifically for use in saltwater environments. The Marine Installation Kit includes accessories needed for VPLGR II installation. It includes a low-loss coaxial cable of either 10m or 30m, a high-gain marine antenna and dual pivot VPLGR II mounting assembly.

Specifications – PLGR II & VPLGR II

Dimensions:	PLGR II: 8"1 x 3.7"w x 1.8"d
	VPLGR II: 3.8"h x 7.7"w x 2.8"d
Acquisition time:	15-17 secs
Acceleration:	9G max
Position accuracy:	SDG PS: <2 metres CEP
WAGE:	<4 metres CEP
PPS:	<12 metres CEP
SPS:	<100 metres CEP
Velocity accuracy:	0.03 m/sec RMS steady rate
Time accuracy:	100 nanoseconds
Battery life:	8 AA lithium, 24 hours
	8 AA alkaline, 16 hours (standard unit)
Storage capacity:	499 usable waypoints
	500 history points
	10 user-definable routes of up to 250 legs each
MTBF:	> 20,000 hours ground mobile
Coordinate system:	10 predefined, 3 user-defined
Datums:	95 predefined, 6 user-defined
Power:	External: 10 v DC to 32 v DC, 5W
Internal:	6 or 8 AA batteries, lithium or alkaline
Temperature range:	Operation –25°C to 70°C
	Storage –57°C to 70°C
Humidity:	0 to 100% (non-precipitation)

MEDICAL KIT

Medical skills are highly valued by Special Forces patrols, who may be operating far from any outside medical assistance for days or weeks at a time. On an operation behind enemy lines it is reassuring, to say the least, to know that one of your colleagues has the skills necessary to treat you should you be injured or fall ill. It is better still to know that your patrol also has good communications with HQ, and can quickly call up a helicopter for casevac (casualty evacuation) if necessary – although this luxury is often denied Special Forces patrols on covert operations. Each four-man patrol will normally include one soldier who is a qualified medic, and who carries a medical pack containing the items which will enable him treat any of the injuries and ailments that the patrol may experience during the operation. That is a tall order: he may have to treat anything from gunshot wounds and burns to snakebite, altitude sickness and gastro-intestinal disorder.

Each Special Forces soldier carries his own FFD (First Field Dressing) or shell dressing, and a small first aid kit for treatment of blisters and the like. His survival kit will also contain one or two items with medical uses – such as potassium permanganate crystals that can be mixed with water to make an antiseptic/antifungal solution, as well as being useful for water purification, firelighting and so on. The patrol medic carries a much larger and more comprehensive kit, to enable him effectively to treat a much wider range of ailments and deal with medical emergencies in the field. Chris Ryan, an SAS medic who was part of the Bravo Two-Zero patrol in the Gulf War, writes in *The One That Got Away* that he carried a medical pack weighing 12lbs in addition to his other equipment. As a result, he says, he took a 12lb M16 assault rifle fitted with an M203 grenade launcher, rather than the heavier, 16lb, Minimi 5.56mm machine gun.

Special Forces soldiers face a range of hazards besides enemy action. Here a group of soldiers receive instruction in jungle survival techniques.
Photo: US Navy.

A medic will make up his own pack, choosing items based on a number of factors: what kind of environmental hazards the patrol is likely to face, the availability of materials in the field for improvisation, the likely delay before a casevac can be arranged, and so on. The equipment is generally carried in a purpose-made pack, divided into compartments arranged to allow easy access in an emergency, while holding items securely and protecting them from contamination. Equipment is grouped logically according to the type of treatment it is needed for, and compartments may be see-through or have mesh panels so that items can be found quickly when needed. The pack itself can be laid flat on the ground and opened out to provide a clean working surface.

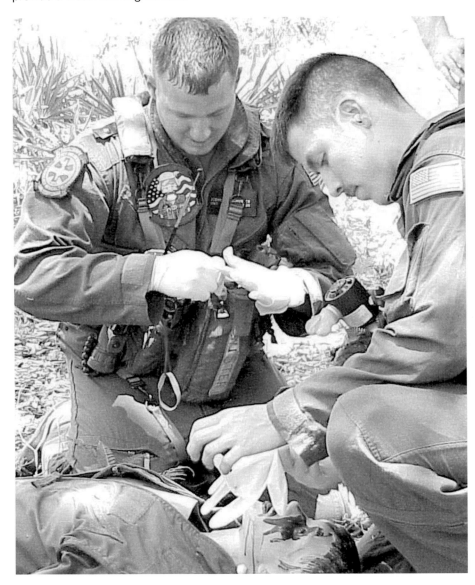

US Navy medics training in procedures for treating a casualty in the field. Special Forces medics must be able to deal with a wide variety of medical emergencies with limited equipment and in difficult conditions. Photo: US Navy.

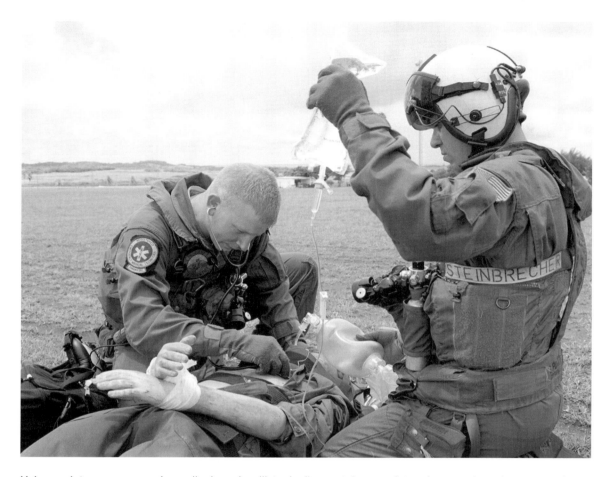

Using an intra-venous drip to replace lost body fluids, a technique which is used to counter the hypo-volemic shock that can result from bullet and shrapnel wounds. Photo: US Navy.

A medical pack will typically contain a variety of general equipment such as: disposable sterile gloves, scissors, tweezers, thermometer, safety pins, electrolyte/rehydration salts, notebook and pencil. There will be a selection of items for cleaning and dressing wounds: surgical wipes, soap, brushes, antiseptic solution, cotton buds, swabs, wound and burn dressings of various sizes, wound closures and rolls of tape. Drugs carried will include antihistamine tablets, hydrocortisone cream, topical anaesthetic/antiseptic ointment, decongestant, antidiarrhoeal tablets, anti-bacterial eye ointment, antifungal cream, antibiotics, lip balm, sunscreen, insect repellant, and a variety of painkillers from aspirin and ibuprofen to the much stronger opiates used in the event of a serious injury. Depending on the environment where the patrol will be operating, the pack may also contain specific items such as malaria drugs, snakebite anti-venom, etc.

The medical kit carried by a Special Forces patrol is broadly similar to the kit carried by any outward-bound-type expedition, for the very good reason that most of the medical problems they are likely to face are of the same kind. The big difference, of course, is that the average outward-bound expedition doesn't get shot at. Special Forces patrols do – and so the patrol medic also carries a trauma pack, containing special equipment for dealing with bullet and shrapnel wounds. After the initial trauma of a bullet wound, one of the biggest immediate threats to the victim's survival is the hypovolemic shock caused by loss of blood volume. This can quickly lead to further tissue damage, and failure of kidneys, heart and lungs. Special Forces medics carry rehydration packs to enable them to treat this in the field. The pack consists of a cannula and bags of HTS (Hypertonic Saline Solution) which is now used in preference to the old-fashioned LRS (Lactated Ringers Solution). Using this pack, the medic can set up an intravenous drip in the field, to restore the victim's lost blood volume.

It should be noted that, as with so much Special Forces equipment, the patrol medic's most important equipment is what he carries in his head – the knowledge and skill that enables him to make the best use of the equipment carried, and improvise with what he can find in the field to get the job done. Special Forces medics spend many hours working in civilian hospitals' A&E (Accident & Emergency) departments, gaining experience in dealing with a wide range of injuries and acute illness – experience that may prove invaluable in the field.

On extended 'Hearts and Minds' operations, Special Forces' medic skills are particularly valuable in treating local people and their livestock, helping to build trust and contacts with the local population.

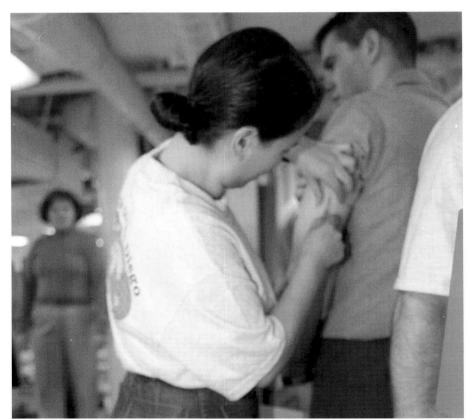

Special Forces medical training helps to build trust with local populations during extended 'hearts and minds' operations. Here, US personnel receive inoculations against the possibility of a biological attack with anthrax. Photo: US Navy.

The following lists detail the contents of a typical expedition medical pack and trauma pack; these examples are supplied by BCB International, a company based in Cardiff, Wales, which specialises in military, aid and disaster relief equipment. As mentioned earlier, each individual medic will tailor his pack to suit the environment and type of operation, as well as his own preferences. The patrol medic will also make up his own list of preferred prescription drugs to be carried on an operation.

BCB International FA312 Extensive First Aid Kit	
2 x No 3 X-Large Ambulance Dressing	1 x Cotton Wool 25g
6 x No 8 Medium HSE (1981) First Aid Dressing	6 x Triangular Bandages
4 x No 9 Large HSE (1981) First Aid Dressing	1 x Pk 100 Mefra 7.5cm Swabs
4 x No 16 HSE (1981) Eye Pad Dressing	1 x Pk 10 Cleansing Wipes
1 x 40 Asst Fabric plasters	4 x 7.5 Conforming Bandage
1 x 20 Asst Waterproof plasters	2 x Crepe Support Bandage 7.5cm
1 x Fabric Strip 6.3cm x 1m	2 x Crepe Support Bandage 10cm
1 x Pk 5 Cutilin 5cm x 5cm	1 x Blunt End Forceps
2 x Pk 5 Cutilin 10m x 10cm	1 x Savlon Spray
2 x Pk 8 Wound Closures 4mm	1 x Ribbon Gauze
2 x Pk 3 Wound Closures 6.4mm	6 x Prs Lrg Gloves
1 x Hypal Surgical Tape 2.5cm x 5m	1 x Spencer Wells
1 x Stretch Fabric Tape 2.5cm x 5m	1 x 150ml Eye Wash
	1 x B/S Scissors
	1 x Vent Aid
	1 x Tuf Cuts
	1 x Penlight

Special Operations Forces Medical Handbook

Although the patrol medic carries in his head much of the information he needs to treat a casualty in the field, it is enormously helpful to be able to refer quickly to standard medical text books while treating a patient. It would be impractical to carry a quantity of books on operations, but recently Skyscape Inc., of Hudson, Mass., has launched a Special Operations Forces Medical Handbook for PDAs (Personal Digital Assistants) such as the Palm series.

The Special Operations Forces Medical Handbook was produced by Teton NewMedia, and the content was created by the United States Special Operations Command, Office of the Command Surgeon, and over eighty medical specialists. It is now the unified reference for Special Forces combat medics in all branches of the US Armed Forces.

This book is specifically designed to help medical personnel make the appropriate diagnoses and administer the proper treatments, even when they may not have access to the methods, drugs and equipment with which they would normally work.

BCB International FA096 Trauma Kit

4 x No 1 Medium Ambulance Dressing	1 x Clip on Sphyg
6 x No 3 X-Large Ambulance Dressing	1 x Tuf Cuts
2 x No 4 XX-Large Ambulance Dressing	1 x Arm Lock (Adult)
	2 x Giving Sets
2 x HSE (1981) Eye Pad Dressing	2 x Venflon Brown
	2 x Venflon White
2 x Pk 5 Cutilin 10m x 10cm	2 x Venflon Pink
1 x Hypal Surgical Tape 2.5cm x 5m	2 x Burn Towels
	1 x Ampoule Opener
1 x Pk 100 Mefra 7.5cm Swabs	1 x Sharps Bin
6 x Triangular Bandages	1 x Stethoscope
1 x ET Tube – Sizes 5, 6, 7, 8, 9	1 x Tourniquet
1 x Catheter Mount	2 x 2ml Syringe
1 x Laryngoscope Handle	2 x 5ml Syringe
1 x Mack Blade – Sizes 1 & 3	2 x 10ml Syringe
	2 x Niko Guard
1 x Medium Intubation Stylet	2 x Burn Bags for Hands
	1 x 500ml Saline Solution

The PDA reference contains the entire content of the book, including 270 images and 50 tables. As well as helping medics in the Armed Forces to access the information they need, it is also a handy reference guide for civilian doctors, nurses and EMTs when they know they will be away from their normal working environment.

The handbook provides treatment protocols organised by symptoms and affected organ system, including speciality areas such as trauma, infectious disease and toxicology. It also has guides for critical procedures, surgeries and basic medical skills, with information on how to handle specific environmental hazards including altitude- and temperature-related illness, chemical injuries and exposures. Through Skyscape's smARTlink technology, the content of the book can dynamically link to content from other medical references, enabling physicians to check drug dosages, drug interactions or refer to speciality texts.

Major Steven Krause, a doctor with the US Army, explains the importance of having a pocket-sized medical reference on operations:

> I am frequently deployed around the world in often very remote locations. I cannot take all my favourite medical text books with me and often find myself at a loss for high quality medical references. Thanks to Skyscape products I can download an endless array of medical texts to my PDA. During my last deployment to the Balkans, I used the 5 Minute Emergency Medicine Consult when taking care of a burn patient. I find Skyscape products easy to use, medically accurate, and my best battle companion.

SURVIVAL KITS

Anyone operating in or flying over hostile terrain risks being caught in a survival situation – where simply staying alive and attracting rescue becomes the main priority. Even relatively mild terrain in a temperate zone can look very different when you are cut off from help. It is all too easy to die of hypothermia in the mountains of Wales; jungles, Arctic regions, deserts and mountains all present their own problems for the downed airman or Special Forces patrol 'bumped' and forced to abandon their equipment.

Special Forces and aircrew train for this eventuality, and develop a range of skills which enable them to stay alive in hostile territory. Priorities for the survivor include shelter, fire, water, medical care, navigation/location and signalling (food is a second-level priority, although important for maintaining the body's performance and the mind's morale). As always, space and weight are at a premium, but Special Forces soldiers carry a basic survival kit containing a range of items that can prove vital in a survival situation.

The size and weight of the kit are kept to a minimum, and where possible items are chosen which are versatile enough to have multiple uses. The kit, for instance, will probably include a small container of potassium permanganate crystals; these take up little space and weigh almost nothing, but can be used to purify water, make an antiseptic solution, help start a fire, and stain snow to signal for help.

A popular combat survival kit is contained in a tobacco tin (lid doubles as heliograph, tin doubles as cooking pot/mug) sealed with sticky tape (reusable, naturally). This tin can be packed into a belt kit, where it will take up very little space and is most likely to remain with the soldier even if he is forced to abandon his other kit. A version of this kit is supplied commercially by BCB International, although some soldiers prefer to make up their own survival kit. The following list is typical of the items that such a kit might contain:

Non-safety matches, waterproofed with candle wax (fire lighting – for warmth, signalling, illumination).
Candle (fire lighting, illumination; wax can also be used as lubricant for zips etc).
Flint and striker (fire lighting – as above).
Cotton wool – a tampon is ideal as it is highly compressed, so takes up little space (used as tinder for fire lighting – see above).
Fish hooks and line (catching fish for food; also for catching birds and small mammals).
Button compass (navigation).
Needles and thread (repair of clothing and equipment; needle may also be used to prick a blister or remove a splinter).
Magnifying glass (fire lighting – see above).
Rabbit snare (catching mammals, birds and fish for food).
Wire saw (cutting timber for shelter, traps, tools, etc).

Scalpel blades (miscellaneous – including preparing game for cooking, cutting cordage, etc).

Spool of dental floss (cordage for fishing, traps, shelter building, etc). Floss is chosen as it is very strong and compact.

Water purifying tablets (to make water safe to drink).

Condom (carrying water).

Antiseptic ointment (prevention of bacterial infections).

Antibiotics (treatment of bacterial infections).

Antihistamines (treatment of stings, bites, etc).

Potassium permanganate (several uses – disinfectant, water purification, fire starting aid, dye for snow, etc).

Sticking plasters (treatment and protection of minor cuts).

Lip salve (protection of lips in harsh environments).

Rehydration salts (treatment of dehydration caused by vomiting, diarrhoea, etc).

Malaria tablets (where needed).

In addition to the survival tin, Special Forces soldiers will ensure that various other items are included in their belt kit, or carried at all times, so that they will always be available even if the patrol has to split up if surprised by an enemy attack. These will normally include: a knife, adequate clothing for the climate, as much water as practicable, a brew kit of fuel and metal mug, spare matches, a bivi bag or poncho, a small quantity of high-energy food such as sweets or chocolate bars, and their personal weapon and ammunition. Cordage is almost always in short supply in a survival situation, so paracord or similar is often pre-wrapped around a knife handle where it takes up little space and is available when needed.

The following are examples of survival kits that might be carried by Special Forces in various situations.

BCB CK420 Air Crew Survival Go Pack Mk4
This kit was designed for the Royal Air Force, and was extensively and successfully used during the 1991 Gulf War. Tightly and compactly sealed in three packs are over twenty essential pieces of kit: Size. approx 20cm x 12cm x 5cm. Weight: 340g.

BCB CK016 Military Survival Tin
This is an excellent survival kit, widely used by Special Forces and others. It contains more than twenty-seven quality items packed in a useful small tobacco tin. Virtually every item has multiple uses, and with the appropriate skills and knowledge will significantly improve a soldier's chances of survival and rescue in a wide range of hostile conditions. Size: 13cm x 8cm x 3cm. Weight: 200g.

BCB CK004 Ultimate Survival Pack
Billed as the 'ultimate' pack, this kit contains a good selection of survival items (listed

below) packed in a quality waterproof aluminium case. The case itself may be used as a cooking pot, etc. Size: 13cm x 11cm x 2.3cm. Weight: 345g.

Water bag	4	Water tablets	10
Cord – nylon	1	Safety pins	6
Compass	1	Tampon/cotton wool	1
Candle	1	Water purification tablets	1
Fire lighter	1	Piriton tablets	20
Fishing set	1	Single edge blade	1
Knife/Blade	1	Salt sachet	1
Matches 10s	1	Paracetamol	8
Book	1	Folding scissors	1
Mirror	1	Potassium permanganate	1
Sewing kit	1	Camo cream	1
Brass wire	1		

E&E

The story of the SAS Bravo Two-Zero patrol during the Gulf War shows how quickly an operation can go wrong, and become an individual scramble for safety. Special Forces soldiers train in E&E (Escape & Evasion) techniques, and carry a small selection of items that will help them to survive and evade capture, even if their other equipment is lost and they are cut off from friendly forces.

Chris Ryan's gripping book, *The One That Got Away*, is the tale of his remarkable escape from Iraq when the famous Bravo Two-Zero patrol went wrong. Reading the book, it is clear that equipment was just one small part of what enabled him to make his way through miles of enemy-held territory, eventually crossing the border and back into the hands of friendly forces. His achievement was made possible by a combination of fitness, training, aggression, courage and a dogged belief that he could do it, despite overwhelming odds.

In such a situation, however, there are a number of items that can give the survivor/evader an edge. The decision whether or not to carry a certain item of survival or E&E equipment must always be based on its potential value versus its weight and bulk. Survival items must be carried on belt kit or even around the soldier's person, so that they are always with him if things go wrong and he has to abandon the rest of his kit. This means that they must be small and light – the smaller and lighter, the better.

Chris Ryan explains that each member of the Bravo Two-Zero patrol carried a silk escape map of the Gulf region, twenty gold sovereigns, and a promissory note in English and Arabic, offering £5,000 to anyone who brought the holder safely into the hands of Allied forces. Each of these items was hidden about the soldier's clothing – the sovereigns stitched inside his belt, for instance – so that they might go undetected in a search, and still be available if the soldier managed to escape after capture.

EPIRBs and Strobes

In a survival situation – a downed aircraft or a patrol that has been compromised in enemy territory, for example – it is important to be able to summon help from friendly forces as quickly as possible. Survivors need to show the SAR (Search and Rescue) team their location precisely and quickly, but without alerting the enemy. There are various items of equipment that can do this, some of which also have applications for civilian expeditions. These generally fall into two categories: EPIRBs (Emergency Position-Indicating Radio Beacons) and Strobes.

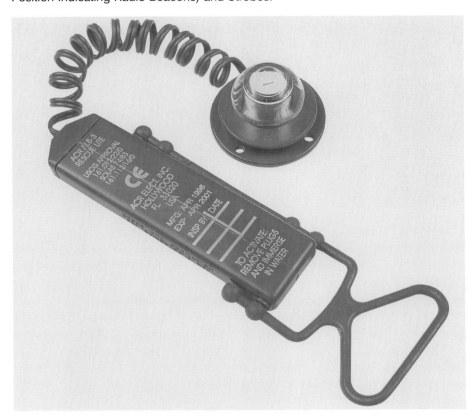

The ACR L8-3 Personal Rescue Light operates when immersed in water. The light is visible for more than a mile, and operates for 8 hours. Photo: ACR.

Signature Industries SARBE & TACBE family

SARBE (Search and Rescue BEacon) is a trade name of Signature Industries in London, a subsidiary of Applied Digital Solutions (ADS). The company was formerly known as Burndept, one of the original founders of the BBC, and has been making Search and Rescue radio equipment for more than forty years. The company makes a range of SARBE units, which are used by civilian aircrew and vessels as well as military users.

TACBE

The TACBE or TACtical BEacon, is based on Signature Industries' highly successful SARBE 5 dual-channel distress beacon. TACBE is a lightweight two-channel ground

A selection of SARBEs (Search And Rescue Beacons) from Signature Industries. The military version, TACBE, is used by a number of Special Forces units as a distress beacon. Photo: Signature Industries.

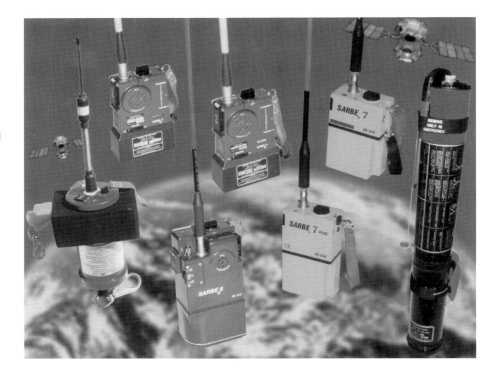

to air communication set for ground forces' use and is also suitable for certain special military 'swimmer' operations. It is a relatively compact device, measuring approximately 130mm x 95mm x 35mm, with an antenna of about 350mm length. It weighs around 250g. It operates as an emergency beacon, transmitting a distress signal on one of the internationally recognised frequencies (VHF or UHF) when a pin is pulled. It can also be used as a simple voice radio, enabling a survivor on the ground to talk to an aircraft overhead, with a choice of two frequencies. The TACBE was carried extensively by Special Forces during the 1991 Gulf War. Unfortunately for the members of the Bravo Two-Zero patrol, however, they were unable to contact Allied aircraft via their TACBEs after the patrol got into difficulties.

SARBE 6

The BE 515 SARBE 6 Personal Locator Beacon (PLB) is designed for use as a survival radio by military and civil air crew. On activation, the beacon provides simultaneous omni-directional beacon transmission on the VHF and UHF distress frequencies. Two-way voice transmission is available on the VHF and UHF distress frequencies. Once activated, a SARBE 6 has a minimum continuous operation time of twenty-four hours. It meets the relevant NATO standards and is CAA Approved.

SARBE 7

The BE 549 SARBE 7 Personal Locator Beacon (PLB) is a compact lightweight radio beacon designed for use as a military or civil survival aid. On activation, the unit provides simultaneous omni-directional beacon transmissions on the VHF and UHF distress frequencies. SARBE 7 is in service in large quantities with military users such as the UK MOD (it is used by the Royal Air Force and Royal Navy), and many commercial users around the world. Like the SARBE 6, it meets the relevant NATO standards and is CAA Approved.

SARBE 7 Plus

SARBE 7 Plus, as the name suggests, is based on the SARBE 7. The main difference is that the SARBE 7 Plus automatically activates after immersion in either fresh or salt water. Once activated, the beacon transmits a digitally synthesised voice message, which may include both text and numbers. The standard message is 'Mayday Mayday, man overboard', followed by the international swept tone distress signal. The unit provides simultaneous omni-directional beacon transmissions on the VHF and UHF distress frequencies.

SARBE 8

The BE 572 SARBE 8 is a multi-role beacon/radio unit which incorporates GPS to provide pinpoint accuracy of personnel. Intended primarily for military users, it is designed for use by both aircrew and ground forces. The SARBE 8 may be programmed to operate either as a standard Search and Rescue Beacon utilising the COSPAS/SARSAT satellite system, or as a Combat Recovery Beacon. In either role, SARBE 8 transmits a pre-programmed identity and current position in latitude and longitude.

In Combat mode the civilian SAR frequencies are disabled and replaced by a secure transmission facility which transmits identity and position data in randomly spaced data bursts which can be decoded by the SARBE 8's dedicated receiver/decoder, SARFIND.

SARBE 8 is also equipped with voice communication in either SAR or CSAR mode for identity verification, recovery assistance or tactical use. A wide range of operating and power management features may be set through the PC-based programming system. SARBE 8 meets the relevant NATO standards.

SARFIND

The BE559 SARFIND is the Decoder Unit for SARBE 8, displaying the identity and position of each SARBE 8 detected. The unit is designed to 'track' the position of all detected SARBE 8s enabling beacon movement history to be studied as an aid to location and pick-up. SARFIND is designed as a 'carry-on carry-off' unit and only requires connection to the aircraft watch receiver and the receiver tuned to the mission operating frequencies. It requires no aircraft modification and can be readily employed on helicopters, fast jets, maritime patrol aircraft and AWACS.

SARBE 10

SARBE 10 Submarine PLB, the newest beacon from Signature, is water-resistant to a depth of more than 250 metres, and is the first of a new generation of Signature beacons to incorporate 406MHz.

Above: The ACR PRC 90-2 is a hand-held survival transceiver with voice and beacon capability on the military distress frequency. It has a ground-to-air range of 60 nautical miles. Photo: ACR.

Above right: ACR's MS-2000 distress marker light is a robust strobe with an IR filter that can block all visible light. It runs on 2 AA batteries and emits a flash visible at more than 6 miles. Photo: ACR

ACR Electronics Locator Beacons and Strobes

ACR Electronics Inc., of Fort Lauderdale, Florida, designs and manufactures a range of safety and survival products including EPIRBs (Emergency Position Indicating Radio Beacons), personal utility lights, marker lights, radios, SARTs and safety accessories. ACR has provided safety equipment to the aviation and marine industries as well as to the military since 1956.

URT-33D Radio Locator Beacon

The AN/URT-33 series radio locator beacon is standard on US fighter aircraft. ACR's newest version, the AN/URT-33D incorporates a range of improvements including automatic activation on ejection. The AN/URT-33 C/M is the standard for the Aces II fighter aircraft seats.

MS-2000 (M) distress marker light

Back in the 1960s, the ACR Firefly was a popular distress marker light – a robust strobe light that, once switched on, would emit a bright flash of light at regular intervals to enable an SAR force to locate a survivor. The MS-2000(M) distress marker light is the modern equivalent of the Firefly, and has become a great deal more sophisticated. There are five distinct versions of the MS-2000(M) that meet the most up-to-date requirements of the military and fit virtually any application:

3990 MS-2000(M)
3991 MS-2000(M) H2O (water activated version)
3992 Photofly (photocell activated version)
3993 Pilotlight (photocell and water activated version)
3994 Doublefly (strobe and incandescent version)

All of the MS-2000(M) models include the following features:

Shield extends/retracts for omni- or uni-directional visibility

Waterproof to 50ft (15.3m); 200ft diver version available

IR filter blocks all visible light (lets through only IR light)

Raised polarity indicators allow correct battery replacement in low or no visibility conditions

New braided steel retainer keeps battery door from being lost

Operates on 2 standard alkaline AA batteries – disposal causes no environmental impact

For extreme cold environments or long term storage, use 2 common lithium batteries

Attached infra-red (IR) filter for Night Vision Goggle (NVG) viewing

Directional, shielded blue filter distinguishes strobe from ground fire when in place.

Raised polarity indicators allow correct battery replacement even when visibility is low

Omni-directional white strobe emits brilliant 250,000 peak lumens

Compact, lightweight and waterproof to 200ft

Large sliding switch for easy operation under any conditions

Specifications

Size:	4.5 x 2.2 x 1.1ins (11.4 x 5.6 x 3.3cm)
Weight:	4.0oz (115g) without batteries
Light output:	250,000 peak lumens per flash
Flash rate:	50 ± 10 per minute
Light dispersion:	White – omni-directional, IR – omni-directional, Blue – uni-directional
Operating life:	8 hours minimum (strobe); 2 hours minimum (incandescent)
Visibility:	Military tested at a distance of 6 miles (9.6km) on a clear dark night
Waterproof:	To a depth of 50ft (15.3m); 200ft (61m) diver version available
Batteries:	2 AA alkaline or lithium batteries (not included)
Case colour:	Black with olive drab flash-guard
Construction:	Case, lens and flashguard – high impact polycarbonate; IR filter – butyrate
Activation:	Spark-proof magnetic reed switch

2 OBSERVATION, SURVEILLANCE, TARGETING DESIGNATION

Satellite imaging can play an important part in locating enemy forces and facilities, but sometimes there is no alternative to placing Special Forces on the ground for a Close Target Recce. Photo: US DoD.

Much Special Forces work involves watching an enemy and collecting intelligence, rather than engaging the enemy directly. Special Forces are skilled in covertly infiltrating enemy territory and setting up OPs (Observation Posts), where they can remain unobserved – for days or weeks if necessary – while gathering intelligence about the enemy's strengths, weaknesses and movements, and sending the information back to their own HQ. Examples include the staking-out of terrorists' homes in Northern Ireland, and the classic Cold War scenario of 'stay behind' Special Forces OPs reporting on Soviet troops as they roll across Europe.

Britain's Special Forces have had the advantage – if that is the right word – of many years' experience in Northern Ireland. The battle against IRA terrorists has provided ample opportunities to develop and refine new techniques and equipment, and gain experience in their practical use in real conditions against a real enemy – just as the USA's campaign against al-Qaeda and the Taliban in Afghanistan has made possible the battle-testing of new weapons and equipment such as thermobaric bombs and miniature UAVs.

Modern warfare is becoming increasingly remote, with precision stand-off weapons such as 'smart' bombs and cruise missiles fired from many miles away and finding their way to a target by means of sophisticated electronics. Modern remote sensing technology makes it possible to locate and track an enemy from satellites and high-flying aircraft, as well as unmanned aircraft. All this has enabled many tasks to be carried out without needing to risk the lives of highly skilled Special Forces soldiers. This is not to say, however, that the need for Special Forces has declined. Indeed, if anything the need is even greater; but the nature of Special Forces' operations is evolving as warfare itself changes.

There is still a need to locate enemy forces, who are becoming adept at hiding from modern surveillance technology such as satellites, and at disguising themselves to blend in with a civilian population. During the Balkan conflicts at the end of the twentieth century, for instance, Serb forces made extensive use of civilian vehicles, hid tanks and other matériel within civilian homes, and would even travel in convoy with refugees. In order to be sure of hitting enemy troops rather than civilians, it was often necessary to have Special Forces on the ground, using equipment such as the Laser Target Designator (LTD) to guide 'smart' bombs onto their targets.

A few years later in Afghanistan, British and American troops found themselves hunting an enemy who looked almost indistinguishable from the civilian population, and would quickly melt away to hide in caves and woodland rather than stand and fight. High-tech weapons such as 'cave-busting' bombs were of value, but searching the caves at Tora Bora, for instance, required troops on the ground to assault the caves and clear them with grenades and assault rifles; some forty US Special Forces troops fought alongside local Afghans to flush out remaining al-Qaeda fighters at Tora Bora.

Warfare will continue to change, with many observers pointing to the increasing polarisation between the high-tech 'industrial' warfare prosecuted by western nations, versus the low-tech guerrilla/terrorist 'human' methods often adopted by enemies as the only viable way to combat them. The term 'Fourth Generation Warfare' has been coined to describe this type of conflict. Special Forces will still have a vital role, albeit a different one to their role in the Cold War of the mid-twentieth century. And observation, surveillance and target designation will continue to play an important part in future warfare.

NIGHT VISION: IMAGE INTENSIFIERS

All things being equal, Special Forces patrols prefer to move at night, and lay up during the daylight hours. Modern night-vision equipment gives an enormous advantage at night – making it possible to see the enemy, while minimising the chance of being seen – particularly when fighting a relatively unsophisticated enemy who is less well equipped. Night-vision kit was in short supply during the Gulf War of 1991, but SAS patrols made full use of the equipment available to them. In more recent conflicts, such as the operations against al-Qaeda in Afghanistan following September 2001, conventional and Special Forces alike have made extensive use of night-vision equipment.

Modern night vision equipment turns night into day, enabling Special Forces to operate around the clock and giving them a significant advantage against a less well equipped enemy. Photo: USMC.

Night-vision equipment falls into two basic types. Image intensifiers magnify the tiny amount of light that exists even on the darkest night (from stars etc.) and form an image on a tube inside. This system is used in weapon sights such as the Kite, as well as in helmet-mounted NVGs (Night Vision Goggles) worn by Special Forces pilots and drivers to enable them to operate in almost total darkness.

The second type of night-vision equipment is thermal imaging: these units form an image of the heat radiated by objects, so that warm vehicle engines, gun barrels and human beings show up brightly against the dark (colder) background.

A true Image Intensification device (as opposed to a Thermal Imager, discussed below) uses light in the visible and infra-red parts of the spectrum. It is a passive system that amplifies the ambient light from man-made and natural sources including the moon and stars – which gave it the nickname 'Starlight Scope' in US military service during the 1962–75 Vietnam War.

As a passive device, Image Intensification does not send a signal, so there are no emissions that an enemy could detect and deduce that he is under surveillance (unlike radar, for instance). Having said that, it is possible to improve the close-range performance of night vision devices by adding infra-red illumination. This light is not visible to the naked eye but can be seen clearly through an Image Intensification device. It is particularly useful in places where there is no natural light – not even the tiny amount needed for a modern Image Intensification device to function – places such as inside buildings, ships and aircraft. Vehicle lights can be replaced with infra-red bulbs for night driving (although the lights may then be seen clearly by an enemy equipped with night-vision devices).

The end of the Cold War released a huge range of low-cost Russian-made Image Intensification equipment on to the civilian market, including binoculars and hand-held systems with IR illumination. First Generation (Gen I) systems such as the T3C2 can now be bought for as little as £100. This has led to the use of Image Intensification equipment by everyday criminals as well as terrorists. Image Intensification can be extremely useful in planning and carrying out a criminal or terrorist attack. One way to combat this threat is to ensure that vulnerable buildings and installations are screened from view by fences, walls or vegetation.

Image Intensification devices have been improved greatly in recent years. The first devices, now known as First Generation or Gen I, produced a murky green image with dancing specks all over. They were badly affected by 'flaring' around light sources, and would be blinded or 'bloomed out' for several minutes by a sudden bright light such as a car's headlights appearing unexpectedly. Blooming out fogs the screen by producing a temporary after-image. These Gen I devices were hardly better than using a decent pair of binoculars, which can be remarkably effective at night once the eyes have grown accustomed to the dark after half an hour or so.

Performance and reliability have been enhanced through three generations of Image Intensification equipment. Second Generation (Gen II) Image Intensification equipment has improved light intensification up to 20,000 times, compared to 1,000 times in Gen I equipment. Filtration is incorporated so that Gen II kit does not 'bloom out' if the user points it at a light source such as car headlights.

Third Generation (Gen III) is a further improvement on Gen II, with better filters helping to give a clearer image in difficult conditions, but the enhancement is relatively

Passive Night Goggles (PNGs) issued to the British Army make it possible to drive a vehicle in almost total darkness. Photo: © James Marchington.

The pilot of this USAF MH-53 Pave Low helicopter is using night vision goggles to fly at night, in operations against Taliban forces in Afghanistan. Photo: USAF.

small for the increase in cost, making it unattractive to all but government agencies.

Image Intensification technology has now moved on a stage further. In 1999 Litton Industries (now Northrop Grumman), one of the US military's major suppliers of night vision and surveillance equipment, delivered the first production quantities of Fourth Generation (Gen IV) Image Intensifier tubes to the US Army Night Vision and Electronic Sensors Directorate (NVESD). Gen IV tubes take Image Intensification performance levels a stage further by taking advantage of new technology, and by rethinking traditional tube design concepts.

The key difference in Gen IV image intensifier tubes is that there is no ion barrier film. In conventional Gen III tubes this barrier prevents damage to the photocathode coating by shielding it from ions backscattered from the microchannel plate (MCP). Northrop Grumman describe this as a significant breakthrough. Gen IV tubes used in night-vision goggles have demonstrated substantial increases in target detection range and resolution, particularly at extremely low light levels.

Northrop Grumman's Gen IV MX-10130E/UV tube will be used in the US Special Operations Command's (USSOCOM) Improved Night/Day Fire Control and Observation Device (INOD) weapon sight, which at the time of writing is undergoing Initial Production Testing.

Image Intensification devices are available in various formats, including monocular viewers, weapons sights and Passive Night Goggles (PNGs). The goggles are particularly suited to driving vehicles or flying aircraft, especially helicopters. PNGs were first used operationally by British helicopter crews in the Falklands War of 1982, to insert Special Forces by night on to the islands. They have since become standard kit for pilots and drivers on the modern battlefield, and are widely used by Special Forces and anti-terrorist operators.

Goggles are available in single- and twin-tube types. The single-tube variety are simpler and less expensive, and can therefore be issued more widely. Dual tubes, however, enable the eyes and brain to perceive depth, using the same stereoscopic method by which we perceive depth with the naked eye in daylight. For certain types of use, such as driving or flying, the depth perception offered by dual-tube goggles is a significant advantage.

There is a splendid story, perhaps apocryphal, of a UK Special Forces flight pilot practising with PNGs prior to being deployed to the Gulf War; he chose to drive a high-performance sports car around the M25 motorway in the early hours of the morning. The police were somewhat baffled when the blacked-out vehicle flashed past at a speed approaching 200mph! True or not, the story demonstrates that with PNGs it is possible to drive or fly at night as though it were daytime – giving a signif-icant advantage over an enemy who is less well equipped.

Northrop Grumman Electro-Optical Systems

Northrop Grumman (formerly Litton Electro-Optical Systems) produce Image Intensi-fication systems for the US Army, Navy, Marine Corps, Special Operations, and many international customers. Products supplied to the US armed forces include AN/PVS-7D Infantry Night Vision Goggles, AN/PVS-14 Monocular Night Vision Systems, and AN/AVS-6 Aviator Night Vision Systems.

Northrop Grumman AN/PVS-7B/D

This goggle is a Second Generation design, with improved performance and ergonomic features. The AN/PVS-7D, adopted by the US Army, incorporates an advanced image tube with very high resolution.

Northrop Grumman AN/PVS-7A/C

The AN/PVS-7A is a rugged, lightweight, compact, single-tube goggle for hand-held, helmet or face mask mounting for the dismounted soldier. It was the first design of this type and offered excellent performance at an attractive cost. It has x1 magnifica-tion for short- to medium-range surveillance, combat, security, law enforcement, search and rescue, etc., while x4 and x6 magnification versions are also available. The AN/PVS-7C is a modified design that is submersible to 20m. Weighing only 0.68kg, it operates from two 1.5v AA alkaline batteries or a single lithium battery, and contains an IR LED (Infra Red Light Emitting Diode).

Northrop Grumman AN/AVS-6

AN/AVS-6 are Rotary and Fixed Wing Aviator's Goggles. The high-performance, high-resolution twin Gen III tube design extends pilots' operational capability into the night. It is helmet-mounted with simple adjustments, fast breakaway and system redundancy for safety. Compatible with most aviator helmets, the AN/AVS-6 features 25mm eye relief, low fatigue design, flip-up stowage, superior light sensitivity and fast flash response.

Northrop Grumman AN/PVS-15

This Gen III twin-tube goggle is a ruggedised Navy qualified system that offers dual-channel depth perception. It can be hand-held or helmet-mounted, and has improved 'flash response' to maintain sharp image detail even through flares or lights. A 25mm eye relief allows its use with masks or goggles.

Northrop Grumman AN/AVS-9 (M949)

While incorporating the same proven operational features as AN/AVS-6, M949 is claimed to be the highest resolution, longest range x1 magnification night-viewing system available today. It uses Northrop Grumman's GEN IV Image Intensification technology, including Filmless MCP, Auto-Gated Power Supply and patent-pending 'Halo-Free' design. The M949 with GEN IV tubes is restricted from export.

PW Allen Nite-Watch

While the Northrop Grumman range described above is typical of the type of night-vision kit issued to land forces in combat, the PW Allen Nite-Watch is the type more typically used for surveillance by police and internal security forces. The Nite-Watch is remarkably light and compact, weighing only 330g (including lens and batteries), making it pocket-sized and easily concealed. The modular construction of Nite-Watch Plus enables it to be swiftly added to most types of SLR, Video and CCTV cameras with a range of adaptors.

When used in low light-level conditions, the Nite-Watch Plus typically provides over 7,000 hours of life, making it more cost-effective than many cheaper alternatives. Typical light intensification is over 20,000 times, compared with a Gen I system with a maximum light intensification of less than 1,000 times.

Nite-Watch Plus is available in two mechanically different forms. The original Nite-Watch form incorporates three miniature lithium batteries, the newer option incorporates two AAA batteries in a 'side-pack' version. The Nite-Watch System is subject to UK Government Export Licensing Regulations, and cannot be exported from the UK without a licence.

Features

Weighs only 330g including lens and batteries	Available with Gen II plus, Super Gen II or Gen III tube technologies
Modular construction	
Covert system	Over 7,000 hours continuous use
Shockproof	Water resistant (ruggedised units only)
Interchangeable lenses	
Push-button or rotary switch	

Specifications

Intensifier type:	Second or Third Generation 18mm channel plate wafer tube
Resolution:	Typically 32 1p/mm
Supply voltage:	2.5 to 3.5v
Supply current:	Typically 18 mA
Battery life:	Typically 30 hours' continuous use from 3 lithium cells type DL1/3N or 2 AAA depending on type
Weight:	Typically 330g (11.64oz) including lens and batteries
Size:	46mm (1.8in) diameter x 120mm (4.7in) long including f/1.4 25mm lens
Objective lens:	Standard C-mount f/1.4 25mm
System field of view:	34° with 25mm lens (42° for side-pack version) 11° with 75 mm lens (15° for side-pack version)
System magnification:	x1 with 25mm lens. x3 with 75mm lens

PW Allen NVSK 1/00 Night Vision Surveillance Kit

The Nite-Watch system forms the basis of PW Allen's NVSK 1/00 Comprehensive Night Vision Surveillance Kit, described as 'a fully comprehensive surveillance kit for night-time observation, intelligence and evidence gathering'. This kit provides all the equipment required to view and record activities by day or night; all the equipment in the kit has been field-proven by security forces in the UK and overseas.

The kit consists of the following items, packed in a rugged case with anti-shock foam inserts:

Gen III Nite-Watch Monocular Sight	Sony Mini Digital Video Camera
SLR Camera Adaptor	Canon EOS IV SLR Camera
SLR Interface Mount	Rangefinder
Mini Digital Video Camera Adaptor	IR Illuminator
Mini Digital Video Camera Interface Mount	Waterproof Case
	Cleaning Kit
75mm f/1.3 Objective Lens	Instruction Manual
75mm f/1.8 Objective Zoom Lens	Spare Batteries 6x AAA

Leica Geosystems

Leica Geosystems of Switzerland produce a range of sturdy, proven night-vision products, including pocket monoculars, night-vision goggles and night binoculars. Export of Leica's night-vision products is subject to Swiss export regulations

Leica BIM25 Night Pocketscope

The Leica BIM25 is a general-purpose, monocular night-vision device in a watertight, nitrogen-filled housing. It provides an actual size image (x1 magnification). There is a choice of image intensifier tube – Gen II, Gen II super or Gen III. It is suited to security and reconnaissance applications, and can also be fitted to a SLR or video camera by means of an adaptor, in order to record intelligence for later use.

Leica BIM35 Night Pocketscope

Leica's BIM35 monocular is identical to the BIM25, except that a larger objective lens provides x3 magnification. This makes it more suitable for observing a target at a distance from a static position such as an OP.

Leica BIG25 Night-Vision Goggles

Leica BIG25 are night-vision goggles suitable for a wide range of tasks such as CTR (Close Target Reconaissance), vehicle driving, navigating and operating various types of equipment in night conditions. The goggles have a single objective tube containing a Gen II or III image intensifier. The intensified image is passed to binocular viewing lenses. The goggles can be hand-held, or worn attached to the head by means of an optional harness – leaving both hands free for driving etc.

Leica BIG35 Night Binoculars

The BIG35 binoculars are similar to the BIG25, but with a x3 magnification object lens. The much larger lens makes it impractical to wear the binoculars with a head harness. The large lens barrel is rubber-covered, giving a good grip, and the binoculars are designed to be used for extended periods without eye-strain. They have rubber eye-cups for comfort, and to prevent light spillage which could give away the user's position.

Specifications – Leica Night Vision Equipment				
	BIM25	BIM35	BIG25	BIG35
Magnification:	x1	x3	x1	x3
Field of view:	>40°	>12.5°	>40°	>12.5°
Focus:	0.25m-inf	10m-inf	0.25m-inf	10m-inf
Weight:	0.43kg	1.16kg	0.55kg	1.19kg

Simrad Optronics

Simrad of Norway offer an array of Image Intensifier night sights for security services and armed forces. As well as image intensifying monoculars, goggles and binoculars, Simrad also produce the KN series, which can be clipped on to existing day scopes or sighting systems without modification. This has the advantage that the existing set-up of a weapons sight etc. remains unchanged, and the sight's performance is retained twenty-four hours a day. The KN system uses Gen II or III image intensifier tubes depending on the customer's requirements.

Simrad KN250 and KN200 Image Intensifiers

The Simrad KN200 and KN250 image intensifiers are add-on units providing a night-time capability to optical day sights. The night-vision image is viewed through the eyepiece of the day sight. This allows the user to retain the same eye position, aiming reticle and magnification for both day and night shooting. The KN series have adjustable focus and variable gain control, and can be supplied waterproofed to 20 metres. A separate laser illuminator and pointer are available.

Specifications – Simrad KN 200		**Specifications** – Simrad KN 250	
Field of view:	10°	Field of view:	12°
Weight (incl batteries):	1.56kg	Weight (incl batteries):	1kg
Magnification:	x1	Magnification:	x1
Dimensions:	127(w) x 192(h) x 220(l)mm	Dimensions:	107(w) x 142(h) x 187(l)mm
Focusing range:	25m to infinity	Focusing:	25m to infinity
Operating temperature:	–40°C to 50°C	Operating temperature:	–40°C to 50°C
Storing temperature:	–40°C to 65°C	Storing temperature:	–40°C to 65°C
Battery:	2 x 1.5v AA cells	Battery:	2 x 1.5v AA cells
Battery life:	>80 h at 20°C	Battery life:	>80h at 20°C

Simrad GN Night-Vision Goggles

Simrad GN Night-Vision Goggles are extremely compact and lightweight binocular goggles, with a flip-up mechanism so they can be worn ready to flip into position at short notice. They have proved popular with a wide range of users, including main-stream infantry units, Special Forces, police, customs and immigration control. At the time of writing, Simrad indicate that they expect shortly to announce an improved goggle that is even lighter and more compact.

Features	
Gen II or Gen III tubes	Head mount or helmet mount
Range focus	Flip-up mechanism
Eyepiece focus	Waterproof to 10m
IR Illuminator	NATO Codified
Lightweight, ergonomic	

Typical applications	
Vehicle driving/commanding	Reconnaissance
Patrolling	Logistical operations
Surveillance	Search and rescue
Weapon handling	Map reading
Parachuting	

Specifications – Simrad GN

Magnification:	x1
Weight (incl batteries):	390g
Field of view:	40°
Size:	155(w) x 73(h) x 58(l)mm
Focusing range:	0.2m to infinity
Weight – head mount:	230g
IR source	LED
Batteries:	2 x 1.5V AA cells
Battery life:	>80h at 20° with IR source off
	>40h at 20° with IR source on

Simrad KDN250 Day/Night-Vision Binoculars

Simrad's KDN250 is a highly useful surveillance tool – a pair of observation binoculars that provide a high-quality image twenty-four hours a day. The binoculars essentially have a two-channel system, with separate night and day optics.

Features

x3.5 magnification	Compatible with 2nd or 3rd generation 18mm image tubes
Lightweight (1.5kg)	
Binocular viewing	Dovetail quick-release mechanism fitted to night channel
Completely passive	
Waterproof to 20m	Focusing wheel on the night channel
NATO codification	
Adjustable interocular distance	

Specifications

Magnification:	x3.5
Weight (incl batteries):	1,550g
Field of view:	12°
Dimensions:	158(w) x 140(h) x 229(l)mm
Focusing range:	25m to infinity
Operating temperature:	–40°C to 52°C
Storage temperature:	–40°C to 67°C
Battery:	2 x 1.5V AA cells
Battery life:	>80h at 20°C

Pilkington Kite Night-Vision Systems

The Pilkington Kite Observation Sight, or KOS, and MAXIKOS or MaxiKite Observation Sight, are the observation variants of the British Army Kite IWS (Individual

Weapon Sight) and MaxiKite Crew-Served Weapon Sight. Having no need to be mounted on a weapon, or used for aiming, the relevant mounting system and aiming marks are omitted, but the working parts and silhouette are identical.

KOS provides x4 magnification and an 8.5° field of view, weighing only 1kg. MAXIKOS is slightly heavier, at 1.3kg, and gives a magnification of x6, with a 5.5° field of view.

Both Kite systems are available in binocular variants, as BinoKite and MaxiBinoKite. These offer similar performance to the monocular Kite and MaxiKite, but are more comfortable to use for prolonged periods of surveillance. All the Kite observation variants can be hand-held or tripod-mounted, and are powered by standard 1.5v AA batteries.

Specifications – Pilkington Kite family

	Kite	MaxiKite	BinoKite	BinoMaxiKite
Magnification	x4	x6	x4.5	x6.7
Field of view	8.5°	5.5°	8.8°	5.2°
Weight	1kg	1.3kg	1.1kg	1.5kg
Power supply	2x 1.5v AA	2x 1.5v AA	2x 1.5v AA	2x 1.5v AA

THERMAL IMAGING

Thermal Imaging technology was readily adopted by the military in general, and Special Forces in particular, as soon as it became available in the 1970s. It presents a picture that shows the different heat patterns produced by men, machines and other objects, whether natural or man-made – making it possible to detect objects that cannot be seen with the naked eye, or even with an Image Intensifier. Since the picture is made up from radiation outside the visible light spectrum, it works equally well in light or dark conditions

Thermal Imaging allows operators to see through visual camouflage and smoke, so a person or vehicle screened by a net or vegetation shows up warm through the cover. Thermal Imaging is extremely useful in search and rescue operations, since operators can find survivors in dense cover or smoke-filled rooms. They can also locate small heat sources, such as a life-raft in the open sea, or a live body in an expanse of snowy hillside. For Special Forces, Thermal Imaging has many applications, from locating enemy troops to watching the movements of a terrorist under surveillance.

Thermal Imaging was first used by the British Army operationally in the Falklands Conflict in 1982, where the heat 'signature' of sheep roaming across the moorland caused some confusion for operators! Improvements to the technology, and operational experience, make it easier nowadays to identify and classify a heat source. Thermal Imaging can be used by day as well as by night, without special filters. As with Image Intensification, Thermal Imaging equipment has become much smaller than the early, cumbersome systems; modern equipment is no more bulky than a video camcorder. It is also a great deal more effective than the early models: modern TI equipment can detect a difference of less than half a degree Centigrade at several hundred yards, making it possible, for example, to see a vehicle's track by the tyres' slight warming effect on concrete or tarmac some minutes after it has passed.

Thermal Imaging is enormously useful, but it does have its limitations. It does not perform well, for instance, in rain or sandstorms. The picture it produces at medium and short ranges has a clearly defined, recognisable shape, but at longer ranges the operator sees just a warm 'blob'. In the Gulf War of 1991, this contributed to some of the 'blue on blue' or friendly fire casualties.

TI equipment is generally bulkier and heavier than image intensification kit, which has somewhat restricted its use. There are, however, much lighter and more compact systems being produced, which will make TI a great deal more versatile and open up new possibilities for its use by Special Forces.

Thermal Imaging was literally a life-saver during conflicts such as the 1991 Gulf War and, more recently, in Afghanistan. With no ambient light on a cloudy night in the desert, Image Intensification equipment is useless. Only HHTI (hand-held thermal imaging) equipment allowed soldiers to locate enemy positions in conditions of total darkness.

Thales Optronics

Thales Optronics Ltd (previously Thomson-TRT) is the UK-based optronics division of Thales, one of the world's largest electronics groups. The company has been at the

Laser-guided 'smart' bombs have revolutionised warfare, making it possible to target facilities such as this one in Iraq, while keeping civilian casualties and collateral damage to a minimum. Photo: US DoD.

forefront of thermal imaging since the early 1970s. Working closely with the UK Ministry of Defence, they have developed a unique capability in the design, development and manufacture of optical and electro-optical sensors for a wide range of applications including navigation, situational awareness, surveillance, target acquisition and infra-red search and tracking.

Thales Optronics is a leading supplier of electro-optical systems and equipment to the UK MoD, including thermal-imaging telescopes and lenses, sensor image enhancement systems, the Battle Group Thermal Imaging system (chosen for the Warrior and CVR(T) vehicles) and STAIRS C thermal-imaging modules.

TARGET DESIGNATION

Modern 'smart' bombs such as Paveway II and III have revolutionised warfare. Until the advent of 'smart' bombs, bombing was an imprecise business. In order to destroy a target such as a missile base or air defence radar station, it would have been necessary to drop dozens or even hundreds of bombs, requiring many aircraft flying multiple operations. If the target was in an urban area, or close to a non-target facility such as a hospital, then civilian casualties were almost inevitable.

Today's technology makes it possible to deliver a warhead with pinpoint accuracy against a target – even to the point of flying a bomb in through the doorway or ventilation shaft of a hardened shelter – using a laser target designator to mark the target and guide the bomb. A powerful laser beam is directed at the target, and the bomb

Smart bombs such as the Paveway series are delivered by modern bombers such as this B2 Spirit, which uses 'stealth' technology to reduce the risk of detection. Photo: USAF.

'rides' the reflected beam down onto the target. This has many advantages over the conventional 'dumb' or 'iron' bombs dropped from aircraft and left to fall unguided. Laser Guided Bombs (LGBs) reduce the risk of collateral damage, and enable the attacking force to do considerably greater damage to enemy resources.

The crucial point, however, is that the target must be illuminated accurately with a laser beam to guide the bomb. The laser may be carried on an aircraft, or it may be deployed on the ground, often by Special Forces operating behind enemy lines to locate targets and 'designate' them for attacking aircraft. This can be particularly valuable when the enemy are using sophisticated camouflage and concealment techniques to hide resources such as mobile missile launchers: Special Forces on the ground can do a CTR (Close Target Reconnaissance) to ensure that a target is genuine and not a dummy, then call up an airstrike and 'illuminate' the target with a laser so that aircraft can target it accurately even though it may be well hidden from view.

Thales LF25 and LF28 Laser Target Designators

For some time British forces have used the Thales LF25 Laser Target Designator, which weighs only 8kg and can therefore be carried by a single soldier, either in its transit case or in a bergen. For use, it is set up on a small folding tripod, and there is a built-in x10 telescope through which the soldier aligns the laser beam. There is also an interface for an image intensifier or thermal-imaging sight, allowing the unit to be used in virtually any conditions, day or night.

The unit is powered by a snap-on battery pack containing either a Lithium battery or a NiCad rechargeable battery. Output is >80mJ, and the beam divergence is <0.25mrad. It has a 3º field of view, and can designate a target up to 10km away.

The LF25 uses solid state electronics, with no need for liquid cooling, and requires no 'warm-up'. It has proved highly reliable in field conditions, with very little maintenance required – usually simply cleaning the objective and eyepiece with a soft cloth.

The latest version of this is the LF28 Laser Designator, produced by Thales Optronics. Like earlier models, the LF28 is suitable for man-portable, vehicle-mounted and airborne applications. It uses Thales's slab laser technology, which offers fast switch-on and allows the removal of the liquid coolant loops found in other laser designators. As a result reliability is increased and maintenance costs are reduced. A modern microprocessor-based control system ensures that the product is flexible and reconfigurable.

Litton GLTD II

The GLTD II is a compact, lightweight, portable laser target designator and rangefinder. The GLTD II is capable of exporting range data via an RS422 link and importing azimuth and elevation. Developed to enable combat soldiers to direct laser-guided smart weapons, such as Paveway bombs, Hellfire missiles and Copperhead munitions, the GLTD II can be implemented as part of a sophisticated, digitised fire control system with thermal or image-intensified sights. Versions of the GLTD II are currently in use by various NATO countries and other armed forces around the world.

Features

Ranges to 20km

Designates to 5km (typical; greater distances can be achieved)

Lightweight: <12.6lbs (5.7kg)

Readily integrated with other day/night observation systems

Range, azimuth, elevation and BIT displays

RS-422 compatible, full duplex

Outputs range

Inputs azimuth and elevation bearings, fire command

Laser boresighting by soldier

Specifications

Laser type:	Nd:YAG
Wavelength:	1.064 micrometres
Pulse energy:	> 80 Millijoules
Pulse repetition frequency:	NATO Stanag Band I/Band II or Programmable.
Weight:	<5.7 kg (12.6 lbs)
Size:	29(l) x 34(w) x 14(h) cm
Operating temperature:	–32°C to 45°C
Storage temparature:	–40°C to 71°C
Operating conditions:	Tested to MIL-STD-810 criteria for vibration, shock, humidity, rain, sand/dust, salt/fog, immersion
Magnification:	x10 (nominal)
Field of view:	Horizontal: 5 degrees (nominal)
Vertical:	4.4 degrees (nominal)
Reticle:	0.2 mrad open cross
Diopter adjustments:	+2 to –6
Exit pupil:	5mm diameter (nominal)
Eye relief:	15 mm (nominal)
Duty cycle:	Continuous operation under most conditions
Ranging:	200 to 19,995m (+/-5 nominal)
Battery power:	Rechargeable NiCad
Vehicle power:	28 volt DC (MIL-STD-1275)

LASER RANGEFINDERS

Special Forces will often need to identify the precise location of enemy troops, vehicles or installations, and transmit this information to a command centre. Laser

Modern GPS and laser rangefinding equipment makes it possible to direct artillery fire with much greater precision. This is one of the British Army's 105mm guns. Photo: © James Marchington.

rangefinding equipment has revolutionised this area of Special Forces work, enabling a soldier to measure the distance to a target with an accuracy of a few metres. He can also measure the compass bearing (azimuth) and angle of elevation from his own position to the target, and – since he knows his own position accurately via GPS – can then provide a very accurate fix on the target which may be used to direct an air strike, call for artillery fire support, etc.

Modern technology has taken this a stage further, with Laser Rangefinding equipment which also measures azimuth and elevation, and interfaces with a military GPS receiver to provide a simple lat-long-alt fix on the target.

Rockwell Viper (Leica Vector)

The Leica Vector Rangefinder Binoculars (known as Viper in the United States) illustrate the potential of today's technology. Weighing 1.7kg, this commercial off-the-shelf instrument features brilliant binocular viewing optics combined with rangefinder, compass and inclinometer functions. It is a Class 1 laser product (eye-safe in accordance with EN 60825-1). A commercial 6v lithium battery is sufficient for 3,000 measurements, which are displayed in the field of view and can be output through the

RS232 interface. On-board processing allows the observer to display further information such as: horizontal distance, height difference and angles – either between his position and a target, or between two remote objects. With its ergonomic, rubber-armoured body, the Vector is a hand-held 'total survey station'. Typical users include scouts, snipers and engineers.

To measure distances greater than 2km, a stable support is required. This is provided by the amagnetic Leica SST3-1 Mini-tripod or the Leica SG12 Digital Goniometer. These combinations are typical for mortar fire controllers and forward observers. MFC and FO generally need target coordinates in UTM grid, rather than range, azimuth, elevation. This transformation is easily computed by the targeting module of the Rockwell Collins PLGR+ GPS receiver, and corresponding software in the Leica Vector.

Leica PLRF Pocket Laser Rangefinder

Leica also produce a 'pocket-sized' Laser Rangefinder (PLRF) which, in spite of its miniature size, will measure distances from 5m to 2,500m to an accuracy of plus and minus 2m.

The Leica Vector, also known as the Viper, combines a laser rangefinder, compass and inclinometer. It links to the PLGR GPS receiver, to give a precise fix on a target. It can be used handheld to measure distances up to around 2km. Beyond that range, it needs to be mounted on a tripod. Photos: USMC & Leica.

Features

Rubber cover	1/4 inch thread hole provided for
x6 magnification	tripod use
Electronic aiming mark	Adaption to night vision
LED range display	IAW MIL-STD 810
5,000+ measurements per	Weight 0.50 kg (1.1lbs)
battery	

Simrad LE7/LP7 and LP10 Laser Rangefinders

The lightweight Simrad LE7 Eye Safe Laser Rangefinder is a high-performance target ranging and observation system with a capability to measure ranges out to 10km. It is simple and fast to operate, can be hand-held or mounted on a support, and can range at night when combined with a Simrad image intensifier.

The LP7, which is still in-service with many armed forces, has now been improved upon to produce the Simrad LP10 Target Locator. This uses eye-safe laser technology, and has an integrated GPS, Digital Magnetic Compass, and a high resolution (VGA) display. The instrument is of modular design and offers a large number of

Right: The Leica PLRF is a handy, pocket-sized laser rangefinder which can nevertheless measure distances up to 2.5km with an accuracy of 2m. Photo: Leica.

Opposite page: The Simrad LP7 uses an eye-safe laser to measure distances of up to 10km with an accuracy of 5m. It has an integrated GPS and digital magnetic compass, and can be used with night vision equipment. Photo: Simrad.

possible configurations to meet customers' specific requirements. The LP10 also interfaces with peripheral equipment such as electronic angulation heads, north finding gyroscopes, external GPS, thermal imagers and image intensifiers. Options include dual magnification, a video camera and a diode laser target designator.

Features	Specifications	
Class 3a eye-safe laser	Magnification:	x7
Simple and fast to operate	Field of view:	7°
Day/night capability	Dimensions:	215 x 202 x 93mm
Immediate range readout		
Digital data output	Weight (incl batteries):	2.5kg
Adjustable minimum range	Resolution:	5m
Multiple target indication and readouts	Operating temperature:	–30°C to 55°C
Eyepiece display	Storage temperature:	–40°C to 70°C
NATO codification	Minimum range:	100m
Optional remote firing	Maximum range:	9,995m
Connector for external power source		

3 COMMUNICATIONS

For a Special Forces patrol in enemy territory, good communications can make the difference between life and death, as well as the success or failure of the mission. Photo: Thales.

Fast, effective, secure communications are vital to every Special Forces operation. Clearly the members of a patrol or assault team must communicate with one another during the operation, but the role of communications goes much further than this. Commanders and their political masters must be kept informed, and their decisions passed back to the men on the ground.

Throughout the chain, the communications systems employed need to be robust enough to overcome the practical problems of distance and difficult terrain (including urban environments which are notoriously troublesome for radio communication), and to resist attempts to intercept or jam the signals.

Modern communications systems are expected to handle much more than simple voice communication. The ability to send data, still images and video enables Special Forces to work much more effectively – for example, sending a picture of a terrorist's meeting with an unknown contact, or the precise location of an enemy missile launcher.

Special Forces operations may involve a range of different agencies, including the army, navy and air force, allied forces, and in the case of counter-terrorist operations, even the police, etc. It is a huge challenge to provide a communications system that enables all these different groups to work together effectively, and make the most of the capabilities of modern techniques.

The systems used should also enable Special Forces to remain covert. Obviously they should not allow an enemy or terrorist target to intercept and overhear the transmissions, and this can be achieved with sophisticated encryption. But also the enemy should not be able to detect the signals at all – encrypted or not. 'Traffic' information can tell an enemy a great deal about who is operating where, and modern DF (Direction Finding) equipment can quickly locate the precise source of a radio transmission. Secrecy is maintained by a combination of technology and SOPs (Standard Operating Procedures).

Modern military radios use 'frequency hopping', skipping rapidly and unpredictably from one frequency to another throughout a transmission. This, combined with the encryption of data, makes it extremely difficult for an enemy to detect that there is any transmission at all, never mind track its source. For still greater security, Special Forces patrols will exercise great caution when transmitting, keeping trans-

The display of a direction finding (DFing) set, which indicates the location of a transmitting radio. Special Forces radio operators take precautions to prevent transmissions betraying their location. Photo: Thales.

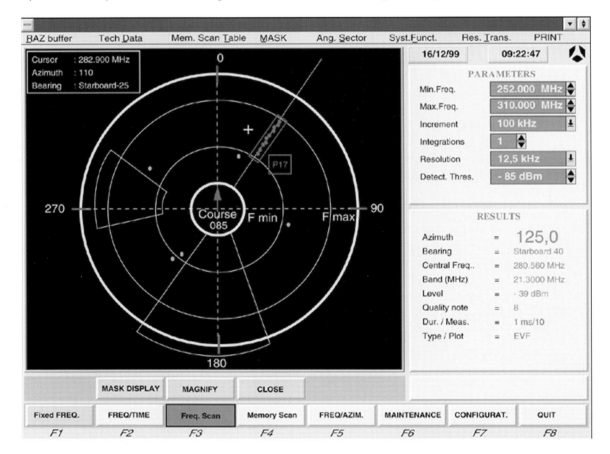

missions as short as possible and communicating only at prearranged times when enemy monitoring is likely to be least effective.

Special Forces use the full range of military communications systems, depending on the requirements of a particular operation. The military uses the full radio spectrum, from shortwave in the area of 2MHz through to microwave frequencies of 10GHz and even beyond, with battlefield communications generally in the HF, VHF and UHF frequencies. A huge range of equipment is available, including small handheld tactical sets, manpack radios and vehicle-mounted sets.

The equipment used by the British Army is typical of the radio equipment used by many forces worldwide. They currently use the somewhat outdated Clansman family of tactical radios, which comprises several different sets operating on HF, VHF and UHF frequencies (between 1.6MHz and 470MHz). This equipment came into general service around the time of the Falklands conflict in the 1980s. At the time it offered significant advantages, notably:

> The audio gear and battery charging equipment can be interchanged between radio sets. This simplifies spares support.
>
> Common operating controls and procedures. This reduces the training time for operators.
>
> Simple maintenance features, which reduce time spent in training and repairs.
>
> Interoperability between different radios.
>
> Several radios can be used in close proximity, even in the same vehicle, without interfering with each other.
>
> Capability of worldwide deployment in rugged conditions.

Among many of the soldiers who used the newly introduced Clansman equipment during the Falklands campaign in 1982, there was considerable enthusiasm. Gone were the problems of 'netting-in' and the constant sound of static in the operator's ears. The PRC-349 section radio was reliable and with its throat microphone enabled section commanders to communicate easily while handling a weapon, notebook or map. The PRC-351 manpack platoon radio was lighter, at 8.2kg, and more reliable than its predecessor. This led to platoon and company commanders carrying radios, which meant that command and control became faster and more reliable.

Clansman has several deficiencies, particularly its vulnerability to electronic attack. The problem of Electronic Counter Measures (ECM) was identified from experience in the Falklands and work in Project Targe in 1983. A number of improvements have been made to Clansman over the years, in particular the introduction of a Tactical Data Encryption System (TDES) known as Kipling. This has brought a major change in the way information is exchanged in the forward battle area – from voice to data transmission. There has also been widespread use of Clansman Secure Speech Harness (CSSH), which allows Clansman to operate in a secure mode.

Regardless of this, Clansman is not and never will be a twenty-first-century tactical radio system. Due to problems with implementing CSSH across the full range of

This truck is fitted with a rotating directional antenna and sophisticated direction finding equipment to locate the source of a radio transmission. Photo: Thales.

Clansman equipment, operators still have to use BATCO (a form of manual encryption by means of sheets issued at intervals) or TDES, which limits their operational effectiveness. It is significant that, during the 1991 Gulf War, when 7 and 4 Armoured Brigades started their short but intense drive across southern Iraq, they dispensed with BATCO since its use slowed operations and had the potential for confusion.

The Clansman system also does not use the electromagnetic spectrum effectively. There is considerable congestion in the VHF part of the spectrum, between 30MHz and 300MHz, used by Combat Net Radio. This is compounded by the limited frequency range of individual VHF sets. This in turn restricts flexibility in frequency management, especially in response to interception and jamming. Clansman has a limited capacity for transmitting and handling data and cannot support the future data distribution requirements of CIS on the battlefield.

Clansman equipment may be integrated with Ptarmigan, the British Army's mobile, secure battlefield communications system. Ptarmigan is computer-controlled and consists of a network of electronic exchanges or Trunk Switches that are connected by satellite and multichannel radio relay (TRIFFID) links, providing voice, data, telegraph and fax communications. Ptarmigan also offers mobile telephone or Single Channel Radio Access (SCRA), which gives isolated or mobile users an entry point into the system.

CLANSMAN EQUIPMENT

The following is not intended to provide a fully comprehensive listing of equipment used with the Clansman system, but to give an idea of the type of equipment used – and still in use with many armed forces worldwide.

TRA-967 VHF Manpack Transceiver

The TRA-967 was primarily designed as a manpack but can be used as a fixed or as a vehicle station. It uses VHF Narrow Band FM in the 36–76MHz frequency range with 25kHz channel spacing. A total of 1,600 synthesiser-controlled channels are available within this frequency selection. The radio includes a pretuned antenna-matching unit, and has a power output of over 1 Watt. Rotary controls allow rapid frequency changes. The frequency digits are lit by tritium beta lights, which require no power supply. The set includes rebroadcast facilities. It is waterproof and is powered by a 12v battery.

PRC-349 VHF Hand-held Transceiver

The PRC-349 is a hand-held VHF FM transceiver intended for platoon-level personal communications under combat conditions. The set is small enough to be carried in a belt holster or in the pocket of a combat jacket. Alternatively it can be worn in an adjustable quick-release holster slung from the shoulder, or worn on the back or chest. The set operates between 37 and 47Mhz, using 400 possible channels with a channel spacing of 25Khz. The PRC-349 features protection from an open or shorted antenna circuit, and an automatic battery-save function. It is powered by a rechargeable or dry battery pack supplying 12vDC. Dimensions: 244(h) x 90(w) x 50(d)mm. Weight 1.5kg.

PRC-344 UHF Manpack Transceiver

The PRC-344 is a lightweight UHF AM radio, used for ground-to-air links between combat troops and their supporting ground attack aircraft, and for control communications for emergency airfields and helicopter landing pads. It is a solid-state set operating between 225 and 400MHz, with channel spacing of 50kHz, giving 3,500 channels. The set can be operated remotely at up to 3km distance, using a 2-core wire. Rebroadcast and homing beacon modes are available. The set has a transmitter output of 2.5W, and offers an operational range of more than 160km. As a manpack the radio is operated from 24v rechargeable NiCad batteries or a hand generator.

VRC-353 VHF Vehicle Radio

When first introduced in the 1970s, the VRC-353 was the world's most versatile and advanced VHF FM vehicle radio system. Manufactured by Marconi Space and Defence Systems for the British armed forces, it has a frequency range of 30–75.975MHz, digitally synthesised, and is capable of handling voice and data. It offers 1,840 channels at 25KHz spacing, or 920 at 25KHz spacing. Output power can be selected on the front panel for 100 mW, 1W, 15W or 50W. The radio is operationally compatible with a range of other Clansman equipment, such as the PRC-77, VRC-12, SEM-25 and SEM-35. The operating voltage is 21.5–34vDC, and typical power consumption is 3A on receive and maximum 10A on transmit, at 24vDC. The set is built in a waterproof die-cast alloy case, and weighs 25kg.

BOWMAN

Having identified the problems with the Clansman system, and set out the requirements for a Future Combat Radio, the British MoD set up the Bowman project. Bowman was intended to provide a whole range of benefits accruing from the latest technology in radio communications, including the following features:

> Making effective use of a congested and hostile EMS (Electro Magnetic Spectrum).
> Incorporation of effective ECM techniques.
> Fully secure.
> Provision of flexible modes of communications (data and voice).
> Interoperability with allies' equipment.
> Capability of surviving in conventional and NBC environments.
> Flexibility, reliability, simplicity of operation, ease of maintenance.

The Bowman project was beset with problems, however, as costs spiralled and the original specification was overtaken by changing requirements and new technology. The project was put back out to tender, and eventually awarded to CDC (part of General Dynamics) in a £1.7bn deal – some nineteen years after the need for a new combat radio had originally been raised. Some 20,000 military vehicles will be equipped and 100,000 personnel will be trained on Bowman by October 2007.

Bowman will provide a secure digital voice and data communication system for the UK armed forces, and will be based on Internet protocol. It will include land-based command and control systems, and will provide the infrastructure to support all digitisation applications over the next thirty years. It will allow voice communications on secure radios over the air and through gateway interfaces to systems using agreed NATO, European and commercial standards and protocols.

Britain is not the only country to find that its military communications systems are lagging behind the needs of its users. During peacekeeping operations in Bosnia in 2002, US soldiers took to purchasing commercial FRS (Family Radio Service – the US equivalent of the European PMR446 service) units, such as the

Motorola Talkabout and Uniden Eco, for squad-level communications. These units were smaller, more powerful and more reliable than the issued equipment such as the AN/PRC-127, AN/PRC-119 and F3S, despite being originally designed for families to keep in touch when hiking or at the shopping mall. Similarly, British soldiers on exercise at Sennybridge or Salisbury Plain have discovered that their personal mobile phone provides an effective way to call up fire support when the combat net is busy – although this would not be an option in a real battle.

JOINT TACTICAL RADIO SYSTEM (JTRS)

Just as Britain has its Bowman programme, the US has an initiative, known as the Joint Tactical Radio System (JTRS), to acquire a family of affordable, high-capacity tactical radios. The cornerstone of JTRS is the development and deployment of Software Defined Radio (SDR) technology through a standardised, open software architecture. This means that radio hardware will be reprogrammable to take advantage of new developments in encryption and security systems.

JTRS will integrate hand-held, manpack, vehicular, base station, maritime, airborne and fixed site radios, enabling them to exchange voice and data –

This graphic from Rockwell Collins shows how the Joint Tactical Radio System (JTRS) integrates a wide range of radio equipment to provide resilient, efficient battlefield communications. Photo: Rockwell Collins.

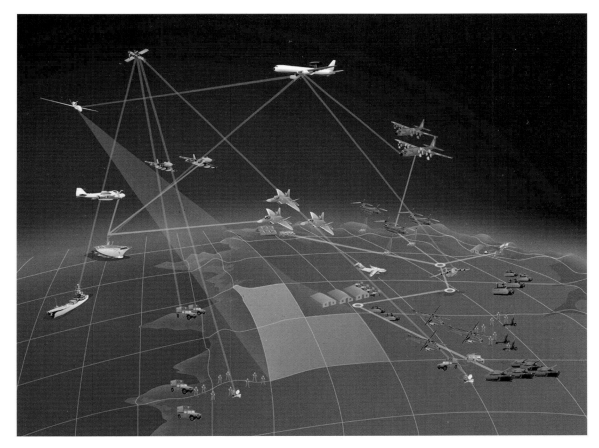

securely and reliably, despite a crowded electromagnetic spectrum and enemy attempts at jamming. The radios will interface with positioning and fire-control systems, improving the speed and efficiency with which forces can engage the enemy.

The following radio sets are given as examples of the type of modern military radio equipment which will form part of systems such as Bowman and JTRS, and which are currently in use with a number of Special Forces units – who generally get their hands on new radio communications kit well before it is widely issued to the country's armed forces.

Harris Falcon II: AN/PRC-117F Multi-band, Multi-mission radio

In November 2002, Harris Corporation of Rochester, New York State, announced that it had shipped the first Low Rate Initial Production (LRIP) high-frequency (HF) radio systems to General Dynamics for integration into the UK's Bowman Tactical Radio Programme. The sets in question were based on Harris's Falcon II HF tactical radio, which is already in use with US, NATO and other armed forces worldwide. They incorporate new hardware and software to address specific UK security and position-reporting system requirements. These product enhancements, and others, support the radio's integration into the fully networked Bowman system, as required by the UK MoD's operational requirements on its path to digitisation. Full production of the UK-manufactured units was expected to begin early 2003 and span a five-year period.

Harris had signed a contract valued at approximately $200 million with General Dynamics United Kingdom Limited, and prototype radio systems were shipped in April, June, and September 2002. Under the terms of the contract, Harris is responsible for providing approximately 10,000 HF radio systems to the UK armed forces.

The Harris Falcon II – also known as the AN/PRC-117F – is described as a multi-band, multi-mission radio. It integrates the capabilities of several distinct radios into one: VHF-FM for combat net radio; VHF-AM for public safety and ground-to-air; and UHF-AM for military ground-to-air and UHF TACSAT communications. With integrated crypto functions, including black-key management and a Crypto Ignition Key (CIK), the AN/PRC-117F(C) is a complete communication package allowing interoperability with all military services in secure and non-secure communication modes.

It can be configured as a manpack, vehicular set or base station. Continuous coverage from 30 to 512MHz fully utilises the frequency spectrum, providing secure ground-to-ground, ground-to-air and SATCOM capabilities. The AN/PRC-117F(C) is interoperable with existing encryption systems and acts as a translator between otherwise incompatible radios. For instance, SINCGARS to HaveQuick, SATCOM and SABER retransmission can be accomplished. The hardware can be reconfigured and software reprogrammed to optimise performance and add capabilities without opening the radio. The digital architecture of the AN/PRC-117F(C) ensures its upgradability into the future.

The AN/PRC-117F(C) has an extended frequency range covering 30–512MHz. This comprehensive coverage includes frequency bands and MIL-STD mandatory modulation modes for combat net radio operations, close air support, long-range patrol, government land mobile radio (LMR) and maritime uses. This makes the AN/PRC-117F(C) suitable for joint ground, sea and air operations.

VHF–FM low-band (30–88)MHz

The AN/PRC-117F(C) provides secure interoperability with SINCGARSICOM, and a host of other tactical radios. It will interoperate with other manufacturers' radios, as well as tactical data terminal equipment with data rates from 2,400 bps through 64 kbps. The detachable keypad/display unit provides on-the-body remote control, facilitating communications on the move. Built-in COMSEC eliminates the need for external tactical encryption equipment.

VHF/VHF–AM (116–150, 225–400MHz) AM, FM, FSK, ASK

Whether on the ground or in the air, the AN/PRC-117F(C) provides secure communications capabilities. In these frequency bands, secure voice and data operation is supported, using either AM or FM modes. HaveQuick I/II ECCM provides support for anti-jam operations. Used in conjunction with the secure black-side-retransmission capability, the AN/PRC-117F(C) enables a seamless interface between HaveQuick and SINCGARS networks when required. The embedded emergency distress beacon can be selected on any frequency, enhancing survivability.

UHF SATCOM (243–270MHz, 292–318MHz)

The AN/PRC-117F(C) provides full interoperability with UHF TACSAT terminals including Demand Assignment Multiple Access (DAMA) protocols, MIL-STD-188-181A, -188-182, and -188-183. Using state-of-the-art modem technology, the AN/PRC-117F(C) can send and receive secure satellite transmissions at data rates of up to 56 kbps. The set's embedded automatic repeat request (ARQ) system provides error-free delivery of data packets. This system offers significantly higher data throughput than legacy systems utilising external data controllers.

VHF/UHF (30–512MHz) FM, AM, FSK, ASK

The AN/PRC-117F(C) provides continuous coverage over the full 30–512MHz band. Multiband scan operations automatically select the appropriate antenna port to deliver the highest levels of performance in scan operations. Support for land-mobile squelch tones (CTCSS) makes the AN/PRC-117F(C) compatible with most repeater systems. Because of these capabilities, joint and civil-military-federal liaisons for both voice and data can be accomplished in one radio.

Secure retransmission operations

The AN/PRC-117F(C) can retransmit across bands – linking SINCGARS nets to Have-Quick nets, HaveQuick to SATCOM and even 12 kbps SABER hand-helds to SATCOM. The black-side-retransmission capability eliminates the need to decrypt and re-encrypt at the repeater site, enhancing performance and security.

Features

HaveQuick I/II ECCM

SINCGARS ICOM ECCM

DAMA MIL-STD-188-181A, -188-183, -188-182

Standard user interfaces – RS232, RS422, MIL-STD -188-114

High-speed SATCOM – up to 64 kbps

High-speed line-of-sight data – 64 kbps

Removable keypad with Crypto Ignition Key (CIK)

Full remote control capability

Longer battery life due to low voltage logic design

Multi-band scanning

100 channel presets

Radio-to-radio cloning

Manpack weight 10lbs. (w/o battery, antenna, handset)

Built-in GPS interface for navigation and time signals

Passes MIL-STD-810E environmental requirements

Software reprogrammable to accommodate evolving waveforms

KY57 VINSON, KG84, KY99/ANDVT COMSEC

Thales AN/PRC-148 Tactical Hand-Held Radio

The Thales AN/PRC-148 is a good example of a modern tactical hand-held radio (THHR). It has been selected by the US Marine Corps under their THHR programme. Weighing less than 2lbs, it is a powerful and capable radio that interfaces well with other radios in a system.

In August 2000, Racal received a $15.7 million order from the United States Special Operations Command (USSOCOM) for production of AN/PRC-148(V)(C) hand-held radios and accessories. This brought the total value of the contract to $32.5 million for the production of over 4,100 radios. The programme, named the Multiband Inter/Intra Team Radio (MBITR), was designed to outfit small teams of Special Operations Forces across all the services with a hand-held means of communicating within and between teams. The order follows the USSOCOM Program Office's receipt of approval to proceed to full production on the MBITR system. Referred to as Milestone III in the Department of Defense acquisitions process, this approval indicates that an item has met a stringent set of operational testing and evaluation requirements and is suitable for fielding and use by combat-ready forces.

The radio operates on frequencies between 30 and 512MHz, using AM or FM, with frequency steps of 5 and 6.25kHz. Output power is selectable between 100mW and 5W, and it can handle voice and data communications, with optional SINCGARS SIP, HaveQuick II, ANDVT, and Retransmit. The set has 100 pre-set memory channels, which can be user-programmed using the front panel, programmed via a PC computer link, or 'cloned' from one radio to another.

Controls include an On/Off/Volume/Whisper/Zeroize Knob, 16-position channel select knob, large tactile PTT (Push-To-Talk) switch, squelch override push-button, backlit 7 button keypad (NVG compatible) and two software configurable option keys. There is a 32 x 80 pixel backlit LCD display showing channel name/frequency, group name, clear/secure mode, key location, battery capacity and transmit power.

The radio offers a variety of standard connectors, allowing it to interface with other equipment such as GPS receivers, antennae, microphones, etc. It offers security to US COMSEC Type 1.

The PRC-119 is one of a new family of SINC-GARS (Single Channel Ground and Airborne Radio Systems) sets which can operate in jam-resistant, frequency-hopping mode. Photo: USMC.

Specifications

Length:	8.44ins (21.44cm)
Width:	2.63ins (6.68cm)
Depth:	1.52ins (3.86cm)
Weight:	30.6oz (867.5g)
Finish:	Matt black, non-reflective
Operating temperature:	−31° to 60° C
Immersion:	20m (AN/PRC-148(V)1(C) version)
Batteries:	Rechargeable Lithium-Ion 3,000 mAH
	>8 hours life at 5W*
	Commercial Lithium Cells
	10 hour life at 5W*
	*Standard duty cycle (8:1:1)
Accessories available:	Vehicle Adaptor
	Radio Holster
	Radio System Carrying Bag
	AC Powered Single Battery Charger
	AC/DC Powered 6-way Battery Charger
	Specialised Audio Accessories
	GPS, Cloning and Data Cables
	PC Programmer
	Special Power Adaptor Interface

Raytheon AN/PRC-119(V)1 SINCGARS radio

Single-Channel Ground and Airborne Radio Systems (SINC-GARS) is a family of VHF-FM radio sets designed to meet the US Army's tactical communications requirements under the new Army operations doctrine. SINCGARS is replacing the AN/PRC-77 and the AN/VRC-12 series radio sets. It is designed for simple, quick operation using a 16-element keypad for push-button tuning. SINCGARS is capable of short-range or long-range operation for voice, frequency shift-keying (FSK), or digital data communications. It may be used for single-channel operation or in a jam-resistant, frequency-hopping mode which can be changed as needed. SINCGARS has a built-in self test with visual and audio read back.

Specifications

Frequency range	30–88MHz	Number of channels:	2,320
Power input:	12v DC	Channel spacing:	25kHz
Power output:	5W	Replaces:	PRC-77

AN/PRC-113

The Raytheon AN/PRC-113(V) is a small, lightweight manpack radio designed to operate in today's military environment, where more radios are operating – closer to one another – in a more threatening environment. The set operates between 116 and 149.975MHz, offering 1,360 channels, and from 225 to 399.975MHz, with 7,000 channels, AM.

The PRC-113's reduced transmitter noise floor and greater receiver dynamic range provides improved communications when located near other radios. The radio is fully qualified to military specifications including Environment, EMI/EMC, TEMPEST, Nuclear Reliability, Maintainability and Human Factors. It is baseband COMSEC (communication security) compatible and is available with or without integral ECCM (Electronic Counter-Counter Measures).

Specifications

Transmit power:	2W/10W
Frequency range:	116.000 to 149.975 and 225.000 to 399.975MHz
Channel spacing:	25kHz
No. of channels:	8,360 (includes 8 Preset and 1 Guard Channel)
Modulation type:	Amplitude Modulation (AM)
Primary power:	24.0v DC (two BB-590 or BA-5590 batteries)
Channel changing time:	7.5 ms
Warm-up time:	10 seconds maximum
Security features:	COMSEC Compatible Baseband Mode
	ECCM Compatible
Power output:	2W or 10W – operator selectable
Frequency accuracy:	±400Hz maximum
Size:	10.4" W x 3.0" H x 12.0" D
	(26.4 cm W x 7.6cm H x 30.5 cm D)
Weight:	With two BB-590s: 18.5 lbs. (8.4 kg)
With two BA-5590s:	15.0 lbs. (6.8 kg)

Raytheon AN/PSC-5D Multi-band, Multi-mission Communication Terminal

The AN/PSC-5D is a multi-band, multi-mission communication terminal with capabilities for UHF/VHF Manpack LOS (Line-of-Sight) and SATCOM/DAMA (Satellite Communications/ Demand Assigned Multiple Access). It supports the Department of Defense requirement for a lightweight, secure, network-capable, multi-band/ multi-mission, anti-jam, voice/imagery/data communications capability in a single package. With all these features, it reduces the operator's burden, while increasing his communications capability. Although this system was originally created as a manpack, its versatile design means that it can be used in other applications such as airborne, vehicular, shipboard and fixed station. The PSC-5D provides all the capabilities of the successfully fielded AN/PSC-5 Spitfire terminal, plus additional capabilities for HaveQuick I and II and SINCGARS anti-jam, receive and transmit over-the-air-rekeying (OTAR). It offers 30–512MHz frequency coverage, high-data-rate in LOS and SATCOM communications and embedded Advanced Data Controller. Options include embedded Tactical Internet and MELP (Mixed Excitation Linear Predictive) Vocoder and SINCGARS SIP AND ESIP.

Specifications	
Frequency range:	30–512MHz
Channel spacing:	5, 6.25, 8.33, 12.5, 25kHz (VHF, UHF, LOS and SATCOM)
Modes of operation:	LOS : AM, FM, FSK, CPM (CPM data rate up to 76.8kbps) Non-DAMA: MIL-STD-188-181B Narrowband (1.2kbps – 9.6kbps) Wideband (1200bps – 56kbps) 5kHz DAMA: MIL-STD-188-182A (75bps – 2.4kbps) 25kHz DAMA:MIL-STD-188-183 AC and DC Modes (75bps – 16kbps)
Programmable presets:	142 for LOS, SATCOM, DAMA and Beacon Operations
ECCM modes:	SINCGARS and SINCGARS SIP (VI) Have Quick I and II
Size (radio and battery case):	3.3" x 10.6" x 13" (H x W x D)
Weight:	11.5lbs. less batteries
Two BB-390A/U batteries:	6.5lbs
Two BA-5590/U batteries:	4.5lbs
Power output (max):	LOS AM (80% modulation) 10 Watts LOS FM 10 Watts (up to 20W selectable in safety override mode) SATCOM 225–400MHz, 20 Watts ±2 dB SATCOM 290–320MHz, 20 Watts min Adjustable Power 1 dB steps down to 0.2 Watts any mode

Rockwell AN/PSC-11 SCAMP

Rockwell's Single Channel Anti-Jam Manportable (SCAMP) is also known as the AN/PSC-11. This terminal uses the Milstar satellite system to provide worldwide secure, jam-resistant, covert voice, data and imagery communications. The radio will support up to four simultaneous Vocoded Voice (VV) channels on the Narrow Spot Beam (NSB), up to two simultaneous VV on Wide Spot Beam (WSB), and up to four simultaneous 75-b/s TTY channels on the Agile Beam (AB). With clear conditions, it will support 4 VV channels on both Spot Beams and the AB or 4 TTY channels on the Earth Coverage (EC) antenna.

Features

EMP protected	Requires user-provided PLGR
½-mile remoting capability	Battery operated
Single operator, easy to use	Self-contained in single transit case
<10-minute setup	

Specifications

Uplink frequency:	44.0Ghz
Uplink bandwidth:	2.0Ghz
Downlink frequency:	20.0Ghz
Downlink bandwidth:	1.0Ghz
Data rates:	75–2,400bps
Voice (ANDVT compatible):	2,400bps
Size (case):	25 x 13.5 x 11ins
Weight:	<44lbs (self-contained terminal with case)
	<34lbs (packed accessories case)
Wind:	20mph winds with 30mph gusts
Rain:	Will survive 2ins/hour rain
Temperature:	Operate –32° to +49°C
Power:	Internal battery, 24 volts DC
	External DC, 20–33v
	External AC110/220v

SATELLITE COMMUNICATIONS

Satellite Communications (SATCOM) systems make it possible to exchange voice and data, securely, to and from nearly anywhere in the world. Operations in the Falklands and Namibia proved the value of satellite communications, and during the 1991 Gulf War and in Afghanistan there was extensive use of SATCOM ground terminals. Now that manufacturers have produced truly manpackable SATCOM terminals, satellite communications are a realistic option – and a very useful one – for remote Special Forces patrols, OPs and the like.

Milstar

Milstar is a joint service satellite communications system that provides secure, jam-resistant, worldwide communications for the military. The multi-satellite constellation links commanders with ships, submarines, aircraft and ground stations. The operational Milstar satellite constellation consists of four satellites positioned around the

Above: Skynet is just one of several military communications satellite systems in orbit around the earth, providing fast, secure communications for Special Forces patrols in remote locations. Photo: BAe.

Right: Even relatively small, man-packable sets can make use of the military satellite communications systems. The AN/PSC-3 set shown here weighs around 16 lb. Photo: US DoD.

Earth in geosynchronous orbits. The first Milstar satellite was launched on 7 February 1994 aboard a Titan IV rocket. Each satellite weighs approximately 10,000lbs (4,536kg) and has a design life of ten years.

Each Milstar satellite serves as a smart switchboard in space by directing traffic from terminal to terminal anywhere on the Earth. Since the satellite actually processes the communications signal and can link with other Milstar satellites through crosslinks, the requirement for ground-controlled switching is significantly reduced.

The Milstar system is composed of three segments: space (the satellites), terminal (the users) and mission control. Responsibility for control and operation of the satellites is split between the US Air Force Space Command's Space and Missile Systems Center at Los Angeles

Air Force Base, the Electronics Systems Center at Hanscom AFB, Massachusetts, and the 4th Space Operations Squadron at Schriever AFB, Colorado.

Specifications	
Power plant:	Solar panels generating 8,000W
Weight:	About 10,000lbs (4,536kg)
Orbit altitude:	22,250 nautical miles (inclined geostationary orbit)
Launch vehicle:	Titan IVB/Centaur upper stage
Unit cost:	$800 million

DSCS III

Air Force Space Command operates ten Phase III Defense Satellite Communications Systems (DSCS) satellites that orbit the Earth at an altitude of more than 22,000 miles. Each satellite uses six super-high frequency transponder channels capable of providing secure voice and high rate data communications. DSCS III also carries a single-channel transponder for disseminating emergency action and force direction messages to nuclear-capable forces.

The system is used for high priority command and control communication such as the exchange of wartime information between defence officials and battlefield commanders. The military also uses DSCS to transmit space operations and early warning data to various systems and users.

The Air Force began launching the DSCS IIIs in 1982. The system is built with single, multiple-beam antennas that provide more flexible coverage than its predecessor. The single steerable dish antenna provides an increased power spot beam which can be tailored to suit the needs of different-sized user terminals. DSCS III satellites can resist jamming and are expected to operate twice as long as the previous generation.

DSCS users operate on the ground, at sea or in the air. Members of the 50th Space Wing's 3rd Space Operations Squadron at Schriever Air Force Base, Colorado, provide satellite bus command and control for all DSCS satellites. Air Force Materiel Command's Space and Missile Systems Center at Los Angeles AFB, California, is responsible for development and acquisition of DSCS satellites and ground systems.

Specifications	
Weight:	2,716lbs (1,232kg)
Power plant:	Solar arrays generating average of 1,500W
Orbit altitude:	22,230 miles (35,887 km)
Dimensions:	Rectangular body is 6 feet long (1.8 metres), 6 feet high (1.8 metres), and 7 feet wide (2.1 metres); 38-foot span (11.5 metres) with solar arrays deployed
Launch vehicle:	Atlas II, later the evolved expendable launch vehicle
Unit cost:	$200 million
Inventory:	4

Covert and special purpose radio accessories

In addition to the general need for communications between fixed and mobile units, command posts, etc., Special Forces operations often require various types of special equipment. Surveillance operations sometimes require operatives to work undercover – maintaining communications with other team members while appearing to be going about their ordinary daily business unencumbered by radio equipment. Assault teams in hostage rescue and similar operations have their own, very specific requirements. Special equipment has been developed for these uses, and is constantly being refined in response to the needs of CRW and SWAT teams.

Davies CT400 communications system

Davies Industrial Communications Ltd was established in 1972 for the design and manufacture of communications equipment. In the late 1980s Davies successfully completed development and trials for a new generation of Special Forces ancillaries known as the CT100 System. Today, Davies is recognised as the world's primary supplier of Special Forces audio ancillaries with their latest range, the CT400 System. CT400 was developed to enhance the quality of communication within Special Forces teams by offering individual users a large range of options to specifically meet their requirements.

Davies Waterproof Special Forces Communications Systems

Davies produces a number of diverse waterproof communications systems that are currently in service with SF teams throughout the world. These systems allow the submersion of most two-way radios to 25 feet (8 metres), whether they were originally manufactured to be waterproof or not. They are particularly suited to waterborne Special Forces operations, and harsh environments such as jungle.

Davies FAST Communications Harness

An important part of the CT400 system is the communications harness, which attaches to the user's body and links the various parts needed to operate the radio while engaged in an operation. The Davies FAST range of Communications Harnesses all incorporate:

- A junction box
- A PTT switch
- A microphone
- An earphone

Some of the FAST systems are designed to be used in conjunction with a respirator, and incorporate a Respirator Microphone Adaptor. This fits onto the external speech port of a respirator such as the SF10, and does not compromise the integrity of the respirator.

FAST Systems that incorporate a Wired Earphone can be used with a wide range of accessories including Ear Hangers, Acoustic Tubes and Electronic Ear Defenders.

Davies Tacmic CT

The TACMIC CT is a Speaker Microphone and Communications Harness in one. There are five models within the TACMIC CT range, each of which features a speaker, microphone, side-mounted heavy duty PTT switch, 3.5mm earphone socket, remote PTT socket and ancillaries socket.

The ancillaries socket allows the connection of a large range of communications headsets, inductors or other types of microphone such as a throat microphone or body microphone.

Certain TACMIC CT models are fitted with an internal inductor for use during covert applications and/or sequential tone signalling. This allows the user to repeatedly press the PTT switch and transmit tone signals instead of speech. The number of presses will translate to a predefined team code.

Davies LASH

The Davies LASH is a throat microphone and earphone in one, and is widely used in the USA. A non-occluding acoustic tube/earmould is fitted to the earphone to direct all received sounds to the user's ear.

Davies Covert Systems

Davies's range of body-worn covert communications equipment uses the latest microcomputer technology to offer advanced features and extend operational capability. Certain systems are fitted with sequential tone signalling. The Covert 500 range comprises four systems, each of which incorporates the following:

- A junction box with built-in tone board (three out of four systems feature sequential tone signalling)
- A PTT/sequential tone signalling switch (where applicable)
- A micro-loop inductive loop with internal microphone or a Collarset I inductive coil with built-in microphone
- An inductive earpiece

Phonak Communications Phonito

Davies Industrial Communications Ltd distributes Phonito, manufactured by Phonak Communications AG. Phonito is a wireless earpiece that fits comfortably and discreetly in the ear and incorporates a volume control, loudness limiting circuit (to protect the user from high sound levels) and a squelch circuit, which silences the receiver totally when there are no speech signals present.

Phonito has been designed to have very low battery consumption. An average battery lifetime is 100 hours and an end-of-life battery circuit produces a warning signal to inform the user when the battery needs changing.

Phonak Communications microEAR

Phonak also produce the microEar, claimed to be the smallest radio receiver in the world. MicroEar is supplied pretuned to the user's selected frequency (VHF narrow

A covert radio rig, here worn over the clothing for purposes of illustration. In use, the equipment would be totally concealed. Photo: Thales.

band FM between 138 and 240MHz). It has a battery life of fifteen to thirty hours, volume control, background noise filter and automatic frequency control, and offers good reception within distances up to a mile, depending on transmitter and radio conditions.

Thales Acoustics RA500 covert audio accessories

Thales Acoustics produce a range of covert radio accessories for use in surveillance work and the like. The system is based around the RA502 Inductive Earpiece, a wireless earphone that receives radio signals from a combined induction coil and microphone that is installed under the user's collar or shirt. The third part of the system is a PTT switch which is held in the user's hand, typically with the cable hidden in the sleeve. The induction coil/microphone and PTT switch are connected to the radio transceiver via a connector block.

The system is designed to connect to most available transceivers. The transceiver itself is worn concealed in a holster under the clothing. The system allows an operator to appear unencumbered with radio equipment, yet remain in constant communication with other team members. If he (or she) cannot talk into the microphone without compromise, pressing the PTT switch a prearranged number of times will make it possible to communicate in a simple code of 'one press means yes, two means no' etc.

Elbit SC3 Sniper Control System

The Elbit SC3 Sniper Control System is designed for situations where a number of snipers are deployed to cover an incident – typically this might be a hostage scenario, where a group of terrorists is holding hostages in a building, train, bus or aircraft.

The system has a camera on each sniper's telescopic sight, which relays the sight pictures to a central point, using either a fixed cable or radio link. The camera fits onto the telescopic sight in thirty seconds, with no effect on the rifle's zero. The camera is connected to an image processor/transmitter contained in a ruggedised box, which will transmit the image in real time for a distance of up to 5km in open country, or about 850m in built-up areas.

The sight pictures are displayed on 4in monitors at the control point, together with a 'ready' indication operated by each sniper. This provides the commander with a constantly up-to-date picture of the situation, and the ability to coordinate the fire of a sniper group in a way that would be impossible with the alternative method of radio checks with each sniper in turn.

Command post

Displays:	4" CRT with brightness and contrast controls
Electrical supply:	12/24v DC, or from mains power with adaptor.

Sniper modules (SP-10)

Weight:	400g
Dimensions:	100 x 55 x 45mm
Transmitted power:	8W
Carrier frequency:	800–950MHz FM
Power supply:	Lithium batteries, life approx 8 hours continuous

---

4 SPECIAL FORCES VEHICLES

Mobility is a vital ingredient of Special Forces warfare, and Special Forces are always quick to take advantage of the most suitable vehicles to get a job done. The British SAS, although conceived as an airborne force, made extensive use of US-made Jeeps in their attacks on enemy airfields in North Africa during the Second World War. Many of the classic early SAS images show Stirling, Mayne, Lewes and others in their Willys Overland Jeeps.

The Jeep proved an excellent choice for this type of operation: it was light, fast and reliable, with good range and cross-country ability, and could carry two or four men plus supplies and weapons. The vehicles were adapted for desert conditions, the modifications including a condenser fitted to the cooling system to conserve water. They were weighed down with jerry-cans, ammunition and other supplies for extended, long-range patrols into enemy territory for attacks on enemy bases and airfields. The Jeeps were typically fitted with twin Vickers 'K' guns mounted at the rear and one at the front, although some vehicles carried a .50 calibre heavy machine gun. There was little if any armouring on the vehicles, so as not to sacrifice speed and agility. Similar vehicles were airdropped into Europe during the latter stages of the war.

Since the 1950s, the SAS have favoured the long wheelbase Land Rover for desert operations. These became known affectionately as 'pinkies' due to the pink-coloured paint used to provide effective camouflage in the desert. These were operated by the

An early picture of an SAS patrol vehicle in North Africa – a modified Willys Jeep armed with twin Vickers 'K' machine guns. Photo: author's collection.

Above: The modern equivalent of the World War II SAS Jeep, a Land Rover Defender 110 stripped down and fitted with roll cage, stowage and weapons mounts. Photo: © James Marchington.

Left: SAS patrol Land Rovers are fitted with a variety of weapons – this one has a MAG 7.62mm machine gun and a .50 cal Browning. Photo: © James Marchington.

Above: A Royal Engineers Land Rover fitted out for operations and hidden from view beneath a camouflage net. Photo: © James Marchington.

Right: US forces in Afghanistan unloading an Intermediate FAV (Fast Attack Vehicle). These light, dune buggy-type vehicles have proved useful for short range operations, but are less suited to long range patrols. Photo: USMC.

Regiment's Mobility Troop and, like the World War Two Jeeps, were typically weighed down with vast quantities of supplies, weapons and ammunition to support extended operations away from base.

In the Gulf War of 1991, SAS Scud-hunting patrols used the latest model Land-Rover, the 110, powered by a 3.5 litre V8 petrol engine. The bodywork is stripped down to bonnet level, and mountings added for a variety of weapons – typically two GPMGs, or a GPMG plus a .50 calibre heavy machine gun, Milan ATGM, or Mk19 grenade launcher. The weapons mountings are incorporated into a roll cage that protects the crew if the vehicle should turn over. Extra stowage racks are fitted for the fuel, water, food, personal kit, weapons, ammunition, communications and other technical equipment carried by the patrol.

The typical crew consists of three – driver, commander and gunner – although on occasions this may be extended to four. Camouflage nets and poles are carried so that the vehicle can be quickly hidden; often the patrol will move at night, using night-vision goggles for driving and observation, and find a suitable spot to lay-up during the day.

During the Gulf War the SAS also experimented with the dune buggy type of vehicle – known as Light Strike Vehicles (LSVs) or Fast Attack Vehicles (FAVs). The Regiment found these unsuitable, however, for Long Range Patrols (LRPs). The Land Rovers, accompanied by a Unimog 'mother' vehicle, were able to operate for weeks at a time, carrying everything the patrol would need, and indeed were active in Iraq

Special Forces have found motorbikes useful in recent operations. A bike such as this Harley-Davidson can be used to recce ahead of a motorised column. Photo: USMC.

Quad bikes, such as this Kawasaki, can be useful as battlefield transport for snipers and the like, but lack the payload needed for patrols behind enemy lines. Photo: © James Marchington.

for the duration of the war with minimal resupply (with the notable exception of one resupply column driven deep into Iraqi territory, which features in Peter Ratcliffe's *Eye of the Storm*). LSVs may be faster and more agile, but they have nowhere near the carrying capacity of a Land Rover, and cannot carry the quantity of supplies needed for extended operations. However, these vehicles were used very successfully by US Special Forces during the liberation of Kuwait, where they were able to operate ahead of the main force, avoiding booby traps and driving around obstructions as they hunted down fleeing Iraqi troops.

Throughout recent history, Special Forces have used a wide selection of other vehicles as required for particular operations. SAS columns in Iraq, for instance, used motor-cycles for their speed and agility, to recce ahead of the main column as well as for communications within a column on the move. The Regiment has also used unmarked Range Rovers (to move CRW teams and their kit around the country), and sanitised civilian vehicles for anti-terrorist operations in Northern Ireland. Indeed, they will adopt and adapt whatever comes to hand when circumstances demand it: members of the ill-fated Bravo Two-Zero patrol on the run in Iraq nabbed a local taxi in their attempt to evade capture and reach the border.

Land Rover SOV

Land Rover vehicles are widely used by military forces worldwide. There are many of the older Series III long and short wheelbase models in service, as well as the more recent 90, 110 and 130 Defenders. These can be found in a wide range of configurations, including military ambulances, weapons platforms, logistics vehicles, command vehicles and many more. The Land Rover Discovery and Range Rover vehicles are also used in military roles. Land Rovers have proved tough, rugged, capable and easy to maintain. They are extremely versatile, and can be readily configured and adapted for different roles – the 'bolt together' construction means that, for instance, a hard top can be converted to a hard top, and weapons mounts added and reconfigured. Land Rovers may be deployed rapidly by land, sea or air, and offer outstanding cross-country mobility in a wide range of difficult conditions, from desert to jungle to arctic terrain as well as arable/woodland in more temperate regions such as Europe.

Based on the Land Rover Defender, the Land Rover SOV (Special Operations Vehicle) is the latest development of the SAS 'Pinkie'. Introduced in 1992, after the 1991 Gulf War, it is a versatile vehicle designed to carry troops across difficult terrain, and provide a highly mobile platform for a variety of weapons. It has a primary

This Land Rover has been adapted by Penman to increase its carrying capacity for extended long range Special Forces patrols – note the six-wheel configuration. Photo: © James Marchington.

weapon mount in the centre of the roll-cage, which can be used for an M60, M240, M2 .50 HMG or Mk19 grenade launcher. There is another weapon mount in front of the forward passenger seat. The SOV has on-board racks that can be configured to carry various types of ammunition and stores; it can also carry mortar ammunition, rockets or ATGMs on side-racks. There are side-bins which can carry land mines or explosive charges. The SOV may be carried inside aircraft such as the C-130 Hercules, CH-47 Chinook, or EH-101 helicopter; it can also be slung under medium and heavy lift helicopters, or dropped by parachute.

The US Rangers have acquired sixty Land Rover SOVs, which they have dubbed the RSOV. They use the vehicle not as an assault vehicle, but to deploy units quickly as needed on the fast-moving battlefield. The RSOV is based on the 110 Land Rover chassis, and is powered by a four-cylinder TDi turbo diesel engine. The Rangers use the RSOV in three main roles: as a weapons carrier, a medical vehicle or a communications vehicle. As a weapons carrier it can carry up to 8,000lbs and six fully armed Rangers.

Specifications – Land Rover Defender 110	
Gross vehicle weight:	3,050kg (standard)
	3,500kg (heavy duty)
Payload:	1,570kg
Width:	1,790mm (70.5ins)
Height:	1,993mm (78.5ins)
Length:	4,599mm (181.0ins)
Wheelbase:	2,794mm (110.0ins)
Track:	1,486mm (58.5ins)
Engine:	4-cylinder 2.5 litre turbo diesel 83kW (111bhp) @ 4,000rpm (5-cylinder 2.5 litre injected turbo diesel also available)
Fuel tank:	75 litres (16.5 gal) standard tank
Fuel economy:	22.7 mpg (12.4 l/100km) urban
	32.4 mpg (8.7 l/100km) extra-urban
Towing:	Unbraked trailer 750kg
	Trailer with over-run brakes 3,500kg
	Trailer with coupled brakes 4,000kg
Clearance:	215mm (8.5ins)
Max. gradient:	45°
Approach angle:	50°
Departure angle:	34° 30'
Traverse:	30°
Wading depth:	600mm (23.6ins) without special preparation
Turning circle:	6.4m (21ft)
Electrical system:	Various options including 12 and 24v military standard systems

Opposite page, top: This Special Forces Land Rover is fitted with an FN MAG 7.62mm machine gun fired from the front passenger seat. Photo: © James Marchington.

Opposite page, bottom: The Special Forces Land Rover is a highly versatile and agile vehicle which can carry a patrol and its supplies over difficult terrain and provides a mobile platform for a variety of weapons. Photo: Land Rover.

Unimog

During SAS operations in Iraq during the 1991 Gulf War, each fighting column of 8 to 12 Land Rovers was accompanied by a Mercedes Unimog truck as the 'mother' vehicle. The Unimog carried the bulk of the column's supplies, fuel, ammunition, NBC equipment, and spares, enabling the columns to stay inside Iraq for the full duration of the war. In *Eye of the Storm*, SAS RSM Peter Ratcliffe describes how a column of Bedford 4-tonner trucks drove from Saudi Arabia to Wadi Tubal in Western Iraq in February 1991 to resupply the Regiment's mobile patrols. With typical panache, the SAS promptly held a sergeants' mess meeting deep behind enemy lines.

The Unimog has a long and distinguished military history. First produced in 1951, it was a simple and practical design, a 3½ metre long 4x4 vehicle with a folding cab. The name 'Unimog' comes from 'Universal-Motor-Gerät' (universal power unit). Over the following years the Unimog was developed and improved, and in 1955 Daimler-Benz produced the first Unimog S (404 series). It featured a long wheelbase and was

First developed in 1951, the Unimog has a long and distinguished military history. Unimogs acted as 'mother' vehicles to the SAS columns in Iraq in the 1991 Gulf War. Photo: Unimog.

designed for military applications. The 'S' continued to be produced for a quarter of a century until 1980, and was used by the French Army and others in addition to the German armed forces who became the major buyer of this version.

The US Army issued a major contract to supply 2,400 U 406 Unimogs to the US Army for use as engineer vehicles in 1986. The latest version of the Unimog is the U 500, which is now marketed in North America and Europe as the basis of specialist vehicles for jobs such as fire-fighting, snow-clearing and verge-mowing as well as military vehicles. The Unimog's chassis, power unit and running gear are highly regarded for their off-road performance and reliability, and are chosen as the basis of several APCs, such as the Panhard and Scarab described later in this chapter.

The Unimog is renowned for off-road performance and reliability, and is used in a variety of roles by the military. The running gear is used in several APCs. Photo: Unimog.

AM General HMMVW (Humvee)

AM General manufactures the High Mobility Multipurpose Wheeled Vehicle HMMWV, pronounced 'Humvee'. Since production of Humvees began in 1985, the company has delivered more than 160,000 of this versatile 4x4 vehicle to the US armed forces and more than thirty other nations. The Humvee is a 1¼ ton vehicle that is fast, agile and highly mobile, and has proved invaluable in a wide range of armed forces deployments, including recent operations in Afghanistan and Iraq. It has permanent four-wheel drive, independent suspension, 16ins of ground clearance and unusually steep approach and departure angles. The Humvee is currently in use with the US Army, Marine Corps, Air Force and Navy as well as various other armed forces around the world.

The Humvee is a multi-purpose platform that can mount a wide range of weapons, including 7.62mm and .50cal machine guns, and the Mk19 40mm grenade launcher. The weapons carrier variant can mount the TOW anti-tank missile system.

The HMMWV or 'Humvee' was widely used by US forces in Afghanistan and Iraq. It provides a fast, agile platform for a variety of weapons, including TOW anti-tank missiles or anti-aircraft SAMs. Photo: author's collection.

The Humvee can be rapidly deployed by land, sea or air. Three Humvees can be carried in the C-130 Hercules, six in the C-141B Starlifter and 15 in the C-5A Galaxy. Under combat conditions, it can be delivered by the Low Altitude Parachute Extraction System without the aircraft having to land. In tactical operations, two Humvees can be slung from a CH-47 Chinook or a CH-53 helicopter, or one from a UH-60A Blackhawk.

The recent A2 series block modification package saw the introduction of a new 6.5 litre naturally aspirated diesel engine with an improved rating of 160hp. The new engine was coupled with an electronically controlled four-speed automatic transmission and a new exhaust emission system with catalytic converter. The A2 vehicles are also capable of accepting a Central Tire Inflation System (CTIS).

There are a number of Humvee variants, including fire-fighting vehicles, ambulances, communications and special operations vehicles. An up-armoured version, the M1025A2, provides protection against 7.62mm ball to the crew, engine and cargo areas, while still maintaining a payload of 2,200lbs. This vehicle can be uprated with underbody protection against anti-personnel and anti-tank mines, and has the option of air conditioning for the crew area.

The Humvee, seen here on operations in Afghanistan, has a 6.5 litre diesel engine and 25 gallon fuel tank. It can ascend a slope of 60% and ford water 30ins deep. Photo: US Army.

The front of this up-armoured Humvee was destroyed by a mine, but the occupants all survived. Photo: US Army.

Specifications – HMMWV

Gross vehicle weight:	4,672kg (M1097A2 Base Platform)
Payload:	1,996kg
Width:	2,180mm (86ins)
Height:	1,830mm (72ins)
Length:	4,840mm (190.5ins)
Wheelbase:	3,300mm (130ins)
Track:	1,820mm (71.6ins)
Engine:	V8 6.5 litre naturally aspirated diesel, 120 kw (160hp) @ 3,400rpm
Fuel tank:	94 litres (25 gal)
Clearance:	390mm (15.3ins)
Max gradient:	60%
Approach angle:	63°
Departure angle:	33°
Traverse:	40°
Wading depth:	760mm (30ins) without special preparation
Turning circle:	7.62m (25ft)

Hägglunds BvS10 ATV(P)

Hägglunds's Bv206D is firmly established and well proven with arctic warfare units of the British and other nations' armies; it is widely used by Britain's Royal Marines, for instance. Some 11,000 units have been delivered to forty countries. Designed to

The Hägglunds
BvS10 ATV.
Photo: Alvis.

transport personnel, support weapons and matériel across snow-enveloped country and uncleared, snow-covered roads, it is configured as two cars, each with a pair of driven tracks. The joint between the two cars enables the vehicle to be steered by articulation between the two. The vehicle measures 2.4m high, 6.9m long, 2m wide, and weighs 4.4 tons unladen or 6.7 tons laden. It has a range of 300km, with a top speed (in favourable conditions) of 52kph and a maximum load of 2.25 tons.

The successor to the Bv206D is the BvS10 Armoured All Terrain Vehicle (Protected) (BvS10 ATV(P)) made by Hägglunds Vehicle AB (Sweden), part of the British-based Alvis group. This vehicle has been developed especially for Britain's Royal Marines. It is an armoured, load-carrying, amphibious, go-anywhere vehicle. It is larger and faster than previous models, with superior mobility in the toughest terrain and enhanced speed and comfort both on- and off-road. It has been undergoing extensive reliability and operational trials with the Royal Marines, who have named the vehicle 'Viking'.

BvS10 ATV(P) is designed for multi-role and worldwide operations in all climates and different types of terrain. Its armour protection makes it suitable for logistic support roles in mechanised units as well as for rapid deployment and peace support tasks. It has excellent tactical mobility and can easily follow modern IFVs and tanks both on roads and in terrain and it is fully amphibious. It is air-transportable in C130 Hercules aircraft, and the separate parts can also be underslung beneath medium and small helicopters

BvS10 ATV(P) is available in several variants such as troop carrier, ambulance, high-mobility load carrier, fuel tanker, water tanker, command post and mortar carrier. Compared to the Bv206, it offers greater protection with enhanced speed and comfort on- and off-road, together with improved load capacity. The Royal Marines have ordered 108 units in three variants: Troop Carrier, Command Post and Repair and Recovery Vehicle. Two trial vehicles were deployed by the Royal Marines in Oman in 2001, where they performed well in the fiercely hot climate, on rugged, soft terrain.

Features

Minimal ground pressure, articulated steering and four-track drive, resulting in excellent off-road mobility in all types of terrain.

Amphibious landing capability.

Carries 12 fully-equipped Royal Marines.

Operational in tropical, desert and arctic environments.

Transportable by C-130 Hercules and CH-47 Chinook helicopter. May also be rapidly separated for transport by lighter helicopters.

High-grade armoured steel construction, providing protection and endurance.

Excellent protection levels and is still mobile if one track is AP mine-damaged.

High reliability, low operating costs.

Available in a range of variants: command, ambulance etc.

Specifications

Length:	7,550 mm
Width:	2,100 mm
Payload:	3,160 kg
Battle weight:	10,600 kg
Turning circle diameter:	12m
Max. road speed:	>65km/h
Max. water speed:	5km/h
Max. gradient (stop and restart) :	100% (45°)
Range on roads:	300km
Operating temperature:	49°C to –46°C
Engine:	Cummins, inline 6-cylinder, diesel
Capacity:	5,900 cc
Max. power:	183kW (250hp)/2600rpm
Max torque:	840Nm/1600rpm
Transmission:	Allison MD 3560 automatic 6-speed forward, 1 reverse
Steering system:	Hydrostatic, articulated, damped
Tracks:	Moulded rubber with cord, 620 mm wide, 4-track drive
Protection:	Armoured steel, direct fire 7.62 AP, anti-personnel mines, NBC, low radar signature

Alvis Supacat

Supacat has been in service with the British Forces since the mid-1980s. It was used in 'Desert Storm' and deployed by parachute to assist in UN operations for humanitarian relief. More recently, Supacat has been deployed in Afghanistan with the British Army's 16 Air Assault Brigade. Supacat is also used by the UK's 5 Airborne, 24 Airmobile and 16 Air Assault Brigades. A fleet has also been delivered to Canada for crisis intervention tasks. The British Army has recently received an additional 64 Supacat Mark IIIs, with self-loading trailers.

Supacat is a fully automatic 6x6, airportable and amphibious ATMP vehicle with a top road speed of 64kph and the ability to climb 45° and traverse 40°. It has remarkable all-terrain capability and can be used as a weapons platform or logistics vehicle, with a 1.6 tonne payload. The Supacat can be used with its specially designed trailer to extend its payload by up to three times, without compromising its performance. Up to eight vehicles can be airlifted in a C130 transport or two fully laden vehicles with laden trailers underslung from a Chinook helicopter.

Supacat III is driven by a 1.9 litre turbo diesel engine and a new steering system. The driver operates the vehicle via a control column, and uses the Ackerman steering (which operates by turning the front wheels like a normal vehicle) for road operation.

The Alvis Supacat, a highly manoeuvrable all-terrain 6x6 with a top road speed of 64kph. It can climb a 45° slope and traverse 40°. This one is fitted with a .50 cal machine gun and smoke launchers. Photo: © James Marchington.

He can switch instantly to skid steering (which locks the wheels on one side to turn the vehicle) when extra control is needed.

Alvis Scarab

The Alvis Scarab was designed as a highly versatile go-anywhere scout and liaison vehicle. As well as its military applications, it is well suited to the armoured scout and patrol car role in internal security operations.

The Scarab is based on the Mercedes Unimog engine and running gear, which gives it good mobility and reliability, and simplifies maintenance and repair. The vehicle's protection is higher than that of other vehicles of its type; it is protected against 7.62mm AP ammunition all round, with armour against heavy machine-gun fire across the frontal arc. Mine protection is built-in against mines up to blast mines containing the equivalent of 7kg of TNT; an enhanced mine protection kit is available.

The Scarab comes in various configurations, the most basic being the Scarab Command, which carries a crew of up to five people and can host a full range of surveillance and communications equipment. The Patrol variant has a one-man turret that can be mounted with a 7.62mm or .50cal machine gun.

Scarab has also recently completed testing at the British Army's Armoured Trials and Development Unit for the UK MoD Future Command and Liaison Vehicle (FCLV) programme. The vehicle was picked out for its excellent off-road mobility and good levels of protection, and performed reliably throughout the trials.

The Scarab's Reconnaissance Mission Suite has been developed in partnership with SAGEM in France. The system is built around a Helio SWARM turret, mounting

The Alvis Scarab scout and liaison vehicle. Based on the Mercedes Unimog running gear, it is armoured against 7.62mm AP all round, and heavy machine gun fire at the front. Photo: Alvis.

Above: The Patrol version of the Scarab has a turret that can mount a 7.62 or .50 cal machine gun. Photo: Alvis.

Left: The Reconnaissance version of the Scarab APC features a Helio SWARM turret with thermal imaging camera and .50 cal machine gun, which can be operated from inside the vehicle. Photo: Alvis.

a 12.7mm machine-gun together with co-axially mounted Sagem Iris thermal imaging camera, which provides detection, identification and recognition ranges of 8,000m, 4,000m and 2,000m respectively. An Avimo eyesafe laser rangefinder and Radamec colour daylight camera are also fitted. A bank of smoke and fragmentation grenade launchers is fitted at the base of the SWARM turret.

The sighting systems are linked to a SAGEM Tactis battlefield management system and SAGEM Sigma navigation system plus GPS inside the vehicle. The whole mission suite is operated and controlled under armour by either the turret operator or the vehicle commander, or both working together. The system enables targets to be identified and located at range on the battlefield. Target information is then fed into the battlefield management system and transferred up the command chain via a secure communications link.

Specifications

Crew:	3–5
Configuration:	Permanent rear-wheel drive, selectable 4x4
Length:	5,283mm
Width:	2,405mm
Height:	1,900mm
Ground clearance:	480mm (axle)
Combat weight:	Up to 11,100kg
Payload:	2,500kg
Engine:	Mercedes OM906LA 6-cylinder injected diesel, with 6-speed automatic gearbox.
Max. road speed:	110km/h
Max. road range:	600km
Approach/departure angle:	44%/42%
Static tilt angle:	45%
Vertical obstacle:	350mm
Armour type:	To 7.62mm AP all round, to 12.7mm AP (horizontal attack) over frontal arc.

Panhard VBL

The Panhard Véhicule Blindé Leger (VBL) was developed in response to the French Army's need for a new light reconnaissance/anti-tank vehicle, and first entered service in 1990. In the intelligence/scout role the VBL is a capable IS vehicle, providing good protection and mobility for a crew of two or three.

The VBL can be fitted with a 7.62mm machine gun and/or a 12.7mm machine gun. Standard equipment includes nuclear/biological/chemical (NBC) protection and passive night-vision equipment. It can also be fitted with a full range of surveillance and communications equipment.

The VBL is fully amphibious, and can be fitted with a single propeller mounted at the rear of the hull, providing a water speed of 5.4km/h. It is fitted with a central tyre-pressure regulation system and power steering, and there is a range of other options

The controls of the Alvis Scarab. The crew are well protected from outside threats, yet have good vision and control. Photo: Alvis.

including an air-conditioning system. The vehicle is extensively used by the French Army, and has been exported to many other countries including Mexico, Nigeria, Oman and Portugal.

Specifications

Crew:	2–3
Configuration:	Permanent 4x4
Length:	3,800mm
Width:	2,020mm
Height:	1,700mm
Ground clearance:	370mm
Armament:	Depending on configuration. Options include 7.62mm and 12.7mm machine guns, cannon and grenade launchers, ATGMs and SAMs
Combat weight:	3,500–4,000kg
Power pack:	Peugeot XD 3T turbo-charged diesel, 95hp, through automatic gearbox
Max. speed:	100km/h on road, 5.4km/h in water
Max. range:	600km, 800km with optional 20 litre tank
Max. gradient:	50%
Side slope:	30%
Vertical obstacle:	0.5m
Fording:	0.9m
Options:	NBC protection, air conditioning, amphibious propulsion, various electronic packages for GPS, radio comms, etc.

Chenowth Advanced Light Strike Vehicles (ALSVs) in Afghanistan. This high performance all-terrain vehicle is based on civilian off-road racing buggies. Photo: Chenowth.

LIGHT STRIKE VEHICLES

When Kuwait City was liberated in the 1991 Gulf War, the first US troops to enter the city were Navy SEALs who rolled in on the same kind of high-performance 'dune buggy' machines that win off-road races such as the Baja 1,000. The desert racers, painted black and equipped with a variety of weapons, climbed over roadblocks and scaled 8-foot-high berms to penetrate the ravaged emirate. Because the hastily constructed obstacles could not hold back the off-road vehicles, the SEALs were able to go where they wanted and avoid traps left by fleeing Iraqi troops. One Kuwaiti citizen dubbed the vehicles the 'Ninja cars'. The so-called Fast Attack Vehicles, or FAVs, raced ahead of US troops to scout out territory, and darted behind enemy lines to assess the size and position of enemy forces.

Britain's SAS, too, experimented with similar Light Strike Vehicles (LSVs) in the Gulf, but found them unsuitable for their type of operations. The vehicles' size and weight make them unsuitable for carrying the sheer quantity of weapons, ammunition and supplies that are necessary for a patrol to operate unsupported for any length of time. Even the Chenowth Fast Attack Vehicle, with its greater range and payload, cannot match up to the Land Rover for this type of operation.

However, for certain types of operation – where speed and mobility are crucial, and the patrols do not have to spend too long away from support – the FAV or LSV type vehicle has become extremely popular with Special Forces, and will no doubt continue to prove its worth in battle.

Chenowth Advanced Light Strike Vehicle (ALSV)

The Chenowth Advanced Light Strike Vehicle (ALSV) is a high performance all-terrain military vehicle designed to penetrate, survive and win on the high intensity battlefield

The Chenowth ALSV carries a .50 cal machine gun or Mk 19 40mm grenade launcher, on a main weapon mounting that has a 360° arc of fire. Photo: Chenowth.

of the future. The 2–4 seat ALSV traverses virtually any terrain with great agility and speed. The ALSV is the successor to the Chenowth Light Strike Vehicle, the only combat-proven production vehicle in its class in the world.

The Chenowth 3-seat Light Strike Vehicle gained renown in the 1991 Gulf War for its ability to operate undetected deep behind Iraqi lines performing reconnaissance and direct action missions for the US Marine Corps and the US Navy SEALs. It is currently in service with the US armed forces as well as with NATO allies, and countries in the Middle East and Central America.

The new generation Advanced Light Strike Vehicle incorporates major improvements to firepower and mobility. The ALSV features a main weapon station with 360° arc of fire, designed to host the M2 .50 calibre machine gun or the Mk9 automatic grenade launcher. The ALSV can also utilise remote control and stabilised platforms to provide accurate shoot-on-the-move lethality. All-wheel drive and an advanced diesel engine are now standard equipment. Greater use of commercial off-the-shelf components assures economical worldwide supportability.

ALSV Mission Roles

Fast Attack/Deep Strike	Special Operations
Surveillance and Target Acquisition	Reconnaissance and Scouting
Command and Control	Peacekeeping Missions

DISCREET OPERATIONAL VEHICLES

In addition to the patrol vehicles described above, Special Forces make use of other types of vehicle, including standard production civilian vehicles which have been adapted for Special Forces use while retaining the appearance of the normal every-day vehicle. These are often referred to as Discreet Operational Vehicles or DOVs, and may be covertly armoured and/or fitted out with specialist weapons and equipment for surveillance, communications, etc.

Clearly a DOV has the advantage that it can pass unnoticed and enable Special Forces to operate undetected while carrying out counter-terrorist operations. This gives the initiative back to the counter-terrorist force, by making it harder for terrorists to determine what measures are being taken and to identify the location and capability of the forces ranged against them. Used to transport a VIP, a DOV can assist in making the target effectively invisible – providing greater security than any amount of armour and weaponry.

DOVs range from police patrol and pursuit vehicles, through VIP limousines and escort vehicles, to specialist surveillance, command and communications vehicles. Although many are converted and supplied 'as new', counter-terrorist forces have been known to purchase privately owned second-hand vehicles and convert them to their own specifications. This tactic was used by undercover forces in Northern Ireland, for example, so that counter-terrorist teams could operate without arousing suspicion in a region where a new or 'foreign' vehicle of any type would have attracted unwanted attention. The conversion work was carried out by the British Army's own specialists, rather than civilian contractors, reducing the chance of a security compromise.

DOV armour and blast protection

The armouring of any vehicle is inevitably a compromise between protection and performance. There is no such thing as total protection against every possible type of threat; given sufficiently heavy weapons, or the time to deploy sufficient force, any armoured vehicle may be compromised. The crucial thing is to assess the threat and provide adequate protection for the occupants – bearing in mind that good intelligence and SOPs will contribute more to security than any amount of armour.

Threat levels are graded according to the type of weapon likely to be used by an enemy or terrorist against the vehicle. Knowing the capabilities of the most powerful weapon that the terrorist can bring to bear, one can then apply armour that is capable of protecting the occupants. Unfortunately there is much confusion over the classification of ballistic threat levels. Different countries around the world apply different standards, with confusingly similar categories denoted by Roman numerals, while some companies appear to have invented their own classification system which by some curious coincidence makes their products sound as though they give higher levels of protection.

Anyone specifying an armoured vehicle (or body armour) should be careful to determine exactly what classification system is in use, and what testing method has been employed. For example, a few millimetres of steel may prevent a high-velocity rifle bullet from passing through, but the spall thrown off the rear surface could be as dangerous to the occupants as a bullet fragment. It is important that the standards applied reflect the actual protection offered in real-life situations.

There are other factors to be taken into account, of course. The vision panels (i.e. windows) should provide the same level of protection as the vehicle panels – there is little point in having superior armour in the doors and body panels, only to be shot through the window. Special attention must be paid to the potential weak areas around door seals and the like. A properly armoured vehicle will have 'splash returns' around the full length of these areas, to catch any bullet or fragment that finds its way through the chink between the door and door pillar.

Perhaps the most reliable indication of ballistic protection is the NIJ standard commonly applied to body armour in the US and elsewhere. The NIJ standards are commonly used to describe the protection provided by vehicle armour, although in fact the NIJ standard does not apply to vehicles. A crucial part of the NIJ standards is the measurement of blunt trauma suffered by the wearer's body, directly beneath the point of impact. This is, of course, not applicable to vehicles. However the spall thrown off the back of the armour – or lack of spall – is crucial in a vehicle, and this is not specified in the NIJ body armour standards. Nevertheless, it is common to hear vehicles referred to as giving 'Level IV protection' etc., and in practice this is taken to mean that it gives adequate protection to the occupants if the vehicle is hit with the equivalent weapon.

This CAV 100 armoured Land Rover hit a land mine which destroyed the front of the vehicle. The occupants escaped unhurt. Photo: © James Marchington.

Various companies worldwide offer armouring of production vehicles, to give protection against small arms fire, bombs and fragments while retaining an outwardly non-military appearance. Photo: © James Marchington.

It is, of course, a mistake to rely too heavily on the nominal protection of a certain type of armour. Only a fool would sit and watch as a terrorist aimed a pistol at his vehicle, thinking, 'That's OK, it's only a 9mm and I've got Level III armour.' For one thing, most types of armour are rated for a single hit at any one point. Although it is unlikely that two bullets will impact on the same point, there is always that possibility. Moreover, there is no guarantee that the terrorists have not acquired a more powerful weapon than the one expected, or will not simply explode a massive land-mine beneath the vehicle as it slows for an obstruction. That said, effective armour is a valuable part of beefing-up security for a VIP, or providing additional protection for counter-terrorist operators – and is routinely used by VIP protection specialists and counter-terrorist organisations worldwide.

There are many companies around the world that provide armoured limousines and 4x4s. Each has its own favoured methods and materials, but the principles remain the same. The process of armouring and protecting a vehicle is likely to include the following:

The passenger/driver area is lined on all sides (including roof and floor) with armour material to resist bullets/fragments.

All window glass is replaced with transparent glass/polycarbonate armour.

The fuel tank is adapted to resist explosion and protect it against bullets/fragments.

The battery and electrical system is hardened to protect it from damage by bullets or fragments.

Run-flat devices fitted to all wheels, including spare.

The suspension is replaced with a heavy-duty system to restore normal handling with the extra weight of the armour and other additions.

The engine is replaced with a more powerful unit to provide adequate performance bearing in mind the additional weight of the vehicle.

Other modifications will depend on the users' requirements, but may include some or all of the following:

Special radio communications equipment, weapons racks, etc. fitted.

Strengthening of front/rear bumper area to protect vehicle in the event of it being used as a battering ram to force through a road-block etc.

Removal of air-bag safety systems which would present a hazard by hindering escape in the event of an attack.

Exhaust modified to prevent tampering causing the engine to stall, or insertion of an explosive device.

Anti-tamper detection system fitted.

Auxiliary battery and electrical system fitted.

Auxiliary fuel tank fitted.

Smoke/tear gas dispensing system fitted.

Intercom/PA system fitted to enable communication from inside the vehicle without the need to open window or door.

Fire-extinguisher system fitted to engine, luggage and passenger compartments.

Compressed-air system fitted to provide positive pressure clean air supply in the event of gas or chemical attack.

Run-flat tyres

The tyres are among the most vulnerable parts of a wheeled vehicle – a bullet or shrapnel fragment can quickly destroy a tyre, causing the driver to lose control and bringing the vehicle to a halt. Likewise, various types of device are designed to be deployed on the road to puncture and deflate a vehicle's tyres. This is clearly unacceptable for an operational vehicle – so run-flat inserts are used in the wheels to enable the vehicle to continue if a tyre or tyres are damaged.

There are a number of different manufacturers of run-flat tyres, but the principle is much the same. An insert of composite material is fitted to the wheel, and the tyre

This cutaway clearly shows the principle of run-flat tyres. A composite insert is fitted around the wheel rim, and is surrounded by the tyre. If the tyre blows, the vehicle can run on the insert. Photo: © James Marchington.

fitted over the top. The insert is basically a 'solid tyre' fitted inside the pneumatic tyre. If the tyre is damaged, it will collapse – but the vehicle will continue to run on the insert. The occupants may have a less comfortable ride, but at least the vehicle can continue with its task, whether that is to whisk a VIP away from a threat, continue a pursuit, or press ahead with an attack.

Hutchinson SNC, of Persan in France, manufacture a range of run-flat inserts. Their CRF is intended for use with a one-piece drop centre wheel and tubeless tyre. It consists of several sectors made of a composite material, locked together with nuts and bolts with opposite threads and secured with a thread sealant. It enables a vehicle to continue, with full driving capability, for 80km or more, despite a flat tyre. There are special variants for high-speed vehicles (in excess of 180 km/h) and for off-road vehicles.

Bomb sensors

The possibility of a bomb being attached to a vehicle while unattended is a constant threat for VIPs and security services personnel. A bomb may be constructed in a

weatherproof container, such as a plastic lunchbox, and include a powerful magnet which allows it to be attached to the underside of a vehicle in seconds. The British Word War Two veteran and politician Airey Neave was killed on 30 March 1979 by such a bomb, planted by the INLA on his car while it was in a car park under the Houses of Parliament in London. The device contained a timer and a mercury tilt-switch; once the timer ran out, the device was armed and any movement of the car could activate the tilt-switch and detonate the bomb. It detonated as Neave's car negotiated the ramp up from the car park to ground level.

Talos, from Vindicator Technologies in Austin, Texas, is a vehicle bomb-detector system which can be fitted to any type of vehicle. It is designed to give a warning if it detects a device attached to the vehicle, or if the vehicle has been tampered with since it was left.

Such a system is not a replacement for standard security procedures such as guarding and visual inspection, but it does give an added layer of protection that can improve the security of high-risk individuals.

This wheel insert developed by Hutchinson is not only a run-flat device, it also deflects the blast of a land mine away from the vehicle cab, helping to protect the occupants. Photo: © James Marchington.

The Talos system is powered by the vehicle's battery, and includes a control unit and eight sensors strategically placed around the vehicle. A display, normally placed on the dashboard where it can be viewed on approaching the vehicle, indicates the system status. The system arms twenty seconds after the last door, hood or trunk is closed, and performs a self-test. If any door is tampered with, or an IED is attached to the vehicle, the system will show an alert.

Land Rover Special Vehicles Armoured Range Rover

At a recent military vehicle exhibition, Land Rover displayed a new discreetly protected version of their Range Rover, incorporating the latest armouring techniques and materials, with ride and handling specially tuned to compensate for the extra weight.

From the outside the vehicle looks indistinguishable from a normal Range Rover, but it has been developed by Land Rover Special Vehicles, working closely with

A discreetly protected Range Rover, developed by Land Rover Special Vehicles and Armour Holdings Group. The vehicle can resist attacks from small arms and hand grenades, and its performance allows a quick getaway. Photo: © James Marchington.

Armour Holdings Group, to resist attack from pistols, rifles, machine guns and hand grenades. Its 4x4 chassis and off-road ground clearance allow a quick getaway from attack or ambush. As Land Rover point out, unlike conventional armoured limousines, the Range Rover can be driven across all terrains, including unforgiving urban obstacles such as high kerbs or even steps. The stiff monocoque body and independent suspension give excellent road holding, enabling the protected Range Rover to evade most threats.

It is available in four levels of protection, up to the European B6+ standard. A variety of armouring materials are used, including steel, Kevlar and non-metallic compounds. The glass is plasma cut and up to 40mm thick. Special 'splash' protection prevents bullet fragments entering the passenger compartment around the door and window edges. The vehicle's battery and fuel tank have extra protection, and the tyres all have run-flat capability.

To ensure that the protected version handles like a Range Rover, Prodrive Ltd have extensively retuned the air-suspension, chassis and braking systems to cope with the extra weight and demands likely to be placed on the vehicle. Options include an internal oxygen system, darkened privacy glass, an intercom system, covert emergency lights and siren. Prices for the protected Range Rover start at £165,000, and the vehicle is available with either a 4.4-litre V8 petrol engine or a 3-litre turbo diesel.

The story of Special Forces from World War Two onwards is closely linked with airborne operations of all types. The first free-fall parachute descent was made in the USA by Leslie Irvin in 1919. He went on to establish a European factory for the mass production of parachutes in England in 1926. Around this time, James Gregory and Sir Raymond Quilter were developing parachute systems for aircrew, and formed GQ Parachutes in 1934. The 1930s saw both companies established as major suppliers of emergency escape parachutes to the world's air forces.

A round-canopy parachute of the type used by paratroops for static line jumps for many years. Photo: US Navy.

US Navy SEALs using parachutes as a method of insertion. Special Forces use a full range of advanced parachuting techniques, including HALO and HAHO. Photo: US Navy.

By 1940, there was considerable interest in parachuting as a method of delivering troops for an assault. Irvin and GQ collaborated to produce the X-Type Paratroop Parachute Assembly, a static line assembly for the new and rapidly expanding Army Airborne Forces. This assembly, with minor modifications, was to be used throughout World War Two and for some twenty years afterwards.

Parachute insertion was a key part of the original concept of Britain's Special Air Service. The original SAS raised in North Africa, which included Lt-Col David Stirling, Lt Jock Lewes and Lt Paddy Mayne, developed and practised parachute techniques as a means of insertion behind enemy lines. Two men died during this training when their parachutes malfunctioned. Typically, Stirling himself was first out of the aircraft on the next training jump.

Military parachuting has become much more sophisticated since those early days. A mass air assault may still consist of hundreds of paratroops jumping with round-canopied static line 'chutes from an altitude of between a few hundred and a few thousand feet. But developments in equipment and techniques have opened up a much wider range of options for Special Forces to insert a small force on the ground without alerting the enemy.

The techniques used include HAHO (High Altitude High Opening) and HALO (High Altitude Low Opening). These methods were developed during the latter half of the twentieth century by individuals such as Richard Marcinko of the US SEAL Team Six.

HALO

SEAL Team Six developed the method of HALO jumping from altitudes of 36,000 feet or more, using oxygen equipment; at that altitude there is very little oxygen in the air, and without an oxygen mask the soldier would quickly lose consciousness. The temperature at this altitude is also well below zero, causing a variety of problems such as goggles freezing up. In addition to all the other equipment carried, a HALO jump requires suitably warm clothing, helmet and goggles, oxygen mask and bottle, altimeter, and a 'chute which is deployed automatically at a pre-set height.

HALO enables Special Forces to be inserted covertly by an aircraft flying literally miles above enemy territory, with very little chance of them being detected: a man falling through the air at 120mph is all but invisible to radar and other surveillance devices, as well as being undetectable by the human eye. By deploying the 'chute at the lowest possible altitude, the chance of being detected at all is minimised.

HAHO

HAHO is a notoriously difficult form of insertion, which requires a great deal of training to be carried out successfully on operations. Typically a HAHO insertion might be done from a commercial aircraft, or military craft with a commercial IFF signature in the normal air traffic lanes. This helps to avoid arousing suspicion. The soldiers exit the aircraft at an altitude of around 30,000 feet, and deploy their ram-jet type parachutes ten to fifteen seconds later, at an altitude of 27,000 feet. The squad forms up in a stack in the air, with the soldier at the bottom of the stack setting the course and acting as the guide.

The squad can fly thirty to fifty miles in formation, navigating to their target with the aid of compass and GPS. Navigation can be tricky as it is necessary to allow for windspeed and direction, which may vary considerably at different altitudes.

Helicopter insertion

The more advanced parachute insertion techniques make it possible to introduce small groups of Special Forces clandestinely, within striking distance of enemy targets. However, they are by no means the only method for Special Forces to 'infil' (infiltrate). Helicopters have become extremely important to Special Forces in recent years, and are frequently used to support Special Forces operations. British Special Forces, for instance, can call on the Chinook HC-2s of No. 7 Sqn, RAF Odiham, Sea

Above: Helicopters are nowadays widely used by Special Forces, especially for infiltration and exfiltration. Special Forces helicopter pilots are trained to fly at very low level, using night vision goggles. Photo: USAF.

Right: Helicopters can deliver Special Forces and their equipment to remote and inaccessible locations. Here a soldier on a motorcycle exits a CH-46E Sea Knight helicopter. Photo: USMC.

King HC-4s flown by 848 Naval Air Sqn at Yeovilton in Somerset, and the Agusta A-109s operated by the Army Air Corps. Other helos, such as the British Army's Gazelle, Lynx and Apache, may be used in support of Special Forces' operations. US and other armed forces have similar units operating with their respective Special Forces.

Where necessary, a patrol can be inserted by landing a helicopter such as a Chinook in enemy territory. Special Forces' flight helo pilots are trained in low-level flying and the use of passive night goggles, and can fly low and fast to avoid detection. 'Decoy' flares are available to help the pilot evade SAMs (Surface to Air Missiles) if they are fired on, and the craft are usually armed with a 7.62mm Minigun or equivalent to engage ground troops. This was the method used to insert Bravo Two-Zero and some other

Above: Fast-roping is frequently used as a quick and effective means of deploying lightly-equipped troops from helicopters. Here marines use the technique from a Chinook. Photo: USMC.

Left: The fast-roping technique is particularly useful for operations such as VBSS (Vessel Board, Search and Seizure), where rapid deployment is essential. Photo: USMC.

patrols into Iraq during the 1991 Gulf War. One of the advantages of this type of insertion is that quite heavy equipment can be landed with the patrol and is immediately available for use – for instance, a Chinook can carry a Land Rover and trailer either inside or underslung.

For rapid delivery of relatively lightly equipped troops, fast-roping has become the favoured option. This method involves the use of a large-diameter rope of 50–100 feet in length. The helo approaches the DZ (Drop Zone) fast and low, to avoid detection by the enemy. Arriving at the target, it hovers and the soldiers slide down the rope, using heavily gloved hands to control their descent. By this method, a team can be on the ground and ready to fight within seconds – even faster than using the rappelling method, with a thinner rope and abseil-type harness. Fast-roping is particularly effective for operations where rapid deployment is important – such as VBSS (Vessel Board, Search and Seizure) and CQB (Close Quarter Battle) operations, for example, where a CT (Counter-Terrorism) team is assaulting a terrorist-held building or craft.

PARACHUTES

Irvin-GQ

Two of the oldest and most respected names in parachutes are Irvin and GQ. These two companies merged some time ago, and have now been acquired by Airborne Systems, part of the Alchemy Group. To meet the varied and demanding requirements of modern airborne operations, Irvin-GQ produces a complete range of parachutes and equipment for Paratroops and Special Forces, including:

> Non-steerable and steerable troop assemblies for massed, tactical
>   parachute assault
> A low-level troop parachute for use at drop heights as low as 250ft (76m)
> Reserve parachute assemblies
> Advanced parachutes for Special Operations and HAHO/HALO missions
> Parachutists' high-altitude oxygen systems

The group is currently developing the XT-11 advanced tactical parachute system (ATPS) for the US Army. This system includes a main parachute developed by Para-Flite and a reserve parachute, produced by Irvin-GQ. The XT-11 will replace the T-10 troop parachute assembly, which has been in use since the 1950s.

The T-10 was principally used for mass tactical parachute assaults, and was designed to handle a gross weight of 250lbs. Today's soldiers are now carrying considerably more equipment, however, and weights are often approaching 400lbs. Typical combat mission drop heights and speeds are more demanding, too – often as low as 500ft and from aircraft flying at speeds of 130–150 knots. In these conditions the new XT-11 parachute reduces the rate of descent by 25 per cent, with a 40 per cent reduction in impact energy. This is expected to cut landing injuries significantly.

FSH Parachutes

FSH (Fallschirm-Service Herbst) of Germany make a range of parachutes, including military models which are used by Special Forces and regular forces. The company developed paraglider type 'chutes in the mid-1980s, and now produces the RS-10T, a tactical military low-level static line parachute, as well as the G-9 Tactical Ram-Air and Multi Mission Parachute/Paraglider System for HALO/HAHO operations, together with a range of high-altitude breathing equipment, and the Nightwing altimeter specifically for HALO/HAHO use.

Specifications – FSH RS-10T Parachute

Type:	Static line, round canopy
Minimum drop altitude:	60m (operations), 200m (training)
Minimum drop speed:	150km/h
Gross weight:	50–150 kg
Canopy area:	66sqm
Rate of descent:	5.0m/s (130 kg)
Self propulsion:	3m/s
Steerable:	Yes
Weight:	11kg
Pack dimensions:	540 x 320 x 200 mm

Specifications – FSH G-9 Parachute

Type:	Tactical ram-air multi-mission parachute/paraglider system
Span:	11.28m (37ft)
Area:	35sqm (375sqft)
Number of cells:	11
Fabric:	1.1 ripstop nylon
Lines:	535kg Spectra
Max. suspended weight:	200kg (440lbs) approx
Test weight:	548lbs
Test speed:	175kn
Glide ratio:	4–6:1 adjustable
Forward speed:	28–48 km/h
Rate of descent:	1.8–4 m/sec adjustable
Ground wind speed:	Max. 13m/sec
Total weight of system:	19kg approx.

Specifications – Oxyjump High Altitude Breathing Equipment

Maximum altitude:	10,000m
Operating temperature:	−45°C to 50°C
Storage temperature:	−65°C to 71°C
Cylinder charge pressure:	200 bar at 1013 mbar/15°C ambient pressure

Regulator:	Supplies 78% to 100% oxygen depending on altitude
Cylinder volume:	80 litres NTPD
Breathing mask size:	Small, Medium, Large
Microphone compatible:	Yes

Specifications – Nightwing

Altimeter developed specifically for night-time HAHO/HALO parachute operations

Measurement range:	0–10,000m
Resolution:	100m
Indicator revolutions:	One
Temperature compensation:	Yes
Illumination:	Integrated, battery-driven, two red light sources
Dimensions:	90 x 108 x 31mm

FIXED-WING AIRCRAFT

C-130 Hercules

Remarkably, the first C-130 Hercules was delivered in 1959 – yet the Hercules and its variants still provide a vital transport and combat role in today's military operations. A rugged, dependable and versatile aircraft, the Hercules can operate from rough, makeshift airstrips, and operate in just about any environment from arctic to desert. It has an impressive load capacity, carrying up to ninety-two fully equipped troops or up to 19,000kg of cargo, which can encompass everything from helicopters, Land Rovers and AFVs to medical and humanitarian supplies. The rear loading ramp and door means that vehicles can be driven straight on (and off) the aircraft, and the ramp can also be used for mass tactical air assaults, with the troops either exiting via the side doors or simply running off the end of the ramp.

The C-130 is used throughout the US Air Force, including Air Force Special Operations Command, as well as by the British RAF and many other armed forces worldwide – it is in service with more than fifty countries. It fulfils a broad range of operational missions in both peace and war. Britain's SAS uses C-130s operated by the Special Forces Flight of 47 Sqn.

There are basic and specialised versions of the aircraft that can perform diverse roles, while the cargo area may be configured for many different types of cargo, including palletised equipment, floor-loaded material, airdrop platforms, container delivery system bundles, vehicles and personnel. It can also be fitted for medical evacuation, or can be armed with a variety of weapons for the close air support role.

The C-130J is the latest version of the C-130, and is gradually replacing ageing C-130Es in US service. The C-130J incorporates new technology to reduce manpower requirements. The J model climbs faster and higher, flies farther at a higher cruise speed, and takes off and lands in a shorter distance. The C-130J-30 is a stretch version, adding 15ft to the fuselage, increasing usable space in the cargo compartment. Major improvements in the J model include: advanced two-pilot flight station with fully integrated digital avionics; colour multifunctional liquid crystal displays and head-up displays; state-of-the-art navigation systems with dual inertial navigation system and GPS; fully integrated defensive systems; low-power colour radar; digital moving map display; new turboprop engines with six-bladed, all-composite propellers; digital auto pilot; improved fuel, environmental and ice protection systems; and an enhanced cargo handling system.

Specifications – C-130J Hercules

Contractor:	Lockheed Martin Aeronautics Company
Engines:	Four Rolls-Royce AE 2100D3 turboprops; 4,591 horsepower Length:
C-130J:	97ft 9ins (29.3m)
C-130J-30:	112ft 9ins (34.69m)
Height:	38ft 3ins (11.4m)
Wingspan:	132ft 7ins (39.7m)
Cargo compartment:	
C-130E/H/J:	Length, 40ft (12.31m); width 119ins (3.12m); height 9ft (2.74m)
C-130J-30:	length, 55ft (16.9m); width, 119ins (3.12m); height, 9ft (2.74m)
Rear ramp:	Length 123ins (3.12m); width, 119ins (3.02m)
Speed:	
C-130J:	417mph/362kts (Mach 0.59) at 22,000ft (6,706m)
C-130J-30:	410mph/356kts (Mach 0.58) at 22,000ft (6,706m)
Ceiling:	33,000ft (10,000m) with 45,000 lbs (17,716kg) payload
Max. take-off weight:	C-130E/H/J: 155,000lbs (69,750kg) C-130J-30: 164,000lbs (74,393kg)
Max. payload:	C-130J: 46,631lbs (21,151kg). C-130J-30: 46,812lbs (21,234kg)
Max. normal payload:	C-130J: 38,301lbs (17,373kg) C-130J-30: 38,812 lbs (17,605kg)
Range with 35,000lbs payload:	
C-130J:	3,062 miles (2,660nm)
C-130J-30:	3,269 miles (2,830nm)
Max. load:	
C-130J:	6 pallets or 74 stretchers or 16 CDS bundles or 92 combat troops or 64 paratroopers, or a combination

C-130J-30:	8 pallets or 97 stretchers or 24 CDS bundles or 128 combat troops or 92 paratroopers, or a combination.
Crew:	
C-130J/J-30:	Three (two pilots and loadmaster)
Aeromedical Evacuation Role:	Minimum medical crew of three is added (one flight nurse and two medical technicians). Medical crew may be increased to two flight nurses and four medical technicians as required by the needs of the patients
Unit cost:	C-130J: $48.5million
Date deployed:	C-130J: Feb 1999

MC-130 Combat Talon

The MC-130 Combat Talon is a Special Forces variant of the C-130 Hercules. It is used to provide infiltration, exfiltration and resupply of special operations forces and equipment in hostile territory. It can also be used for secondary missions including psychological operations and helicopter air refuelling.

There are two variants: MC-130E Combat Talon I and MC-130H Combat Talon II. Both aircraft have terrain-following and terrain-avoidance radars capable of operating as low as 250ft in adverse weather conditions. Changes from the basic C-130 include an in-flight refuelling receptacle, and strengthening of the tail to allow high speed/low-signature airdrop. Their navigation suites include dual ring-laser gyros, mission computers and integrated GPS, enabling the aircraft to locate and either land or airdrop on small, unmarked zones with pinpoint accuracy, day or night. An extensive electronic warfare suite enables the aircrew to detect and avoid potential threats.

The Combat Talon first flew in 1966 and saw extensive service in South-east Asia, including the attempted rescue of Americans held at the Son Tay PoW camp in 1970. Combat Talons landed in the Iranian desert in April 1980 in support of Operation Eagle Claw, the attempt to rescue American hostages held by Iran. The aircraft saw combat in Grenada in 1983, and in Operation Desert Storm. The Talon also conducted numerous aerial refuellings of special operations helicopters involved in combat search and rescue operations.

MC-130P Combat Shadow

Another variant of the C-130 Hercules, in service with US armed forces, is the MC-130P Combat Shadow. This aircraft is fitted out to fly clandestine, or low visibility, single or multi-ship low-level missions penetrating politically sensitive or hostile territory to provide air refuelling. It can deliver Special Forces and equipment by airdrop. With the use of night-vision goggles, radar and infra-red sensors, the Combat Shadow primarily flies missions at night to reduce the probability of visual acquisition by ground and airborne threats.

Recent modifications to the MC-130P have provided improved navigation, communications, threat detection and counter-measures systems. The aircraft has a fully integrated inertial navigation and GPS, forward-looking infra-red, radar and missile warning receivers, chaff and flare dispensers, night-vision goggle compatible head-up displays, satellite and data-burst communications.

Following Desert Storm, the MC-130P was involved in operations Northern and Southern Watch, supporting efforts to keep Iraqi aircraft out of the no-fly zones.

AC-130H/U Spectre and Spooky Gunships

The AC-130H Spectre and AC-130U Spooky Gunships are heavily armed versions of the C-130 Hercules, intended to provide close air support for troops on the ground. The aircraft have a variety of powerful side-firing weapons, integrated with sophisticated sensor, navigation and fire-control systems to provide surgical firepower or area saturation during extended loiter periods, at night and in adverse weather. The sensors allow the gunship to identify friendly ground forces and targets at any place and time.

The AC-130 gunship is a heavily armed version of the ubiquitous C-130 Hercules. It carries a powerful arsenal of side-firing weapons which can be used to support Special Forces operations. Photo: USAF.

The AC-130 Gunship's combat history dates back to Vietnam, where gunships destroyed more than 10,000 trucks and were credited with many life-saving close air support missions. During Operation Urgent Fury in Grenada in 1983, AC-130s suppressed enemy air defence systems and attacked ground forces. During Operation Desert Storm, AC-130s provided close air support and force protection (air base defence) for ground forces. Gunships were also used during operations Continue

Hope and United Shield in Somalia, providing close air support for United Nations' ground forces.

More recently, the gunships have played an important part in operations against Taliban and al-Qaeda forces in Afghanistan.

A-10 Thunderbolt II

The A-10 Thunderbolt II is a heavily armed and armoured fixed-wing aircraft designed for close air support of ground forces. Its 30mm GAU-8/A Gatling gun can fire 3,900 rounds a minute and can defeat tanks and other armoured vehicles. The aircraft can also fire AGM-65 Maverick and AIM-9 Sidewinder missiles.

It is a twin-engine jet aircraft with excellent manoeuvrability at low air speeds and altitude, and provides a highly accurate weapons-delivery platform. It can loiter near battle areas for extended periods of time and operate below 1,000ft. Using night-vision goggles, A-10 pilots can conduct their missions during darkness.

The aircraft can survive direct hits from armour-piercing and high-explosive projectiles up to 23mm. It has self-sealing fuel cells protected by internal and external foam. Manual systems back up the redundant hydraulic flight-control systems, so that pilots can still fly and land even if hydraulic power is lost.

The Thunderbolt II can be serviced and operated from bases with limited facilities near battle areas. Many of the aircraft's parts are interchangeable left and right, including the engines, main landing gear and vertical stabilisers.

An A-10 Thunderbolt II 'Tankbuster'. Photo: US DoD.

Avionics equipment includes communications, inertial navigation systems, fire-control and weapons-delivery systems, target penetration aids and night- vision goggles. The weapons-delivery systems includes head-up displays that indicate airspeed, altitude, dive angle, navigation information and weapons-aiming references.

The A-10 proved to be a valuable asset to the United States and its allies during Operation Desert Storm. In the 1991 Gulf War, A-10s flew 8,100 sorties and launched 90 per cent of the AGM-65 Maverick missiles used in the conflict.

Specifications – A-10 Thunderbolt II

Contractor:	Fairchild Republic Co
Power plant:	Two General Electric TF34-GE-100 turbofans
Thrust:	9,065lbs each engine
Length:	53ft, 4ins (16.16m)
Height:	14ft, 8ins (4.42m)
Wingspan:	57ft, 6ins (17.42m)
Speed:	420mph (Mach 0.56)
Ceiling:	45,000ft (13,636m)
Maximum take-off weight:	51,000lbs (22,950kg)
Range:	800 miles (695 nautical miles)
Armament:	One 30mm GAU-8/A seven-barrel Gatling gun; up to 16,000lbs (7,200kg) of mixed ordnance on eight under-wing and three under-fuselage pylon stations, including 500lbs (225kg) of Mk-82 and 2,000lbs (900kg) of Mk-84 series low/high drag bombs, incendiary cluster bombs, combined effects munitions, mine-dispensing munitions, AGM-65 Maverick missiles and laser-guided/electro-optically guided bombs; infra-red counter-measure flares; electronic counter-measure chaff; jammer pods; 2.75in (6.99cm) rockets; illumination flares and AIM-9 Sidewinder missiles.
Crew:	One
Date deployed:	March 1976
Unit cost:	$9.8 million

HELICOPTERS

CH-47 Chinook

Just as the C-130 Hercules is the fixed-wing workhorse of many armed forces, so the CH-47 Chinook is ubiquitous as a heavy-lift cargo helicopter, carrying out a wide range of tasks including the infiltration and exfiltration of Special Forces patrols, often

The CH-47 Chinook helicopter is used for infiltrate and exfiltrate of Special Forces patrols, and can be flown at high speeds at night at very low level to avoid detection by enemy forces. Photo: US DoD.

flying at extremely low level at night to avoid detection. The craft is easily recognised by its distinctive twin-rotor configuration, and has a readily identified 'wop, wop, wop' rotor sound which is very different from that of any other craft.

The US Army has operated a variety of CH-47 Chinook models since first taking delivery in 1962. Shortly afterwards, Chinooks were deployed to Vietnam, where CH-47A, B and C models served with distinction for a decade until the war's end in 1975. The CH-47D is the current standard Chinook in service with the US Army. This model features composite rotor blades, an improved electrical system, modularised hydraulics, triple cargo hooks, avionics and communication improvements and more powerful engines that can handle a 25,000lb useful load, nearly twice the Chinook's original lift capacity. The CH-47D was a central element in US Army operations in the 1991 Gulf War, where more than 160 Chinooks carried US and Allied troops in history's largest aerial assault to outflank Iraqi forces and cut off their retreat from Kuwait.

Famously, it was a Chinook that flew the ill-fated Bravo Two-Zero patrol into Iraq during the Gulf War, in one of many operations carried out by Special Forces Flight Chinooks during that conflict. Infamously, it was also a Chinook – flight ZD 576 – that crashed on the Mull of Kintyre in Scotland in 1994, killing twenty-nine people including many senior figures in Britain's security and intelligence services. The crash has been surrounded by controversy ever since; officials stick doggedly to the RAF Board of Inquiry's verdict of pilot negligence, while others insist that problems with the Mk11's FADEQ computerised engine control system were a contributory factor. It seems unlikely that the full story will ever be made public, but there is no doubt that the Chinook, in its various models, will continue to be an integral part of conventional and Special Forces operations for many years to come.

US Army Special Operations Forces operate thirty-six Special Operations Chinooks, designated MH-47D and MH-47E, for low-level, high-speed flight for infil-

The Chinook can carry considerable loads either inside or underslung – these two are lifting Humvees weighing over 4,600kg each. Photo: US DoD.

tration and exfiltration of Special Operations teams at night and in adverse weather. The E model is one of the most advanced rotorcraft in operation today. It has a fully integrated digital cockpit; forward-looking infra-red, terrain-following/terrain-avoidance radar; long-range fuel tanks; and aerial refuelling capability. The MH-47E's integrated avionics system (IAS) permits global communications and navigation. The MH-47E is required to complete a 5.5-hour covert mission over a 300nm (556km) radius, at low level, day or night, in adverse weather, over any type of terrain, and do so with a 90 per cent probability of success.

Specifications – CH-47D/F Chinook

Power plant:	Two Textron Lycoming T55-L712 engines
Rotor system:	Two hubs, three blades per hub
	Fibreglass construction
	Manual folding blades, 60ft diameter
Speed:	225rpm
Cruise speed:	143kts (at 50,000lbs)
Rate of climb:	1,522ft/min (at 50,000 lbs)
Range:	230nm
Cockpit-crew seats:	2
Cabin seats/stretchers:	33/24
Max. gross weight:	50,000lbs
Empty:	23,401lbs
Overall length:	99ft (rotors tip-to-tip) 51ft (fuselage) 39ft 2ins hub-to-hub.
Height:	18ft 11.5ins (to highest point of rotor blade)

MH-53 Pave Low

The MH-53J Pave Low III heavy-lift helicopter is the largest, most powerful and technologically advanced helicopter in service with the US Air Force. It is used for low-level, long-range, undetected penetration into denied areas, day or night, in adverse weather, for infiltration, exfiltration and resupply of special operations forces.

The MH-53 is equipped with highly sophisticated terrain-following and terrain-avoidance radar, forward-looking infra-red sensor, inertial navigation system with GPS and a projected map display. These systems enable the crew to follow terrain contours and avoid obstacles, making low-level penetration possible.

The MH-53J flew numerous missions in Panama during Operation Just Cause in 1989, inserting and transporting Special Forces. In 1991, it was used during Operation Desert Storm. Pave Lows were the first aircraft in Iraq, leading the Army AH-64 Apaches in destroying Iraqi early warning radar to open a hole in enemy air defences. In addition to infiltration, exfiltration and resupply of special forces teams throughout Iraq and Kuwait, the Pave Low provided search-and-rescue coverage for coalition air forces in Iraq, Saudi Arabia, Kuwait, Turkey and the Persian Gulf.

Following the 1991 Gulf War, Pave Lows supported operations Provide Comfort and Southern Watch, and participated in operations Provide Promise and Deny

Flight, the humanitarian relief effort and no-fly zone security in the Balkans. MH-53s also played a significant part in operations against Taliban and al-Qaeda forces in Afghanistan.

The MH-53 Pave Low is used for low-level, long range penetration into denied areas in adverse weather, day or night. Photo: USAF.

Specifications – MH-53 Pave Low

Manufacturer:	Sikorsky
Power plant:	Two General Electric T64-GE/-100 engines
Thrust:	4,330 shaft horsepower per engine
Length:	88ft (28m)
Height:	25ft (7.6m)
Rotor diameter:	72ft (21.9m)
Speed:	165mph (at sea level)
Ceiling:	16,000ft (4,876m)
Max. take-off weight:	46,000lbs
Range:	600nm (unlimited with aerial refuelling)
Armament:	Combination of three 7.62mm mini guns or three .50cal machine guns
Crew:	Six: two pilots; two flight engineers, two aerial gunners.
Date deployed:	1981
Unit cost:	$40 million

6 SEABORNE OPERATIONS

Many of the world's best-known Special Forces specialise in seaborne operations: France's CASM (Commando D'Action Sous Marine) combat divers and Britain's SBS (Special Boat Service) are just two examples. Such forces have a long and distinguished history of using every conceivable means of reaching targets via the sea and inland waterways. This ranges from canoes like the folding Klepper, used by the SBS since the 1950s, to inflatable boats like the Gemini, to larger patrol and assault craft, to submarines and 'stealth' diving equipment.

The US Navy Seals are one of the world's most highly trained Special Forces. Although they use a variety of insertion methods (SEAL stands for SEa, Air, Land), the unit's origins lie with the US Navy frogmen of the World War Two. The SEALs' selection and training places great emphasis on seaborne operations. Trainees must pass a tough diving medical, and perform long swims and diving exercises, as well as demonstrating an aptitude for underwater demolition work. SEALs practise 'wet' drops into the sea with full equipment, from a variety of aircraft, and learn to operate a variety of small surface craft and mini-submarines. The SEALs' entire selection and training process may last up to a year – twice that of army Special Forces.

Although there are specialist seaborne units, other Special Forces also make use of a variety of water transport. The SAS has its Boat Troop, for instance, who use a

The US Navy SEALs are just one of many Special Forces around the world that specialise in seaborne operations. Photo: USMC.

Left: Submarines provide one means of covert infiltration for seaborne Special Forces. This one is a British Vanguard class sub. Photo: BAe.

Below left: Underwater demolitions is the bread-and-butter of seaborne Special Forces operations. Photo: US Navy.

Below: Britain's SBS specialise in seaborne ops, but other units will use boats when necessary; the SAS has a specialist Boat Troop. Photo: author's collection.

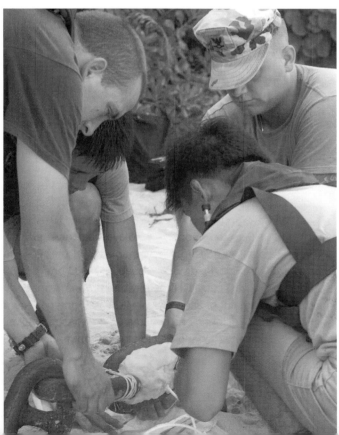

The littoral zone is crucial to modern warfare, and a wide variety of vessels are employed. This hovercraft is used by the US Marines. Photo: USMC.

Diving equipment enables Special Forces teams to make a stealthy approach from a vessel well out to sea. Photo: USMC.

wide range of small boats to operate in rivers, lakes and coastal regions. During the Falklands War, the SAS used Gemini inflatable boats to land on South Georgia, and Rigid Raiders in their diversionary attack on Port Stanley harbour.

The littoral zone remains crucial to modern warfare, and aircraft carriers and other ships are a vital component of 'force projection'. Consequently, seaborne Special Forces' operations will continue to be of huge importance in warfare and 'operations other than war' in the foreseeable future.

Rebreathing apparatus is used to avoid the release of exhaled gas, which leaves a clearly visible trail of bubbles on the surface.
Photo: US Navy.

DIVING EQUIPMENT

The use of diving equipment opens up a whole world of operations for Special Forces. Divers can covertly exit a submarine, or use a swimmer delivery vehicle, to approach an enemy vessel or coastline completely undetected. Modern Special Forces' diving equipment enables divers to remain underwater for extended periods, allowing them to enter the water beyond the range of today's sophisticated night and

A diver wearing specialist equipment by Divex of Aberdeen, one of the world's leading suppliers of military diving apparatus. Photo: Divex.

day surveillance equipment. 'Rebreather' apparatus minimises the release of spent gases to the surface, which might be observed by an alert enemy.

Divex

Divex, based in Aberdeen in Scotland, is a world leader in the design and manufacture of diving and subsea equipment for civilian as well as military divers. The company is the largest supplier of diving equipment to the UK Ministry of Defence and Royal Navy. Divex designs, manufactures and supports more than 11,000 products, ranging from the smallest of washers to a complete saturation diving system. Their range of military diving apparatus encompasses EOD (Explosive Ordnance Disposal) and Special Forces' requirements, including the Stealth Rebreather.

Divex Oxygen Combat Swimmer

Divex supply a range of equipment for combat swimmers using oxygen rebreathers at shallow depths of 0–10m. This type of equipment is typically used for operations such as placing explosive charges on enemy shipping or conducting a recce of a shoreline prior to amphibious landings. Equipment used for such operations includes the oxygen rebreather unit and mask, a buoyancy jacket, a compass swimboard for navigation, depth gauge and watch, fins and drysuit.

Shadow Oxygen Rebreather

Divex Shadow is a long-endurance, chest-mounted oxygen rebreather which can allow the diver to remain underwater for six hours or more, depending on his oxygen

The Divex Shadow oxygen rebreather allows the diver to remain underwater for more than six hours. Note also the compass swimboard held in the diver's left hand. Photo: Divex.

Divex equipment is designed to be compatible with the other kit that a combat swimmer needs to carry; this diver is wearing belt pouches and could also add a backpack. Photo: Divex.

consumption. Careful design and the use of modern high technology lightweight materials have enabled Divex to make this unit no bigger or heavier than similar systems that offer much less endurance time. The Shadow rebreather has been designed to interface easily with other equipment such as the company's Digicom underwater communications system and the Divex Stealth Full Face Dual Mode Mask

(DMM), enabling the diver to access on-board gas supplies such as Swimmer Delivery Vehicle (SDV) systems.

Shadow Buoyancy Jacket

The Divex Shadow Buoyancy Jacket is designed for use with a rebreather, and enables the diver to adjust his buoyancy. It is tailored to be compatible with the field equipment worn by a combat swimmer, and provides a clear back area for field packs. The design incorporates a single or double inflation cylinder, oral inflation device, overpressure relief valve, integrated weight pocket system with quick-release, and a small backpack for carrying ancillary equipment.

Digicom 3,000m Diver Through Water Communications

Communication with and between divers presents severe technical difficulties, and often Special Forces divers have had to rely on basic, short-range methods such as 'buddy lines' and hand signals. The Divex Digicom provides an effective, long-range radio communications system for divers, enabling them to communicate with each other and surface-based observers and commanders. This means that divers can be kept updated on the tactical situation at the surface.

Long-range through-water communications enables combat swimmers to remain in touch with commanders on the surface. Photo: US Navy.

The Divex Digicom Diver Through Water Communication (DTWC) system is compatible with oxygen/mixed gas rebreathers or open-circuit Self Contained Underwater Breathing Apparatus (SCUBA). During field trials this system enabled clear speech communications in excess of 4,500m. As well as its use on operations, it adds significantly to safety when training student divers.

The Digicom DTWC is in service throughout the UK Royal Navy, UK Army and various Special Forces units. It is NATO codified, and has been adopted by various other countries.

Compass Swimboard

The Divex Compass Swimboard is a small, lightweight combat swimmer's board with a built-in compass. The markings are luminescent to permit underwater navigation, and a depth gauge and watch can be fitted.

Force Fins

These fins are specially designed to improve swimming efficiency and are now the choice of Special Forces around the world.

Combat Drysuit

The Divex Combat Drysuit's easy-glide material is water-repellent and smooth, offering minimum resistance while swimming. The suit comes with hard soled boots as standard but may be fitted with latex socks if required.

Divex Special Forces Mixed Gas Diver

For operations where the diver needs to go deeper than the safe depth for oxygen rebreathers, it is necessary to use a mixed gas rebreather. For Special Forces divers this might include covertly exiting and re-entering submarines, or piloting swimmer delivery vehicles. Divex's Special Forces Mixed Gas Diver equipment enables Special Forces divers to operate at depths of up to 120m, with a dive duration of six hours. Air can be used as the diluent to provide a nitrox mixture for depths up to 54m. For deeper diving a heliox (helium and oxygen) mixture or tri-mix (oxygen, helium and nitrogen) may be used. Divex's mixed gas rebreather allows a 'no decompression' depth of 18m – meaning that there is no need for the diver to go through a decompression routine when exiting the water in order to avoid the decompression problems commonly known as 'the bends'. This makes the system ideal for submarine or swimmer delivery vehicle (SDV) insertions.

Stealth Dual Mode Mask

The Divex Stealth Dual Mode Mask is a full face mask fitted with a changeover valve which enables the diver to switch between rebreather closed-circuit mode to an open-circuit gas supply such as an external emergency bale-out cylinder or an Auxiliary Life Support System (ALSS) within a Swimmer Delivery Vehicle (SDV). The mask may be interfaced with most types of rebreather, and is in service with the UK Royal Navy and Royal Marine Commandos, as well as various NATO navies.

Stealth SF Closed Circuit Mixed Gas Rebreather

The Divex Stealth SF Closed Circuit Mixed Gas Rebreather is a highly advanced, versatile unit. It was developed for Special Forces diving operations below the safe depth permitted by oxygen. Oxygen levels are maintained electronically to provide the optimum breathing mixture regardless of depth. Stealth SF has an endurance of six hours, and has simple pre- and post-dive procedures. The 'no decompression' depth is 18m. This makes it an ideal system for shallow-water Special Forces operations such as locking-out of submarines or Swimmer Delivery Vehicle (SDV) pilots and navigators. Stealth Mixed Gas Rebreathers are in service with the UK Royal Navy and Royal Marine Commandos, the Federal German Navy and the Italian Navy.

Subtug Diver Propulsion Vehicle (DPV)

Subtug is a heavy-duty two-man diver's tow designed specifically for military operations. The propulsion system is encased within an exceptionally strong torpedo-shape body surrounded by a protective aluminium frame. The frame provides extra hand-holds for divers and fastening points for equipment.

Divex Marine Counter Terrorism Equipment

Maritime counter-terrorist operations require Special Forces to assault any water-borne terrorist stronghold – which might be anything from an offshore oil rig to a luxury cruise liner. Obtaining access to such a wide range of vessels and installations from the water line, in adverse weather and sea conditions, presents enormous problems – all the more so when it must be done covertly. Divex supply a range of equipment for such operations, all of it designed to be lightweight, extremely robust and able to function after long salt-water exposure.

Plummet Grapple Hook

The Plummet Grapnel uses compressed air and is capable of propelling 8mm climbing rope to a maximum height of 20m or 6mm rope up to 30m.

Carbon Fibre Poles

These are available in two lengths: 3m and 5m. The superior design of Divex's poles eliminates the whipping effect of conventional poles, permitting the MCT diver greater control while establishing ladders during rough sea operations.

Aluminium Wind-Up Pole

The wind-up pole is used from pursuit craft to establish ladders, allowing assault troops to establish a foothold on a vessel that is underway. The pole is available in two sizes: 13.2m and 15.2m.

Wire-Rope Ladders and Titanium Hooks

Attached to the target vessel with the aid of a pole, a wire-rope ladder enables the assault swimmer to climb aboard from the water line. Divex wire-rope ladders are available in lengths of 15m and are constructed of 3mm stainless steel wire, with a distance between rungs of 250mm or 300mm. Weight 5kg. Titanium hooks are light-weight and extremely strong. They are available in different designs for attachment to a variety of fixing points, and can be tailor-made to suit customers' requirements.

SUB-SEA VEHICLES

Advanced SEAL Delivery System (ASDS)

For many years British and American Special Forces have used the Swimmer (or SEAL) Delivery Vehicle (SDV). This is a wet submersible that transports six to eight combat swimmers. The SDV has been used by the British SBS and US Navy SEALs,

US Navy divers training in the use of the Seal Delivery Vehicle (SDV). The vehicle is a very tiring means of transport – the divers are pummelled by cold water throughout the journey. Photo: US Navy.

among others, since its introduction in the early 1980s. US Navy SEAL teams are carried by converted nuclear submarines, such as the USS *Kamehameha*, and launched from platforms attached to the deck of the vessels, called dry-dock shelters, while submerged. This is an effective way of transporting a team to their target, but it has considerable drawbacks. The divers travel on the SDV in full diving gear, and are exposed to cold ocean water for the duration of the journey – an experience described by Capt. Joe Fallone, programme manager for the Navy Sea Systems Command, as like 'being locked in the trunk of a car in full dive gear, with a fire hose on you'. After extended exposure to this treatment, even the fittest swimmer cannot perform at his best.

The US Navy has recently introduced the Advanced SEAL Delivery System (ASDS). Built by Northrop Grumman Corporation, the ASDS is an improved version of the SDV for clandestine insertions and extractions of SEAL squads into high-threat environments. The ASDS is a manned, dry-interior, combatant submersible with the necessary range, endurance, speed, payload and other capabilities for SEAL operations in a full range of hostile environments.

'The ASDS will offer us enhanced undersea mobility capabilities for a wide range of special operations,' explained Lt. Cmdr Bob Wilson, executive officer for SEAL Delivery Team One. 'We will be able to take the SEALs over a longer distance with more equipment and get them there dry. They will be fresh for the operation and have that much more capabilities.'

The ASDS is driven by a battery-powered electric motor. It is 8ft in diameter, 65ft long, and weighs about 55 tons. The vehicle will carry 8–16 personnel, can submerge to depths of 245m (800ft) and travel 125 nautical miles at a speed of 8 knots. It can be launched from navy submarines, and is air transportable by C-5 or C-17, and land transportable on specially designed trailer-trucks. The USS *Charlotte* (SSN 766) and USS *Greenville* (SSN 772) have been specially configured to serve as host ships for the ASDS vehicle. New Virginia-class submarines are being designed to carry ASDS.

Specifications – ASDS	
Length:	65ft
Beam:	6.75ft
Height:	8.25ft
Dry weight:	55 tons
Range:	125+ miles
Speed:	8+ knots
Propulsion:	67hp electric motor (Ag-Zn battery)
Diving depth:	245m (800ft)
Crew:	Two: pilot and navigator
Masts:	Two: Port–periscope. Starboard – communication and GPS
Sonar:	Forward-looking – detects natural/man-made obstacles. Side-looking – terrain and bottom-mapping, mine-detection
Passengers:	Up to 16 SEALs, depending on equipment loads

SURFACE CRAFT

Zodiac

The story of Zodiac goes back to the end of the nineteenth century, when the company was involved in the development of early airships and aircraft. In the 1930s the company invented the concept of the inflatable boat, an idea that Special Forces

were quick to latch on to. In the 1960s Zodiac worked with the UK Lifeboat service to develop the Rigid Inflatable Boat (RIB), a design that is now widely used by the armed forces of many countries, as well as professional and leisure users outside the military.

Zodiac F470 CRRC (Combat Rubber Raiding Craft)

The Combat Rubber Raiding Craft is a massively strong rubber inflatable which is used by SEALs and other units for coastal insertion/extraction, including over-the-horizon operations, and in riverine actions. Light and easily handled by a squad, the CRRC can also be airdropped out of a helicopter or C-130 Hercules, the SEALs themselves also dropping into the sea from the aircraft.

The CRRC measures 15ft 5ins (4.7m) long, and is powered by single or

Left: US Navy SEALs return to their ship in a Zodiac inflatable rubber boat. The CRRC is light and easily carried by a squad. Photo: USMC.

dual 35hp outboards, or a single 55hp outboard. It is capable of about 20 knots when carrying eight combat-loaded marines. Significantly, a number of marines have been injured by the engine/propeller after falling from CRRCs – the 'bounciness' of the craft makes it possible for a coxswain or passenger to be thrown out during sudden manoeuvres or in rough seas if they fail to remain seated.

In 2002 Zodiac unveiled Armorflate, a new bullet-resistant system for the CRRC, claimed to turn the F-470 into a 'bulletproof boat'. Made with soft armour from a ballistic material provided by Simula Inc., it folds and stores on the inflatable tubes, taking

Below: The Zodiac CRRC is powered by single or dual outboard motors, and is capable of 20 knots when carrying eight combat-loaded marines. Photo: USMC.

up minimal space. When needed, it can be inflated in about forty seconds to provide armour protection for the occupants, the boat and its engine. Hard armour panels can be inserted in pockets on the soft armour panels to provide upgraded protection.

Zodiac Hurricane RIBs

Zodiac produce a range of RIBs (Rigid Inflatable Boats) which have proved popular with Special Forces for seaborne operations. The range falls broadly into two groups: outboard and inboard models, with lengths from 15ft 5ins to 33ft.

The ZH 850 is an example of an outboard-powered RIB. It is 28ft long, with an aluminium hull, and is used as a fast commando boat as well as for SAR. Its compressed air tanks and special fuel tanks allow it to be airdropped. Radar arches, T-tops, and self-righting frames are designed to fold down for loading into aircraft. It is regularly used with dual 300hp outboards.

The ZH 920 is an inboard-powered RIB, driven by dual 150hp diesel stern drive engines. It has an aluminium hull and offers a versatile platform that can carry troops or supplies. Quick-release components such as seats and bolsters can easily be removed to provide cargo space, and folding superstructures allow the craft to be loaded on to aircraft for rapid deployment. It can be supplied with dual divers' doors.

Gemini inflatables and RIBs

Gemini inflatables were first created in 1979, and have become synonymous with seaborne Special Forces operations. Small three-man Gemini inflatables with 40hp outboards were used by the SAS and SBS in the Falklands War, and have been used in many Special Forces operations since. The company are careful not to disclose details of their military products, but their development team has a strong military

A British Navy Rigid Inflatable Boat (RIB) is brought aboard. RIBs are fast and manoeuvrable, and used by Special Forces for a variety of operations. Photo: US Navy.

background, including former members of UK forces, South African military and the Australian Navy.

Inflatables built by Gemini range in size from 3m to 5.3m and can be airdropped. They are part-inflated, leaving the middle two chambers empty so that they can be folded in half. A swimmer follows the boat out of the aircraft, and uses a high-pressure cylinder to inflate the middle chambers.

Gemini inflatables are strongly made, using Hypalon 1670 DTEX military specification fabric. The tubes can be supplied in a variety of colours, for either high visibility or covert ops.

Rigid Raider

In service with the UK Royal Navy and Army, the Rigid Raider is a fast patrol craft used for patrolling coastal and inland waterways. There are two models in service: the 5.2m Mk1 and the 6.5m Mk2. The Rigid Raider has a flat 'cathedral' fibreglass hull which gives it a very shallow draught and good handling characteristics; in favourable sea conditions it will plane on the water's surface, giving greatly increased speed and improved range. Powered by a single or twin 140hp outboards, it can carry up to ten men and 1,500lbs of equipment, plus a coxswain who sits or stands at the steering console towards the aft end of the boat. Weight of the Mk2 version is 1.31 tons, and it is capable of 30 knots when fully laden.

The Rigid Raider is a fast patrol craft that is well suited to coastal and inland waterways. The flat hull gives it a very shallow draught, and enables it to plane on the water's surface. Photo: author's collection.

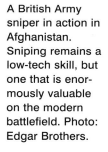 SNIPER WEAPONS AND EQUIPMENT

There are those who say that snipers are not truly 'Special Forces'. Strictly speaking, they may be correct, depending on which definition of the term 'Special Forces' you care to use. However, the military sniper is 'special' in any normal and military sense of the word, and this book would be incomplete without including a section on sniping. In any case, many of the sniper's skills are used by, and useful to, other types of Special Forces such as behind-the-lines patrols, OPs and the like.

The sniper has the skills, ability and equipment to move unnoticed into a position with a good view of the enemy, close enough to shoot accurately, and remain watching for hours or even days without being detected. When the time comes, he may take out a carefully selected target with a single shot at extreme range ... or he may simply fade away like a ghost, to report back the details of an enemy who never knew he was there.

Snipers are by no means a cure-all for every military problem, but used wisely they can have an effect out of all proportion to their cost and numbers – even on today's high-tech battlefield. Sniper units are fond of quoting figures to support this. A sign at the USMC Sniper School reads: 'The average rounds expended per kill with

A British Army sniper in action in Afghanistan. Sniping remains a low-tech skill, but one that is enormously valuable on the modern battlefield. Photo: Edgar Brothers.

the M16 in Vietnam was 50,000. Snipers averaged 1.3. Cost difference: $2,300 vs. 27 cents.' Another way of looking at this is that the average (US) soldier will hit a man-sized target with one shot in ten at 300 metres. The US Army standard for snipers is a 90 per cent first-round hit at 600 metres.

The history of sniping is littered with commanders who failed to understand how best to use snipers. All too often, the sniper has been seen as merely a marksman – an assassin who can hit targets at extreme ranges. On the modern battlefield, snipers are much more than that. Used well, a handful of snipers can halt an entire battalion, by targeting key personnel and communications equipment. They can deny ground to the enemy, destroy the enemy's ability to use key weapons, or buy time for the deployment of additional forces.

Sniping is basically a low-tech skill. A man, dressed in a ragged hessian-covered ghillie suit and handfuls of foliage, crawls into position and uses a simple, one-shot weapon to fire a single bullet at a target. The basic techniques, and even much of the equipment, would be familiar to a Victorian deer stalker: ghillie suit, bolt-action rifle, telescope, compass, map, binoculars. As the battlefield becomes more high-tech, and equipment more sophisticated, it is tempting to think of the sniper as an anachronism, doing a job that can be done more efficiently by modern surveillance equipment and guided munitions. And yet the sniper remains a valuable resource on today's battlefield.

With the development of thermal imaging equipment, it was widely predicted that the sniper's days were numbered. An enemy would be able to spot the sniper simply by sweeping a hillside with a thermal imager, which would instantly show up the sniper's warm body. The 'invisible' sniper would have lost his cloak of invisibility. It didn't work like that, however. The sniper's tactical skills, such as using dead ground, are equally effective against thermal imaging equipment. Snipers have developed further skills to defeat modern surveillance equipment, such as using a camouflaged 'umbrella' to shield their thermal signature, and making use of modern thermal camouflage materials which are designed to dissipate the heat of a human body and make it less visible through a thermal imager.

Sniper rifles themselves have changed little in recent years. Snipers still choose a bolt-action mechanism rather than semi-automatic, and sniper rifles retain the basic stock-receiver-barrel configuration seen on, for instance, the World War Two sniper rifles such as the Lee-Enfield No 4T. Wooden stocks have given way to modern plastics-based materials that are less affected by extremes of moisture and temperature. Modern manufacturing methods permit better-quality barrels and actions that can shoot more accurately. But basically the rifle and its ammunition are largely the same as fifty years ago. Sighting systems have improved enormously, however, with the introduction of high-quality optical and electro-optical sights permitting much greater accuracy in a wide range of conditions.

Snipers have adopted many of the modern electronic aids to navigation and positioning. A sniper pair today would typically be equipped with a GPS receiver and rangefinding binoculars. Other equipment is generally kept to a minimum, but one item that is well worth its weight and bulk is a small electronic anemometer for measuring the strength of the wind. Wind is a constant problem for the sniper, whose bullet may drift several inches, or even feet, as it travels to a distant target under a strong side-wind. A modern pocket anemometer is convenient to carry and gives an accurate indication of wind strength, as well as other useful information such as temperature and barometric pressure – which also influence the performance of the ammunition and need to be taken into account in precision long-range shooting.

Some of the equipment typically carried by a sniper pair is also used by other Special Forces, and therefore appears elsewhere in this book: this includes, for instance, rangefinding binoculars and GPS receivers.

SNIPER RIFLES

British Army L96A1/Accuracy International AW

The British Army's current in-service sniper rifle is produced by Accuracy International in the UK. This is the Accuracy International AW, which has also been selected by thirty-five other countries worldwide, including Sweden and Belgium. It fires the 7.62 x 51mm NATO round, and is a single-shot bolt-action magazine-fed design. The barrel is made from stainless steel and is the floating type, being fitted to the receiver only at the threaded breech end. The stock consists of two halves bolted together, which allow access for maintenance and cleaning. The bolt has been specially designed to resist cold conditions (the 'AW' designation originally meant Arctic Warfare) and will operate at temperatures down to –40°C.

The rifle is fitted with a detachable bipod, which is fully adjustable and can be used in conjunction with a spike at the toe of the butt to form a tripod if the sniper needs to maintain his position for long periods. The stock is adjustable for length by fitting or removing spacers.

The Accuracy International AW is the standard sniper rifle of UK armed forces. It is a single-shot, magazine-fed bolt-action weapon in 7.62mm calibre. Photo: Edgar Brothers.

A variety of telescopic and electro-optical sights can be fitted, depending on the operation, but typically the rifle will be used with a x6 or x10 telescopic sight with rangefinding military graticule. For night-time operations and other specialist uses, the normal telescopic sight can be replaced with an imaging intensifying or thermal imaging sight.

Accuracy International have also produced versions of the AW in other calibres, including .338 Super Magnum and .50. There is a suppressed (silenced) version of the 7.62mm model, with a reduced muzzle velocity to provide effective noise suppression.

The British Army recently acquired nearly 100 Accuracy International .338 Lapua Magnum rifles, although many of these are intended for use by soldiers without full sniper training. It is reported that these rifles will be fitted with Schmidt & Bender 3–12x50 scopes, with mildot and rangefinder stadia reticle.

Specifications	
Manufacturer:	Accuracy International, England
Model:	AW (British Army designation L96A1)
Calibre:	7.62 x 51mm NATO (.308 Win), also available in .338 Lapua Mag and .50 BMG
Action:	Single-shot bolt-action
Feed:	10-round magazine
Sights:	Rail mounting system enables use of a variety of telescopic, optical and electro-optical sights
Weight:	6.5kg (14.3lbs)
Muzzle velocity:	2,756fps (840m/s)
Barrel:	655mm, 4 grooves, RH twist, one turn in 12ins (305mm)

USMC M40A3 (Remington 700 series)

The M40A3 is the latest military sniper incarnation of the Remington 700, a well-proven action that has formed the basis of the US Army and USMC's sniper rifles – among many others – for a number of years. Its predecessor, the M40A1, served the USMC well for years, and the M40A3 shows only relatively minor changes and improvements.

It is based on the Remington 700 Short Action, and built by USMC armourers at Quantico, Virginia. With a simple, rugged bolt-action mechanism and composite stock, it is a tough, resilient and highly accurate rifle. It is fitted with a Harris bipod, Unertl x10 telescopic sight and McMillan Tactical A4 stock that is unaffected by moisture.

Specifications	
Calibre:	7.62 x 51mm NATO (.308 Win)
Barrel:	Schneider Match Grade SS7, 24ins (610mm), 4 grooves, RH twist, one turn in 12in (305mm)

A USMC sniper in action in Afghanistan, using the M40A1 rifle built on Remington's 700 Short Action, a simple and rugged bolt-action design. Photo: USMC.

Action:	Single-shot bolt action with 5-round box magazine
Muzzle velocity:	2,540fps (775m/s)
Length:	44.25ins (1,124mm)
Weight:	16.5lbs (7.5kg)
Trigger:	Adjustable between 3 and 5 lbs
Sight:	Unertl x10 with mildots and BDC
Stock:	McMillan Tactical A4
Max. effective range:	1,000 yards (915 metres)

Armalon PR series

In addition to the US Army and Marine Corps' sniper rifles, there are many other variations and customisations based on the Remington 700 action. One example is the Armalon PR series of rifles, produced by Armalon Ltd in the UK.

The Armalon PR is a high-precision magazine-fed bolt-action rifle, available in 7.62 and 5.56mm calibres. The rifles are normally fitted with an HS Precision composite stock, which has an integral high strength 7075 alloy skeleton chassis and bedding block encapsulated within the carbon fibre, Kevlar and GRP outer shell structure of the stock.

The PR series rifles use a fluted barrel, which retains the stiffness and shot to shot consistency of heavier, round-profile barrels, while improving the barrel's heat dissipation. An optional 'mirage band' can be fitted above the barrel to reduce the mirage effects of air passing over a hot barrel. An optional muzzle brake can be fitted to reduce felt recoil and muzzle deflection on firing. This helps the shooter to retain the scope picture of his target between shots, and watch the fall of shot.

The Armalon PR series of rifles have achieved many notable successes in competition shooting, such as the NATO Services Championships.

Barrett M82A1 'Light Fifty'

The Barrett 'Light Fifty' is the heavyweight among sniper rifles, and one with an awesome reputation. It fires the devastatingly effective .50 calibre Browning Machine Gun (.50 BMG) round, with an effective range of nearly two kilometres and the power to stop a soft-skinned vehicle in its tracks or demolish a lightly fortified position. Needless to say, the effect on the human body is lethal, regardless of any body armour worn.

The rifle is a semi-automatic, air-cooled, box magazine-fed weapon that operates on the short-recoil principle. It has standard iron sights for emergency use, but is normally fitted with a telescopic sight and a bipod. The rifle is considered to have an effective range of around 1,800m, although in sniping terms the maximum effective range is usually limited by tactical or environmental factors rather than the sheer distance a bullet will travel.

The 'Light Fifty' was conceived as an anti-matériel weapon, that is to say a weapon that could be used to knock out enemy assets such as trucks and aircraft

The Barrett M82A1 'Light Fifty' is an awesome sniper weapon, firing the .50 cal Browning Machine Gun round which will defeat any body armour and has a range of 2km. Photo: US DoD.

from a distance of over a kilometre, and deny ground to enemy forces. In this role it has certainly proved its worth, but experience has shown it is a valuable tool in other ways too.

In peacekeeping operations, such as those in the Balkans towards the end of the twentieth century, the 'Light Fifty' was used as an effective anti-sniper weapon. Snipers armed with standard .30 calibre weapons would hide in buildings or lightly fortified positions giving a commanding view of an area, and cause havoc among the opposing civilian population. With one or two well-placed .50 rounds, a peacekeeping force sniper could effectively discourage this and make the enemy sniper's position untenable. In the 1991 Gulf War and elsewhere, EOD operators have found the 'Light Fifty' useful for neutralising unexploded ordnance from a safe distance.

The weapon has been shown to have a significant psychological effect, causing a serious loss of morale among troops who know that their enemy possesses a .50 calibre sniping capability. When the IRA obtained a small number of 'Light Fifties' in the 1980s, the weapon was much feared by British troops stationed in Northern Ireland, and for a while even conventional sniper attacks were attributed to the .50 calibre weapon.

Specifications	
Manufacturer:	Barrett Firearms Manufacturing Inc., Tennessee, USA
Model:	M82A1 (Barrett 'Light Fifty')
Calibres:	.50 BMG (12.7 x 99mm NATO)
Action:	Recoil-operated semi-automatic.
Feed:	10-shot detachable box magazine
Sights:	Normally fitted with telescopic sights
Weight:	28.5lbs
Length:	57ins overall
Barrel:	29ins, rifled 1 turn in 15ins

The Barrett M82A1 'Light Fifty'. Photo: Barrett.

TELESCOPIC SIGHTS

There are many different manufacturers of telescopic sights around the world, although not all are suitable for military use. Scopes favoured by military snipers include Schmidt & Bender and Leupold.

Schmidt & Bender scopes

The German company of Schmidt & Bender produce rifle scopes that are highly respected for their superb optics, exceptional lens coatings and rugged quality. These scopes are used by deer stalkers and other sport shooters in all types of climate and conditions, and have long been one of the top choices for snipers and military and police marksmen.

The company produces a range of dedicated scopes intended for snipers, SWAT and tactical teams, police marksmen and the like. The latest versions of these are known as Police Marksman II, or P/M II. The scopes are available in a range of specifications, including a fixed magnification 10 x 42 scope and two variable models, 3–12 x 50 and 4–16 x 50. The variable models have a 34mm main tube (cf 30mm for the 10 x 42). The knurled adjustment knobs are easy to turn, with a positive feel to each precise click. Each click moves the point of impact 10mm at 100m (.358ins at 100 yards). Each second click is marked with a white line, while each tenth click is marked with a number. For example, number 1 represents 10 clicks or 100mm at 100m (3.58ins at 100 yards).

The oversized adjustment turrets allow quick, precise adjustment for windage and elevation. A third turret controls the parallax adjustment – claimed to be more convenient than the normal ring on the objective bell of the scope. Non-adjusting scopes have the parallax set at zero for 300 yards. In the S&B illuminated reticle model, the third turret controls the reticle brightness.

The scopes are threaded to accept either a soft rubber shade (with aluminium base) or a hard aluminium shade, to reduce glare, protect the front lens from rain etc., and minimise reflections from the lens which might compromise the sniper (although scrim or similar material is usually placed over the lens to prevent this).

Leupold scopes

Leupold is a US-based company well known for its range of quality rifle scopes, including tactical military and police models that are used by many Special Forces, SWAT teams and the like. Leupold scopes are renowned for their robustness, accuracy and optical excellence. The tactical scopes in Leupold's range consist of the fixed magnification Mk4 models, and the variable magnification Vari-X II and III scopes. Several of the variable magnification models are designated 'Long Range' and incorporate a number of features specifically designed for longer-range tactical shooting.

Leupold Mark 4 Scopes

Leupold Mark 4 scopes are noted for edge-to-edge optical sharpness and excellent low-light capability. They have a side focus knob which enables the shooter to adjust parallax from fifty yards to infinity while in the shooting position. All Mark 4 scopes come with a lens shade and Butler Creek 'Flip Open' lens covers.

The oversized adjustment knobs on Mark 4 M1-10 x 40mm and Mark 4 M1-16 x 40mm give audible and tactile confirmation of each 1/4-MOA (MOA = Minute Of Angle – 1 MOA is equivalent to approximately 1in at 100yds) click. The elevation knob has a horizontal scale for counting adjustment revolutions. The Mark 4 M3-10 x 40mm has bullet-drop compensation marks, 1-MOA elevation clicks and 1/2-MOA windage clicks. The windage and elevation dials can both be set to show zero after the scope is sighted-in, simplifying the allowance of windage and elevation in the field – the shooter simply calculates the amount of adjustment needed, and turns the dial the correct number of clicks away from the 'zero' point on the dial.

■ Mark 4 M1-10 x 40mm ■ Mark 4 M1-16 x 40mm ■ Mark 4 M3-10 x 40mm

Leupold Vari-X-II and Vari-X III Tactical Scopes

The Vari-X range are variable power scopes, with 1/4-MOA adjustment clicks. (MOA = Minute of Angle – 1 MOA is equivalent to approximately 1in at 100 yards) Each full revolution of the windage or elevation dial gives a 15-MOA adjustment. These scopes give an extremely high-quality sight picture, adding to the shooter's confidence and control.

Some of the scopes in the range, such as the Vari-X III 3.5–10 x 40mm Tactical and the Vari-X III 4.5–14 x 40mm Adj. Obj. Tactical, have built-in range estimating, employing the standard duplex reticle and rear-facing numbers on the power selector ring to approximate the distance to targets. Like all Leupold tactical scopes, these models are available with a mildot ranging reticle.

Vari-X II 3–9 x 40mm Tactical
Vari-X III 3.5–10 x 40mm Tactical
Vari-X III 4.5–14 x 40mm Adj. Obj. Tactical

Specifications – Leupold Vari-X III 3-5-10 x 40

Actual Magnification:	3.3(3.5x) 9.7(10x)
Length:	13.50ins (343mm)
Eyepiece length:	3.0ins (76.2mm)
Objective length:	4.30ins (109mm)
Objective diameter:	1.80ins (46mm)
Objective lens diameter:	1.575ins (40mm)
Eyepiece diameter:	1.60ins (41mm)
Tube diameter:	1.18ins (30mm)
Weight:	19.5oz. (553g)
Eye relief:	4.6ins (117mm) at x3.5, 3.6ins (91mm) at x10
Max. adjustment:	65ins at 100yds
	1.81m at 100m

Field of view:	x3.5: 29.5ft at 100yds	x10: 10.7ft at 100yds
	x3.5: 9.8m at 100m	x10: 3.6m at 100m

Leupold Long-Range Scopes

Long-range tactical situations are especially demanding, with no room for error. Leupold's 'Long Range' scopes are built to particularly high standards, and include features to help the sniper achieve the best possible accuracy. The Vari-X III 3.5–10 x 40mm Long Range M1, for instance, has oversized adjustment knobs and elevation adjustments in 1/4-MOA clicks for precision adjustments and is available with an illuminated reticle for use in low light situations. All the long-range models have turret-mounted side focusing and 30mm main tubes. The Vari-X III 3.5–10 x 40mm Long Range M3 has specially calibrated adjustment dials that are interchangeable for bullet drop compensation. A side parallax adjustment dial allows parallax elimination from a shooting position.

Vari-X III 3.5–0 x 40mm Long Range M1
Vari-X III 3.5–10 x 40mm Long Range M3
Vari-X III 3.5–10 x 40mm Long Range M1 Illuminated Reticle
Vari-X III 3.5–10 x 40mm Long Range M3 Illuminated Reticle
Vari-X III 4.5–14 x 50mm Long Range M1
Vari-X III 6.5–20 x 50mm Long Range M1

SNIPER WEAPON NIGHT SIGHTS

Simrad KN200 and KN250 Image Intensifiers

The Simrad KN200 and KN250 image intensifiers are clip-on units that provide a night-time capability to optical day sights. The night-vision image is viewed through the eyepiece of the day sight. This allows the user to retain the same eye position, aiming reticle and magnification for both day and night use.

The Simrad image intensifying night-sight gives the sniper the ability to shoot to 400m and beyond at night. The sight has a magnification of x1 and piggy-backs on to the rifle scope (daysight). This means that the daysight never has to be removed, resulting in no loss of zero. The Simrad can be boresighted to the daysight and also allows the daysight to be used if required, by flipping down a small rubber cover. The sight is powered by two 1.5v AA batteries giving up to eighty hours' use.

Features

Clip-on system for rapid mounting	No requirement for boresighting
Focus control	Variable gain control
Waterproof to 20 metres, (option)	Laser illuminator and pointer, (options)
NATO codified	

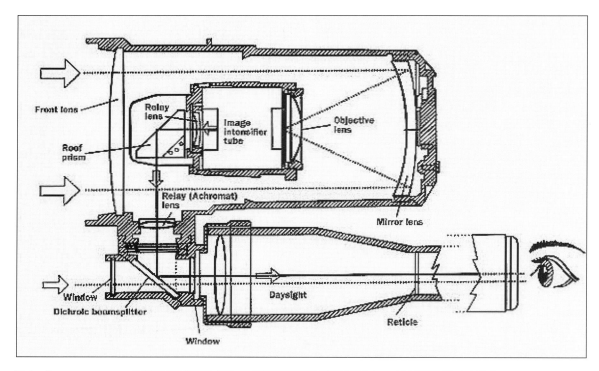

Front lens

Relay lens

Image intensifier tube

Objective lens

Roof prism

Relay (Achromat) lens

Mirror lens

Window

Dichroic beamsplitter

Daysight

Reticle

Window

This diagram shows the workings of the Simrad KN200 image intensifier, which attaches to a standard riflescope to provide a night-time capability. Photo: Simrad.

Specifications – KN 250	
Dimensions (w x h x l):	107 x 142 x 187mm
Weight (inc. batteries):	1kg (approx)
Field of view:	12°
Magnification:	1x
Focusing:	25m to infinity
Battery:	2 x 1.5v AA cells
Battery life:	>80h at 20°C
Operating temperature:	–40°C to 50°C
Storage temperature:	–40°C to 65°C

SNIPER AMMO

High-quality ammunition is important to the sniper, who demands the highest precision in order to shoot accurately at the limits of his, his rifle's and his ammunition's capabilities. Most sniper rifles are chambered for the 7.62 x 51mm NATO (.308 Winchester) round, which has been the standard for a good many years, and is considered to have a useful range of around 800m. This round is well proven in combat, and has been the subject of much research and development work during that time. This familiarity is important to snipers, who through practical experience have developed rules of thumb governing how the round will perform in the field. This enables them to make quick adjustments for changes in wind, target speed and the like, backing them up with more detailed calculation if time permits.

Various manufacturers produce the type of high-quality match-grade ammunition required for sniping. British military sniper ammo is generally provided by Royal Ordnance, and is headstamped 'RG' to indicate it is made at the company's Radway Green manufacturing facility. The round fires a 143grain FMJ (Full Metal Jacket) bullet, which is sometimes criticised as too light for long-range sniping; many snipers prefer a 150grain (9.7g) or even 170grain (11g) bullet, such as those produced by Lapua.

For certain police and urban situations, a sniper will choose to use the 5.56 x 45mm NATO round (as used in assault rifles such as the M16 and SA80). This round does not have the range or knock-down power of the larger 7.62mm, but has the advantage that it is less likely to penetrate walls, vehicles and the like, possibly endangering members of the public.

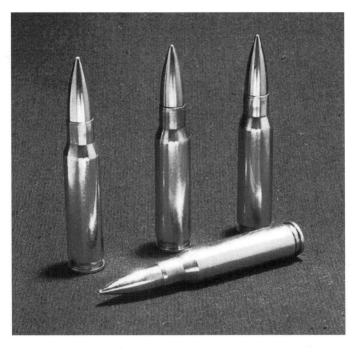

Snipers are very particular about their ammunition – a top quality 'match grade' round gives better consistency from shot to shot. Photo: Nammo.

At the other end of the scale is the .50 BMG (12.7 x 99 mm) cartridge, used in anti-matériel sniper rifles such as the Barrett 'Light Fifty'. Precision-made .50 BMG calibre rifle ammunition has a maximum effective range up to 2,000m, and is a powerful round that is more than capable of knocking out a soft-skinned vehicle or aircraft at that range. The .50 calibre rifle is big, heavy and not very manoeuvrable, however, and has considerable noise and muzzle blast which can easily compromise a sniper who is trying to remain hidden.

Filling the gap between the 7.62mm and .50 calibre is the .338 Lapua Magnum (8.6 x 70mm). This round has an effective range up to 1,500m, and is fired from a rifle of similar weight and dimensions to the 7.62. The .338 is powerful enough to defeat most types of body armour, and can be used effectively in the anti-matériel role against vehicles and aircraft. For most military applications, the .338 ammunition of choice will be match grade ball ammunition with a 16.2g (250grain) FMJBT (Full Metal Jacket Boat Tail) bullet. Lapua themselves produce such a round, with their Streamlined Lock Base bullet. This has an excellent ballistic coefficient, and it maintains its velocity well at ranges beyond 1,000m. There is an AP (Armour Piercing) version of this round (as with other calibres), known as AP 485. This bullet can be effectively used against fortifications, light armoured vehicles and personnel wearing body armour. It will penetrate 15mm (0.6in) of hardened steel (hardness HB400) at a distance of 500m.

ANEMOMETER

There are many factors that can affect the 'fall of shot' – the point where the sniper's bullet strikes – at a given range. These include temperature, pressure, humidity and wind, all of which affect the way the bullet flies through the air and modify its trajectory. Of these, wind is generally the biggest problem. A 10mph side wind at 90° to the bullet's path will deflect it by around 0.7in at 100yds, and 3in at 200yds. This may not sound a lot, but at 800yds the same 10mph wind produces 64ins of drift – more than 5ft – and twice the wind will produce twice that amount of drift. The precise figures depend on the round used – heavier, faster bullets are deflected less than lighter ones. Military snipers carry tables to show the allowance needed to compensate for the effects of wind.

The Silva Alba Windwatch gives the sniper an accurate measure of wind speed, enabling it to calculate the bullet's drift downrange. It also measures pressure and altitude. Photo: Silva.

Snipers practise estimating the wind strength (which may vary between the firer and the target) by watching its effects on foliage, dust, water and the like. A 'fresh' wind of 15mph (24kph), for instance, will raise dust and paper, and cause small branches on trees to be in constant motion. For the most accurate results, however, it is best to use a pocket anemometer such as the Silva product shown below.

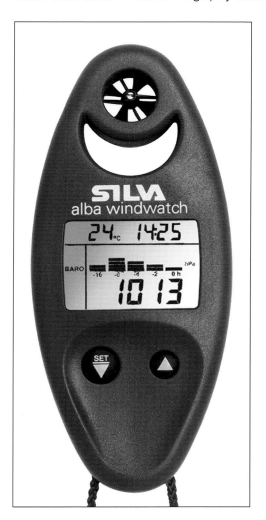

Silva Alba Windwatch

The Silva Alba Windwatch is made in Switzerland by the company better known for their compasses. It is essentially a combination instrument, which can measure wind speed, barometric pressure/altitude and temperature – all factors that are useful to the sniper in calculating the allowances necessary for an accurate shot. The instrument is contained in a rugged ABS plastic casing, which is waterproof and will float if dropped in water.

The pressure sensor gives an accurate reading of current barometric pressure, as well as trend data for the past sixteen hours and information about current altitude. The impeller gives the wind speed in m/sec, knots, kph, mph or Beaufort scale. Readings can be shown as current, peak and average wind speed over a selected period. While not in use the wind sensor impeller is fully protected by a simple twist of the casing. The device can also calculate the wind chill based on ambient temperature and wind speed. Temperature readings for the range –20°C to 55°C (–4°F to 131°F) can be shown in either °C or °F.

The highly versatile Windwatch has proved popular with civilian target shooters as well as military snipers, and offers a mine of useful information at little cost in terms of weight and bulk.

Specifications

Weight:	55g
Dimensions:	10 x 4 x 1.8cm (3.93 x 1.57 x 0.70in)
Altitude indication:	0–10,000m (0–30,000ft)
Resolution:	1m (3ft)
Barometric pressure indication:	hPa or inHg
Resolution:	1hPa/0.01inHg
Wind speed indication:	m/s, knots, km/h, mph, Beaufort
Resolution:	0.1m/s
Averaging for wind speed:	5 to 60 sec, in steps of 5 sec.
Operating range, wind speed:	0.1m/s to 40m/s (ca 140kph)
Accuracy for wind speed:	+/–4%
Temperature range:	–20°C to 55°C (–4°F to 131°F)
Temperature display:	Celsius or Fahrenheit
Accuracy for temperature:	+/–2% .
Resolution of temperature:	1°C or 1°F
Clock:	Quartz clock gives time in hours and minutes
Casing:	High impact ABS
Water-resistant:	IP64
Battery type:	3v lithium battery, type CR 2032
Battery life:	Approx. 1 year (with low battery warning)
Lanyard:	Included
Warranty:	2 years

OBSERVATION

Leica Vector (Viper) binoculars

Snipers are typically issued Leica Vector (Viper) rangefinding binoculars, as described in Chapter 3. These have excellent optics for observation, will give an accurate range measurement – essential for precision shooting – and can interface with the Rockwell Collins PLGR series of GPS receivers for accurate location of enemy forces. See Chapter 3 for details of these binoculars.

Leupold 12–40 x 60mm Variable Power Spotting Scope

The sniper and his spotter will generally be issued with some sort of spotting scope, which offers greater magnification than the binoculars or telescopic sight available to them. This is helpful for identification of targets at long range, range estimation, and adjusting the fall of shot.

The Leupold 12–40 x 60mm spotting scope is a popular choice. Its configuration effectively compresses the performance of a long spotting scope into a compact package measuring 5.5 x 11.3ins. The Leupold scope gives high-quality optical performance, with a reticle of mildots and stadia enabling accurate rangefinding. The tough, light magnesium body is coated with a protective rubber armour, and it is nitrogen filled and sealed to guarantee waterproof performance. Optically, the scope has multiple lens coatings, a light-absorbing interior finish to suppress glare, and an efficient lens and mirror optical system combine to transmit the maximum amount of available light to the user's eye. The result is a sight picture that is bright, crisp, and rich in visual detail.

Specifications		
Minimum focus distance:	12yds	
Height:	5.5ins	
Length:	11.3 in at min diopter	
Weight:	929g (32oz)	
Objective diameter:	60mm	
Setting:	x12	x40
Magnification:	x 12.7	x 40.0
Exit pupil diameter:	5.0mm	1.5mm
Field of view (angular):	3.4°	1.1°
Field of view (linear) at 100yds:	17.8ft	5.8ft
Field of view (linear) at 100m:	5.9m	1.9m
Eye relief	31.1mm	29.2mm
Twilight factor	26.8	48.9
Relative brightness	25	2.3

Clothing, camouflage and hide building

The sniper pair will generally wear ghillie suits, which they will construct themselves by attaching strips of hessian to a camouflage jacket, then 'distressing' it. Every sniper has his favourite method for this, including tumbling it in a dryer, dragging it across country behind a vehicle, and giving it a good beasting with a wire brush. The ghillie suit was developed in Victorian times by Scottish gamekeepers for lying in wait to catch poachers, and the principle has since been adopted by snipers throughout the world. Local vegetation is built in to the ghillie suit to add to the camouflage effect.

Snipers must pay great attention to personal camouflage, including details such as wearing brown-soled boots (since black soles can show up against lighter vegetation), camouflaging the rifle barrel and action, and placing scrim netting over the optics of riflescope and binoculars. Failure to take obsessive care over such detail can lead to the sniper being spotted, and mistakes are likely to prove fatal.

In some tactical situations it may be necessary to construct a hide, which can involve anything from minor modifications to a bush, to digging a sophisticated underground hide. The sniper pair will carry a small selection of tools for hide-building, typically comprising a digging tool (tri-fold entrenching shovel), pruners and folding saw. Where the enemy are known to be using thermal imaging equipment, thermal sheeting and the appropriate support poles etc. may also be carried.

The ghillie suit was invented by Scottish game-keepers for ambushing poachers. Today it is used by specialist sniper units around the world. Photos: USMC.

Fibrotex multi-spectral camouflage systems

The Fibrotex multi-spectral camouflage net is a lightweight system which provides full operational protection against sensors in the visual, infra-red, thermal and radar spectrums.

The netting is produced in flat sheets or made up into coverall suits. It combines camouflage pattern material with high-tech coatings that reflect back the infra-red, thermal and radar signature of the surroundings, effectively hiding the sniper from all types of sensors in use on the battlefield.

ASSAULT AND RAPID-ENTRY EQUIPMENT

At 7.23 pm on a Bank Holiday Monday, 5 May 1980, the British SAS (Special Air Service) stormed the Iranian Embassy in Prince's Gate, London. The assault, named Operation Nimrod, was watched live by a massive TV audience, thrusting the SAS unwillingly into the media spotlight.

The siege had begun five days earlier, at 11.25 a.m. on 30 April, when six armed Iranians overpowered police constable Trevor Lock, who was on duty outside the embassy. Inside they took twenty-six hostages, mostly embassy staff, and began making their demands: the release of ninety-one political prisoners in Iran, and a plane to fly themselves out of the UK. During the tense negotiations that followed, press photographers and TV news crews set up outside the building; the crisis became a real-life TV drama.

When the body of a hostage, Abbas Lavasani, was pushed out of the embassy door, it was clear the time for negotiations was over. Twenty minutes later, the SAS assault team went in. Within fifteen minutes, five of the six terrorists were dead. All but one of the hostages, killed by the terrorists, were free. The SAS team were on their way back to Hereford, and the legend of 'The Embassy Siege' was born.

It was not the first such operation; three years earlier, on 13 October 1977, a GSG9 team aided by the SAS had successfully stormed LH181, a Lufthansa Boeing 737 at Mogadishu. Significantly, stun grenades provided by the SAS were used to initiate the assault. Three of the four Palestinian terrorists were killed, and all the hostages were released.

Operation Nimrod was unique, however, in that it was watched live by millions on TV. British newspapers published detailed graphics showing how the assault had been carried out, together with photographs of the SAS teams moving into position on the embassy roof, abseiling down to the windows and placing frame charges, and finally handling the hostages (and one surviving terrorist) on the small patch of grass at the back of the building. In the months and years that followed, the whole area of CRW (Counter Revolutionary Warfare) attracted massive public interest, spawning a host of books, videos and films featuring dramatic scenes of hostage rescue.

In some ways the high-profile nature of Operation Nimrod, and the continuing interest in hostage rescue, has been unhelpful to Special Forces and SWAT teams. The advantage of surprise is largely lost if hostage-takers know what to expect. They can obtain special protective equipment to prepare themselves for an attack supported with stun grenades, CS gas and 9mm SMGs. On the other hand, it sent a clear message to terrorists around the world, and has certainly acted as a deterrent against similar hostage-taking attempts. It has also encouraged a number of people (not all of them suitable, of course) to seek a career in Special Forces at a time when recruitment has proved difficult.

Before going into details of the equipment used in hostage rescue and similar operations, it is worth reiterating that, as elsewhere in this book, we have been careful to avoid giving details of equipment and techniques that could be of use to terrorists. All the information that follows is in the public domain, and available from unrestricted sources. Certain equipment and information has been deliberately omitted, in order not to compromise operational security.

SURVEILLANCE

In any hostage situation, one of the security forces' first tasks is to gather information: about the terrorists, the hostages, the building or craft in which they are being

This hostage-taker is unaware that he is being closely watched by the surveillance team with high-tech video and audio equipment. Photo: PW Allen.

held, and any other intelligence that may be relevant. One aspect of this involves drawing on other departments' resources – such as immigration records, police and security services' files, architects' plans, etc. It is also vital to get a look inside the besieged building to ascertain the numbers and positions of terrorists and hostages, the type of weapons used, the terrorists' morale and state of readiness, and so forth.

After the Iranian Embassy assault, it was widely reported that various surveillance devices had been deployed. These included microphones lowered down the embassy chimneys, and miniature video cameras inserted in holes drilled through the walls from adjoining buildings. Indeed, the kidnappers quizzed PC Trevor Lock about the sounds of drilling (he blamed the sound on mice in the walls!). Aircraft heading for London's Heathrow Airport were diverted over the embassy so that the noise would mask the sound, and 'workmen' began drilling noisily in the street near by. The information gained from these devices was vital in preparing the assault plan, and undoubtedly helped to preserve the lives of the hostages and assault team members.

Today, more than twenty years on, the equipment available to security forces has become more sophisticated, smaller and more reliable than anything available at the time of the Iranian Embassy siege. The principles remain much the same, however: specialised cameras and audio equipment are used to gain a clear picture of what is happening inside the besieged building, without alerting the kidnappers.

Without going into unnecessary detail, the security forces will also ensure that they control communications in and out of the besieged building, whether by land-line or by RF (radio frequency) communications. They will also take control of services such as water, gas and electricity into the building, as well as the supply of food, cigarettes, medical supplies etc. to the terrorists and their hostages.

Wall/ceiling scopes

There are various scopes available for viewing through a hole drilled in a wall or ceiling. A typical example is supplied by P. W. Allen, and comes as a kit that includes the endoscope itself, a mounting bracket suitable for various types of wall, drill bits and centring bushing, and a carrying case.

The endoscope probe measures 2.5mm in diameter (approximately 1/10in – about the size of a match head) and is available in lengths of 180mm and 280mm. It has an offset mirror that gives a 55 degree field of view, and can be rotated to cover an 85 degree view of the interior of the room under surveillance.

The scope gives a bright, sharp image that can be viewed directly through an eyepiece, or remotely by coupling the device to a video camera by means of an adaptor. It can also be used with an infra-red camera to provide an image if the room under surveillance is in darkness.

The through-ceiling scope is a shorter version of the through-wall scope. It is set up in the same way, being inserted through a 2.5mm diameter hole drilled in a ceiling tile or plasterboard ceiling. As with the through-wall scope, it provides an offset 55 degree field of view.

Under-door viewer

Another device for covertly viewing the interior of a room is the under-door viewer. P. W. Allen supply such a device, which slips easily under a door with a gap as small as 6mm. The device has a 55 degree field of view, and can be adjusted once in position to survey the entire interior of the room. The kit also includes a right-angle adaptor that provides a clear view of the inside surface of the door. This enables the user to examine any barricades or booby traps that may have been set up.

The PW Allen under-door viewer is slipped under a door to view the interior of the room beyond. An adaptor makes it possible to check the door for booby traps. Photo: PW Allen.

The under-door scope has a C-mount so that a video camera can be attached, or the picture can be viewed directly with a detachable eyepiece. As with the through-ceiling and through-wall scopes, the under-door scope can also be used with IR viewing equipment if the room is in darkness. An IR light source is available to provide illumination.

Peephole viewers

Many houses and flats have a peephole viewer on the main entry door. The optical design of this type of viewer allows a person inside to see clearly anyone standing outside the door, but it is hard to see through the other way, into the building. However, by using a scope with specially designed optics, it is possible to view the interior.

P. W. Allen supply two types of peephole viewer. One is a small diameter scope, similar to a small telescope, that is held to the eye and looked through directly. The other consists of a miniature low-light video camera, with a specially designed video lens. The camera has a bracket that fits quickly onto standard interior and exterior door peephole viewers. The picture relayed by the camera can then be viewed on a monitor, or recorded for use as evidence. The angle of view depends on the optics inside the peephole viewer itself, but usually allows a good view of the room behind. The camera is powered by a standard 9v battery, or a mains adaptor.

Audio probes

When a terrorist group is holding hostages inside a building, aircraft or vessel, obtaining real-time pictures of the scene inside is clearly a huge advantage for negotiators, and for planning an assault. However, pictures tell only part of the story; having audio as well can provide a great deal more intelligence. Audio will help to assess the terrorists' state of mind as well as their level of preparedness and their plans – as they discuss events, give orders to one another, or argue among themselves. It will also help to determine how the hostages are likely to react when an assault takes place.

P. W. Allen supply an audio surveillance probe designed to be used in conjunction with their through-wall and through-ceiling video probes. It consists of a 4mm diameter stainless steel microphone probe that can run in the same drill bush mounting as the video probe.

The audio probe has an electret microphone characterised by its wide, flat frequency response, high sensitivity and low noise. It is ruggedly housed to withstand severe conditions, and being pushed through brick and plasterwork. The microphone is normally used in conjunction with the matched battery-powered amplifier and headphones supplied in the kit, but provided the microphone is connected to a suitable power source (0.9–1.6v DC) it can be connected to any compatible amplifier and recording equipment.

Dog collar camera

Sandia in the US have been evaluating the potential of a wireless video 'K-9' camera attached to a dog's collar for use in hostage negotiations and rescues. The project was inspired partly by the April 1999 Columbine High School attack, when officers lacked the reliable information they needed to safely enter school buildings. Work on the project, funded by the NIJ, began in April 2001.

The system consists of a camera attached to a collar worn by a trained police dog. The dog is sent into a building where terrorists or criminals are believed to be hiding. The video image collected by the camera is transmitted to a hand-held video receiver; the signal will pass through the walls of a target building.

The project received a field test rather sooner than planned. Shortly after the World Trade Center attack on 11 September 2001, NIJ project officials contacted Sandia to see whether the kits could be deployed rapidly to aid the Federal Emergency Management Agency's (FEMA) Urban Search and Rescue (US&R) teams as they scoured the rubble for survivors.

Sandia project leader Richard Sparks spent twenty-two days at the site helping the US&R teams outfit their search dogs with the cameras and radios attached to special collars carried by the dogs. The kits were in use twenty-four hours a day for several weeks. The real-life situation provided valuable information about the K-9 cameras' potential uses not only in law enforcement, but also in emergency response, and helped suggest needed improvements.

Other surveillance methods

In a hostage or siege situation, the security forces will remain flexible and use any surveillance equipment and methods that may prove useful in the circumstances. Any of the equipment described in Chapter 2 may be deployed as appropriate, in order to gain the maximum intelligence about the terrorists and hostages, and any physical information about the building and obstacles that may have been emplaced by the terrorists. For a team planning an assault, details of a building's layout and construction (materials and thicknesses of walls, doors, etc.) are vital in deciding how best to carry out the assault.

Snipers will be deployed early in the operation, positioned to provide good all-round surveillance of the target building, craft or vehicle. A good sniper will provide a constant flow of valuable intelligence about the terrorists' locations and actions, as well as details of weapons carried, level of alertness, etc.

All these sources of intelligence will be collected and collated at the command post, and will aid commanders in preparing their plans and choosing between the various options.

LADDER SYSTEMS, VEHICLE PLATFORMS, ABSEIL EQUIPMENT

When an assault is made on a building, aircraft or vessel, speed, aggression and surprise are vital to the success of the operation. The terrorists should have no idea that an assault is about to take place until the assault team are in and shooting. Even a few seconds' delay could give them time to kill hostages, detonate a bomb or fire back at the troopers.

Clearly this means that the assault team must be in place at the entry points, ready to enter immediately they are breached (in the next section we will look at the

equipment used rapidly to breach doors, windows and walls).

As millions saw in May 1980, abseiling from a roof is one way to gain access to windows above ground level. Once a team is in position on the roof, they can quickly and covertly drop to the level of the target window, emplace frame charges, throw in stun grenades and swing inside. Of course things do not always go smoothly, as in Operation Nimrod, where one SAS trooper became entangled in his abseil rope above a burning window. He suffered severe burns before his colleagues cut him down; to his credit he promptly entered the building and shot a terrorist dead.

The architecture of the Iranian Embassy lent itself to an assault. The building was not especially high, and there were balconies and balustrades on which the assault team could assemble ready to enter the building. Other types of buildings, not to mention ships, aircraft, trains and buses, present a range of problems. The SAS and other counter-terrorist forces constantly practise techniques for assaulting every kind of situation where their specialist skills might be called for. In conjunction with various manufacturers,

Abseiling (or rappelling) allows the assault team to gain access quickly and with minimum disturbance. The technique can be used from a roof or, as shown here, a helicopter. Photo: author's collection.

they have developed a range of specialist equipment for the job. The equipment is designed to be as adaptable and versatile as possible, as there is no knowing where terrorists may strike.

Camlock PDE vehicle system

The PDE vehicle system has been developed by Camlock Engineering Ltd of Hereford, England, in conjunction with British Special Forces. The system may be fitted to a prepared vehicle in minutes, and can deliver fully equipped troopers at various heights, with the added advantage of cover from other personnel positioned on the vehicle. Camlock's ground assault ladders can also be carried on the vehicle, providing a highly effective system for Special Forces troopers to assault a variety of buildings, vehicles and aircraft. Naturally, a number of suitably equipped vehicles can be used simultaneously to attack the target at multiple entry points.

The system can be fitted to any suitable vehicle – typically a powerful 4x4 on/off road vehicle such as a Land Rover, Range Rover, Toyota Land Cruiser or Mercedes

A CAV100 Land Rover fitted with the Camlock PDE vehicle system for assaulting a hijacked aircraft. Photo: NP Aerospace.

G-Wagen. The basis of the system is a rigid main deck, mounted on the roof of the vehicle. Clamp hand wheels secure the platform to the vehicle in seconds, and anti-slide pins prevent it slipping, even under heavy braking or acceleration.

The platform is fitted with grab handles and hand-rails so that personnel can cling on safely even if the vehicle has to travel over rough ground or perform sudden manoeuvres. Side ladders with sniper platforms allow additional personnel to be deployed at the sides of the vehicle, to provide cover for the main team. The side ladders are attached to the vehicle with heavy-duty steel hooks and secured with a ring-pin. There is a bonnet protector so that troopers can deploy quickly to the ground from the main platform by stepping on to the bonnet – the protector's surface is ridged to provide a good grip even in wet conditions.

The ladders are attached with special fixings that are easily adjustable, yet can be quickly locked in position with a cam-lock system (hence the name). This makes it possible to set up the system very quickly to assault a target with entry points at just about any height.

DOOR, WINDOW AND WALL BREACHING EQUIPMENT

Once the assault team is in position, it is essential to gain entry very quickly indeed, so that the terrorists do not have time to kill their hostages, attempt to escape or mount a counter-attack. There are a wide variety of rapid entry tools available for breaching the many different types of doors, windows, walls, etc. that may be encountered.

As in Operation Nimrod, explosives may provide the fastest and most effective means of gaining entry. They have the added advantage that the sudden noise, blast, dust and smoke of an explosion can help to disorientate the terrorists – especially if charges are emplaced at multiple entry points around the target building and the detonations are synchronised.

Practical experience and trials have made it possible to predict accurately the size and type of charge most suitable for a wide range of different walls, doors, window frames, etc. Clearly it is important to gauge this correctly: too weak a charge will simply warn the terrorists of impending attack, while too strong a charge may injure hostages or members of the assault team, or leave parts of the building dangerously unstable. In his book *Fire Magic*, former SAS trooper Barry Davies, BEM, describes how on an exercise he added the favourite ingredient 'P for Plenty' – and completely flattened the house they were supposed to be assaulting!

For a combat engineer skilled in such work, it is relatively straightforward to rig up a frame charge for a specific task, using commonly available materials and military explosives such as PW4 Plastic Explosive and Linear Cutting Charge. Knowing the thickness and type of material to be breached, he can refer to tables showing the correct weight and configuration required to achieve the desired result.

Explosive Wall Breaching System
P. W. Allen supply a purpose-made Explosive Wall Breaching System, which is designed to provide a rapid method of entry for Special Forces assault teams through walls and other obstacles. The unit consists of a plastic shell with a frame to support the explosive and a container for water to surround the explosive. The unit is placed against a wall and fired; the water tamps the explosive and directs the energy forward, cutting a hole in the wall.

The unit has two channels for explosive: one around the perimeter, which defines the size of the hole; and another vertical channel down the centre of the unit, which

on thicker walls helps to push out the building material to leave a clean, open hole through which the assault team can enter quickly.

The amount and type of explosive used depends on the task. For a thin, internal wall a single length of detonating cord may be sufficient. For thicker, more strongly built walls, it may be necessary to use multiple lengths of det cord, or flexible linear cutting charge for a more directional effect. The water jacket surrounding the explosive helps to quench the hot gases and reduce the danger from fragments.

Door rams

The door ram is widely used by police and fire services around the world for breaking through inward opening doors quickly and with minimum fuss. There are a variety

The Explosive Wall Breaching System provides a rapid means of entry through walls. The plastic shell contains explosive and water, and instantly blows a man-sized hole through the wall. Photo: PW Allen.

The Enforcer door ram will break open almost any door with a single blow. They come in various sizes and weights. Photo: PW Allen.

of sizes and designs available, but the principle remains the same. A good example of this type of tool is the Enforcer, supplied by Sigma Security Devices of Dover, England. Many thousands are in use worldwide. This 16kg (35lb) steel ram consists of a tube with a solid block at one end. Two handles are fitted, the forward one of which has a D-shaped guard to protect the user's hand.

The Enforcer is designed to be used by one man, either left- or right-handed. It is swung against the door near the lock, providing an impact of more than 3.5 tons. This is sufficient to break open most residential doors, even reinforced ones, within a couple of seconds. Experience has shown that the Enforcer can open doors with up to seven different locks, bolts and chains with a single blow. The Enforcer measures 58cm (23in) long, and is also available as a kit with protective mitts and forearm protectors. A back pack is available for carrying the Enforcer while keeping both hands free for abseiling, climbing, etc.

The Disrupter, also supplied by Sigma Security Devices, is a more powerful version of the Enforcer, weighing 18kg. Like the Enforcer, it measures 58cm (23in) long. The design is improved, with the front handle further back. This ensures that impacts are higher and more effective, while also making the ram safer to use.

A smaller version, the Firecracker, is only 46cm (18in) long and weighs 16kg (35lbs). It can be stowed and carried more easily, and can be used in more confined spaces such as corridors and small entry halls, yet packs the same punch as the Enforcer.

For very sturdy and reinforced doors, there is a Two-Man Enforcer, with a length of 140cm (55ins) and weighing 33kg (72lbs). This tool requires plenty of space to be swung effectively by two men, but generates huge power to open any inward-opening door.

Door rippers and 'hooligan' tools

While a door ram is the answer to an inward-opening door, a different approach is required for outward-opening doors. A specially designed Door Ripper is supplied by Sigma Security Devices. This has a blade that can be slipped or driven with a hammer into the gap between the door and its frame. Pulling back on the handle will normally break any locks and bolts, and force the door open at the first attempt. A ratchet mechanism allows the blade to be worked behind the door to improve the leverage and overcome resistance. The Ripper weighs 6kg (13lbs) and measures 79cm (31ins) long.

There are a large variety of 'hooligan' tools available for general purpose use in breaking open locks, windows, grilles, gates and the like. The standard Hooligan Tool measures 107cm (42ins) long and weighs 6.4kg (14lbs). It consists of a straight, high-alloy steel shaft, with a claw at one end and a dual head at the other.

The head has a sharp, tapered spike that can be inserted behind locks and latches, and a broad, flat 'duckbill' wedge for levering open doors and windows. The claw is designed to fit over locks and hasps, allowing them to be broken quickly. An alternative model has a can-opener-type claw, which can be used to cut openings in vehicles and metal containers. The tool is particularly effective at breaking through windows. The glass can be knocked out quickly with the end of the tool, and the frame then ripped out with the hooked end.

Rapid entry personnel may also use a variety of more general-purpose tools such as axes, sledgehammers and pry-bars, as well as specialist tools designed to over-come specific makes of locks and hinges. The pump-action shotgun, firing a special cartridge known as a Hatton Round, is also employed to breach locked doors by blowing out the locks or hinges.

The door ripper is used to break open an outward-opening door. The blade is slipped into the gap, and a single pull on the handle will smash any locks and bolts. Photo: PW Allen.

Hydraulic and pneumatic door breakers

Where a door is strengthened and reinforced, it may take too long to break down with an Enforcer-type tool. To be sure of gaining entry rapidly, and maintaining the element of surprise, a hydraulic or pneumatic door breaker can be used.

The Hydraulic Ram can exert 5 tons of pressure, reliably breaking open steel-reinforced inward-opening doors. The ram is placed over the door, at the level of the main lock. Pumping the handle forces apart a pair of jaws, which bite deep into the frame and secure the device, at the same time pushing the door frame apart and loosening any bolts, locks and catches. Once ready, a valve is operated to activate a ram that forces the door open. The manual hydraulic system is virtually silent in operation, and the entire operation can be completed in thirty to forty seconds. The Hydraulic Ram kit comes with three claws for all standard door widths, in a heavy-duty carrying bag, and weighs 25kg (55lbs).

The Blower is a pneumatic door ram advertised as the most powerful door-breaking system in the world – it exerts 5 tons of force across the door frame, and 11 tons against the door itself. The first part of the Blower system is basically the same as the Hydraulic Ram. It has a pair of claws that are forced apart by a hand-pumped hydraulic system to embed themselves into the door frame at either side, exerting up to 5 tons of pressure. This then forms a firmly anchored cross-beam. A specially designed air-bag is then slipped between the beam and the door itself, and inflated rapidly with compressed air from a cylinder. The sudden force of up to 11 tons will blow open just about any door, even heavily reinforced steel doors. The task takes less than one minute from start to finish, and is virtually silent until the final blow that bursts the door open instantly.

The Blower is supplied as a self-contained kit in a heavy-duty carrying bag, complete with air-bag, air-hose and compressed air cylinder with shoulder strap. It weighs 27kg and comes with three claw lengths: 16, 19 and 22 ins.

STUN GRENADES

When GSG9 and SAS troopers stormed LH181 at Mogadishu in October 1977, the assault was initiated by throwing in a number of 'stun grenades', designed to stun the occupants with a combination of a loud report and a very bright flash. The SAS had been experimenting with the devices, nicknamed 'flashbangs', as a means of adding to the surprise and disorientation of the terrorists. Barry Davies describes in *Fire*

This new variety of stun grenade has been developed by Sandia National Laboratories to reduce the risk of injuring a hostage. Photo: Sandia.

Magic how he brought a case of stun grenades with him to Mogadishu and instructed the GSG9 troopers on their use.

The stun grenade is designed specifically for use by Special Forces during hostage rescue. It is classified as a diversionary assault grenade, producing noise and brightness levels sufficient to induce disorientation in the terrorists. The grenade itself consists of a case with a firing mechanism and operating lever fitted to the top. It is roughly similar to a soft drinks can in size and shape – approximately 100mm high by 50mm diameter, with a weight of around 150g.

The grenade contains an ignition and delay mechanism, and a quantity of flash composition – typically a mixture of aluminium powder and potassium perchlorate. To operate the grenade, the trooper pulls the ring, taking care to hold the flip-up lever against the body of the grenade. The grenade is then thrown, allowing the lever to flip up and operate the ignition system. After a short delay (approximately one second) the flash composition ignites, emitting a loud bang and bright flash via the blow-out base of the grenade.

An alternative version contains a number of sub-munitions to provide a 'fire-cracker' effect of multiple flashbangs. The first report starts within one or two seconds of initiation, followed by fifteen or so loud reports in quick succession over the next few seconds. This type of grenade is typically of similar dimensions to the 'single' type, or slightly larger, and a little heavier at around 175g.

There has been much work carried out over the years to reduce the risk to hostages from stun grenades. If a conventional stun grenade detonates close to a hostage it could cause permanent injury. Sandia National Laboratories in the US have recently developed a new type of stun grenade that reduces this risk.

The new 'flashbang' creates the same blinding flash and deafening bang as a conventional stun grenade, but this is achieved with an airborne powder that fans out before igniting, making it less dangerous to hostages. The new grenade is also reusable, making it more suitable as a training aid.

The new grenade is made of plastic, and contains only metal powder, without any potassium perchlorate or other oxidising agent. The particles of powdered metal are forced out like a burst of talcum powder through sixteen 1/4in diameter holes in the base of the canister. The ejected particles hang momentarily in the air, forming a sheet of metal dust about 5ft in diameter, before igniting by combining with oxygen in the air.

The spread of the powder means that the pressure in the immediate vicinity of the device is lowered to a safer level. The canister remains undamaged, and can be reloaded for a few dollars.

CS and other gases

CS and other types of gas are options that will always be considered when an assault team is planning a hostage rescue operation. These carry a number of risks, however. Russian Alpha anti-terrorist personnel pumped incapacitating gas into the Palace of Culture Theatre in Moscow on 26 October 2002, where some fifty Chechen terrorists were holding around 800 hostages. Some of the terrorists were wearing

explosives strapped to their bodies, and had threatened to detonate them if the theatre was attacked. The gas rendered the terrorists unconscious before they had time to carry out their threat.

The operation was a success, in that the siege was broken, the terrorists were killed and the majority of the hostages freed. More than 110 hostages died due to the effects of the gas, however, and many more were critically ill in hospital.

PROTECTIVE CLOTHING

In any hostage-rescue assault operation, all the personnel are potentially exposed to a whole range of risks, from fire and explosion to bullets and fragments. It is important that they are protected, so far as is practical, against all these. The standard assault kit is nowadays instantly familiar from countless pictures, books and films. In addition to protecting the trooper from multiple threats, it also has a very intimidating appearance. This helps in psychologically overwhelming the terrorists.

Sandia's new 'flashbang' contains powdered metal which is ejected from the casing and oxidises when mixed with air. The canister can be reloaded for re-use. Photo: Sandia.

The standard assault kit has a very intimidating appearance, which gives a psychological advantage over the terrorists. Photo: NP Aerospace.

Barry Davies puts it well in *Fire Magic*:

For maximum psychological advantage, these men are dressed to look evil ...
They advance rapidly towards the terrorists with the sole aim of blasting their
brains out ... A terrorist's instinctive first reaction is to stop the invading beast
bearing down on him. It takes only micro-seconds to choose between resistance and surrender, but he will be dead before he ever makes that choice.

A further advantage of the anonymous black kit, with faces hidden by insect-like
respirators, is that there is no chance of a trooper being identified if the assault is
caught on film or video, as with Operation Nimrod.

The standard kit makes extensive use of fire-resistant Nomex material. GD
Specialist Supplies produce a full range of flame-retardant underwear and overgar-
ments, including a hood to cover the parts of the head not protected by the respirator. The assault suit incorporates felt pads on knees and elbows, to provide additional

The assault
team's clothing
makes extensive
use of fire-resist-
ant Nomex mate-
rial, including a
hood to protect
parts of the head
and face not
covered by the
respirator.
Photo: author's
collection.

This US soldier is dressed for MOUT (Military Operations in Urban Terrain), and is wearing camouflage fatigues and protective goggles rather than the typical CRW black overalls and SF10 respirator. Photo: US Army.

protection when it is necessary to crawl across hot surfaces, as well as protecting against blows and sharp objects.

The respirator of choice is the Avon SF10, which was developed from the military S10 specifically for Special Forces use. The SF10 incorporates an internal microphone and clip-on anti-flash lenses, and protects against CS and other irritant gases as well as aerosols and smokes. It is compatible with the CT400 communications system described in chapter 4. Body armour, as described in chapter 10, is worn.

An assault belt kit or assault vest is used to carry the various items of equipment needed for the operation: CS and stun grenades, pistol, spare magazines, communications equipment, forced entry tools, etc. Traditionally this type of load-carrying equipment was made of leather, but increasingly modern fabrics are being used, as in the Blackhawk range of tactical nylon equipment. This company, based in Chesapeake, VA, USA, offers a huge range of holsters, pouches, assault vests and similar equipment in their catalogue, and online at www.blackhawkindustries.com.

Special forces are renowned for using whatever weapon is available and best suited to the job in hand, and are constantly testing and evaluating new weapons and techniques. There is hardly a weapon in existence that has not been tried by Special Forces at some time or another, including the full range of military weapons as well as improvised weapons – such as incendiaries mixed from a cocktail of household chemicals, man-traps built of sharpened bamboo and cordage, or the apocryphal 'rock in a sock'.

It is not the purpose of this book to serve as a primer on improvised weapons, however, so we will restrict ourselves to the weapons commonly issued to Special Forces, particularly those of the UK and USA. It is worth noting that, although each unit has its preferred weapons for specific tasks, problems such as availability and resupply may force them to use a different weapon on specific operations.

Special Forces, whose work may place them in hostile territory for days or even weeks on end, must be familiar with their enemy's weapons as well as their own; they may need to use a captured weapon if their own fails or ammunition runs low. The SAS, for example, train with a variety of weapons, including the ubiquitous Kalashnikov AK47 and 74, and the RPG-7 rocket launcher and its successors. This means that, in a combat situation, a soldier can pick up a weapon dropped by a fallen enemy

Special Forces train in the use of a variety of weapons, as well as unarmed combat – as in this Cold War era propaganda shot of Russian Spetsnaz forces. Photo: author's collection.

Right: All Special Forces have their favoured weapons – these soldiers are using the Diemaco C7FT variant of the M16A2 – but also familiarise themselves with enemy weapons. Photo: Diemaco.

Right: All Special Forces have their favoured weapons – these soldiers are using the Diemaco C7FT variant of the M16A2 – but also familiarise themselves with enemy weapons. Photo: Diemaco.

Opposite page: Bagram, Afghanistan. Princess Patricia's Canadian Light Infantry (3 PPCLI) Battle Group armed with the C7 variant of the M16A2. Photo: Cpl Lou Penney, 3 PPCLI BG

and immediately put it to use, without having to work out where the safety catch is and how to operate it.

It is interesting to note that firearms have changed little in the last fifty years or so. Materials and manufacturing methods have been improved, but today's weapons still fire jacketed lead bullets from brass-cased cartridges containing a primer and propellant powder. The rounds are housed in a box magazine, and fed into the chamber by the operation of a bolt or slide. The ubiquitous H&K MP5 SMG – still favoured by most

counter-terrorist forces around the world for hostage rescue – was first developed in the mid-1960s, and fires a round created decades earlier.

Special Forces are not slow on the uptake when it comes to adopting new technology. They were among the first to use GPS navigation, satellite communications, and a host of other new technology. But they stubbornly stick with the old tried-and-tested firearms such as the Vietnam-era M16 assault rifle, and the 1960s H&K MP5. This is not nostalgia; it is a choice based on sound, practical reasons.

The Special Forces approach is to use overwhelming firepower. This van, used by the IRA in an attack on the RUC station at Loughall in May 1987, was ambushed by the SAS and riddled with more than 600 bullets, killing all the occupants. Photo: author's collection.

In close-quarter battle, what really matters is 100 per cent reliability, and a combination of shape, weight and balance that provide intuitive handling. Having the latest bit of clever technology is irrelevant. At the vital moment, when it is kill-or-be-killed, all that counts is having a weapon you can rely on to drop the enemy – fast. Just watch someone fiddling with the controls on one of the latest 'ergonomically designed' electronic cameras; if taking a photograph first meant life or death, you would choose a simple manual camera every time.

SUB-MACHINE GUNS

Heckler & Koch MP5 Series

Since it was first developed in the 1960s, the Heckler & Koch (H&K) MP5 sub-machine gun has become the favourite of anti-terrorist forces around the world. It is carried by police firearms teams, internal security forces, SWAT teams, hostage

rescue assault teams and many others – including the British SAS and police, and Germany's GSG9. The sight of SAS troopers using MP5s to assault the Iranian Embassy in 1980 was a powerful advertisement, of course. But there is much more to it than that. The MP5 really is in a class of its own.

The MP5 is correctly described as a sub-machine gun. It fires what is basically a pistol round on fully automatic in a weapon designed to be held two-handed. But it is a million miles from the crude, inaccurate 'spray 'n' pray' weapons that are typical of sub-machine guns. The MP5 is a sophisticated weapons system that is really a high-quality selective fire carbine, which just happens to fire the 9mm Parabellum round.

The MP5 appears in a number of variants; it is, in fact, a family of weapons rather than a single weapon. It comes with a fixed or folding buttstock, and with the option of single-shot, three-round burst and fully automatic fire. There is a special silenced model, and a short K (for *kurz* – 'short' in German) model. The various combinations of these options produce a long list of variants, all designated by a combination of letters and numerals. So an MP5 A5, for instance, has a telescoping buttstock, 225mm barrel and three-round burst option.

At the time of Operation Nimrod, the SAS had already decided that the MP5 was the ideal weapon for hostage-rescue assaults. Its 9mm Parabellum round is suffi-ciently lethal at short range to produce an instant knock-down of a terrorist, especially if he/she is struck with multiple hits from burst or fully automatic fire. Yet it does not

French comman-dos and US Navy SEALs practice with 9mm sub-machine guns and a 9mm pistol during Operation Desert Storm. Photo: US DoD.

The Heckler &
Koch MP5 series
sub-machine gun
is the firmly
established
favourite of
counter-terrorist
forces worldwide.
It fires the 9mm
Parabellum round
at around 800
rounds per
minute. Photo:
author's collec-
tion.

carry the problems of over-penetration that would occur with rifle calibres, where rounds could pass through a wall or aircraft skin, possibly injuring a passer-by a kilo-metre or two away.

The MP5 is outstandingly accurate for a sub-machine gun, and can be fitted with various sighting and target illumination devices to aid target acquisition and aiming. The weapon is compact and handles well, making it simple to carry when undertak-ing difficult insertion techniques. It has also proved to be exceptionally reliable. With normal routine maintenance, a jam is virtually unheard of when using good-quality metal jacketed ammunition.

It is also well supported by the manufacturers, now part of Britain's BAe Systems, who provide a high level of after-sales service including spare parts, armourers' courses, etc.

The MP5's mechanism is unusual for a sub-machine gun in that it fires from a closed, locked bolt – this enables it to achieve its excellent accuracy and reliability. The bolt is locked by a roller mechanism. The bolt is in two parts: the bolt head, which lies against the cartridge head; and the larger mass of the main body of the bolt. When the bolt is closed, inclined planes on the bolt body press against the rollers, pushing them outward into recesses and locking the bolt head against the breech.

On firing, there is a slight delay as the main body of the bolt begins to withdraw, allowing the rollers to unlock. The two parts of the bolt then travel rearward together, extracting and ejecting the spent case. Spring pressure drives the bolt closed again, collecting the next round from the magazine and loading it into the breech before the rollers lock again and the mechanism is ready to fire. That might sound like a long, slow process, but it happens in the blink of an eye, and the MP5 is capable of firing at a rate of 800 rpm (rounds per minute) – emptying a 30-round magazine in 13.5 seconds.

The controls on the MP5 have been designed so that they are simple and intuitive to operate. The cocking lever travels in a slot in the upper left quarter of the receiver, and has a large three-quarter moon knob that is easily operated even with gloved hands. The combined safety catch and selector switch is located above the trigger, and can be operated by the thumb of the trigger hand without changing grip on the weapon. The magazine catch is at the rear of the magazine well, where it is easily operated by the thumb of the hand grasping the magazine.

The basic sights are similar to those on the H&K G3 rifle from which the MP5 was developed. There is a blade foresight contained within a protective ring. The rearsight consists of a rotating turret offering apertures of different sizes to suit various conditions.

An entire industry has grown up supplying specialised sighting and target illumination systems for use with the MP5. Laser systems that project a red dot onto the target have become popular for anti-terrorist operations. In some circumstances, simply shining the dot onto a kidnapper may be sufficient to persuade him to surrender, resolving the situation without the need to fire. Alternatively, the laser light may be invisible to the naked eye, but visible through night-vision goggles worn by the assault team.

There are many different night-vision scopes, optical scopes and other aiming devices that can be mounted on the MP5. This type of scope is popular with police firearms teams such as Britain's SO19, who may find themselves in a stand-off where they must cover a kidnapper at ranges of up to 100 metres for some length of time. For hostage-rescue assault operations, however, where snap-shooting is required, it is normal to use the standard fixed sights in conjunction with a target illumination device and perhaps a red-dot laser sight; the longer-range accuracy provided by a scope is not required, and the scope would simply get in the way.

Target illumination systems have come a long way since Operation Nimrod, when the assault team had D-cell Maglite torches fixed above their MP5s' receivers like telescopic sights. Nowadays the preferred torch is much smaller and gives a more precise, even beam. There are various mounts available which replace the standard MP5 fore-end to provide a housing for torches such as the Sure-Fire. The torch may be fitted with an IR filter, so that the beam is visible only through night-vision goggles, to give an added advantage to the assault team who will certainly have cut all electrical power to the target building or craft before initiating the assault.

Specifications	
Manufacturer:	Heckler & Koch, West Germany (part of BAe Systems)
Model:	MP5 series sub-machine gun (Specifications refer to MP5 A2 except where indicated)
Introduced:	1965
Calibre:	9mm Parabellum
Action:	Roller-locked delayed blowback, selective single shot/3-round burst/fully automatic
Feed:	15- or 30-round box magazine
Rate of fire:	800rpm
Sights:	Blade and aperture open sights, rearsight with revolving turret to allow selection of aperture size. Various target illumination and laser pointer systems available
Weight:	2.55kg
Length:	680mm (telescoping butt variants 490mm with butt retracted, K variants 325mm)
Barrel:	225mm (115mm on K variants)
Variants:	MP5 A2 – Fixed stock, 225mm barrel
	MP5 A3 – Telescoping stock, 225mm barrel
	MP5 A4 – No buttstock, 225mm barrel
	MP5 A5 – As A3 with 3-round burst option
	MP5 SD1 – No buttstock, silenced
	MP5 SD2 – A2 type buttstock, silenced
	MP5 SD3 – A3 type buttstock, silenced
	MP5 SD4 – As SD1 with 3-round burst option
	MP5K – Short variant with 115mm barrel and no butt stock. Broom handle type forestock
	MP5K A1 – As MP5K but with low-profile sights
	MP5K A4 – As MP5K with 3-round burst option
	MP5K A5 – As MP5K A1 but with 3-round burst option
Service:	In service with British Special Forces and Police firearms teams. Used by similar forces worldwide.

Uzi

The Uzi sub-machine gun was developed in 1949 by Lieutenant Uziel Gal of the Israeli Army, and has since become one of the best-known SMGs in the world. It is still in widespread use, both with Israeli armed forces and elsewhere. It is instantly recognisable by the ribbed, box-shaped receiver, and the magazine housed in a vertical hand-grip.

The Uzi's mechanism uses a principle known as advanced primer ignition. The round is fired while the bolt is still travelling forward, allowing the bolt to be made lighter and giving a high rate of fire. The bolt is also overhung, which improves the weapon's balance and handling characteristics. The Uzi fires from an open bolt – the bolt is cocked and remains in the open position until the trigger is pulled. On firing, the bolt flies forward, collects a round from the magazine and pushes it into the chamber.

The friction of the round in the chamber is sufficient to push it back against the firing pin, igniting the primer and firing the round just before the bolt is fully closed. As the bolt reaches the closed position the pressure is building up to drive it back again, drawing out the fired case with an extractor claw. An ejector lug knocks the

The basic MP5 has open sights consisting of a blade and tunnel foresight and a rotating turret aperture rearsight. However, there are many specialist sighting systems that can be fitted. Photo: © James Marchington.

An Uzi sub-machine gun. Photo: Pageant-Pix.

fired case clear through the ejection slot, as the bolt continues rearward against spring pressure. At the full extent of its travel, the bolt reverses direction and the cycle begins again – unless the trigger is released, in which case the sear engages and holds the bolt back in the cocked position ready to fire again.

The cocking handle travels in a slot on the top surface of the box-section receiver. A grip safety prevents the bolt moving unless the grip is held in the hand. A combined safety catch/fire selector is located at the top of the left grip. It is a sliding catch which can be operated with the thumb of the trigger hand – back for 'safe', forward one click for single shots and two clicks for fully automatic fire. The magazine catch is at the bottom of the left grip.

Specifications	
Manufacturer:	Ta'as Israel Industries (formerly Israeli Military Industries), Israel
Model:	Uzi
Calibre:	9mm Parabellum
Action:	Advanced primer ignition blowback, selective fully automatic
Feed:	32-round box magazine
Rate of fire:	950rpm
Sights:	Post and aperture sights, with flip rearsight graduated for 100 and 200m
Weight:	3.7kg
Length:	470mm with folding buttstock folded; 650mm extended
Barrel:	260mm
Service:	Israeli armed forces, and others worldwide

Steyr AUG 9mm Para

The AUG Para is a 9mm version of the futuristic-looking Steyr AUG assault rifle, which was developed to fire the NATO 5.56 x 45mm round, and has been adopted by the armies of Australia, New Zealand, Ireland, Saudi Arabia, Oman and other countries.

The assault rifle can be converted to fire the 9mm Parabellum by means of a kit, which consists of a replacement barrel, bolt group, magazine adaptor and magazine. The conversion turns the AUG into a 9mm blowback weapon, with a one-piece bolt assembly. It has a separate firing pin, and fires from a closed bolt.

Controls are the same as on the standard assault rifle. There is a cross-bolt safety catch above the trigger. Fire selection is by trigger pressure: first pressure gives single shots; further pressure provides full automatic fire. The magazine catch is at the rear of the magazine adaptor/housing. The cocking handle is on the left side of the receiver.

Specifications	
Manufacturer: Steyr-Mannlicher, Austria	
Model:	Steyr AUG Para
Calibre:	9mm Parabellum
Action:	Blowback, closed bolt, selective fully automatic
Feed:	32-round magazine
Rate of fire:	700rpm
Sights:	1.5x optical sight
Weight:	3.3kg
Length:	665mm
Barrel:	420mm

Beretta Mod 12S

The Beretta Model 12 SMG was originally designed in the 1950s, and although it has been developed over the years the current Model 12S is largely the same in appearance and operation. It is the standard SMG of Italy's armed forces, and has been sold to a number of other countries, including Saudi Arabia, Nigeria, Libya and Brazil.

The weapon operates on the blowback principle: the chamber gases blow the bolt back on firing, ejecting the fired case and cocking the mechanism. The bolt returns, under spring pressure, collecting a new round from the magazine and loading it into the chamber. If the trigger is still pulled, the hammer falls and the cycle begins again.

The Model 12S uses a 'wrap around' bolt – much of its bulk is forward of the breech at the moment of firing. This improves the balance of the weapon, reduces vibrations and counters any tendency for the weapon to climb when fired on full automatic.

The cocking handle travels in a longitudinal slot on the left side of the receiver. To cock the weapon, it is pulled back and released. There is a grip safety which prevents the weapon firing unless the grip is firmly held in the hand. A safety catch above the left grip also provides fire selection – up for 'safe', middle position for single shots, and down for full automatic fire. The magazine catch is on the underside of the trigger guard, just behind the magazine itself.

Specifications

Manufacturer: P. Beretta, Italy

Model:	Model 12S
Calibre:	9mm Parabellum
Action:	Blowback, selective fully automatic
Feed:	20- 32- or 40-round magazine
Rate of fire:	650rpm
Sights:	Blade and aperture open sights, with flip-up aperture rearsight
Weight:	3.2kg
Length:	418mm
Barrel:	200mm

FN P90

The FN P90 was conceived as a cross between an assault rifle and a sub-machine gun – a personal weapon for support troops. It should be compact enough to be carried by signals engineers, drivers, medics and similar personnel without getting in the way, yet provide enough firepower to be effective when needed. Being neither assault rifle nor sub-machine gun, it has been assigned to a special category of Personal Defence Weapon (PDW).

None of the available rounds fitted the PDW concept, so FN created a new round, the 5.7 x 28mm. This offers greater range, accuracy and stopping power than the 9mm Parabellum sub-machine gun round, yet is smaller than the standard NATO assault rifle round, the 5.56 x 45mm. The 5.7 x 28 uses a sharply pointed projectile known as a boat-tailed spire-point. This weighs 2.02g and achieves a very high muzzle velocity of 715m/sec. It has an effective range of 150m and gives outstanding penetration, passing through 48 layers of Kevlar at 150m.

The tip of the FMJ bullet has a steel penetrator followed by an aluminium core heavier than the forward tip. This causes the bullet to tumble in soft body tissue after two inches of penetration, causing a larger wound cavity and much greater damage than a 9mm Parabellum bullet.

The weapon itself looks and handles unlike any other weapon. Its bullpup design gives a squat shape, with fat, curved plastic grips and a very short barrel. It measures just 50cm long and weighs 3kg with a full magazine of 50 rounds. The combat sling allows it to be carried close to the body, where its shape and size mean that it can be forgotten about while the user gets on with his primary task – yet be ready for use almost instantly if an enemy appears.

The body casing of the P90 is a one-piece polymer shell which houses all the main parts, offering good protection from physical damage, moisture, dust and debris. The design incorporates a thumbhole semi-pistol grip, a forward grip which doubles as the trigger guard, and a hand protector that prevents the user letting his leading hand stray in front of the muzzle – potentially a problem with such a short

weapon. The design and balance of the P90 means it can be fired effectively with one hand, like a pistol, as well as held to the shoulder with two hands like a rifle.

The sights are mounted on a raised platform over the forward end of the barrel. Recent models have been fitted with a British made 1x magnification Ring Sight collimating sight, with a day/night graticule. This can be used with one or both eyes open. A laser pointer can be fitted to the hand-protecting spur beneath the muzzle, with a switch in the hand-grip.

The magazine is as unusual as the rest of the P90. It is located on top of the receiver, parallel to the barrel, and holds 50 rounds stacked at 90 degrees to the bore. The rounds are fed by spring pressure along a curved track that turns them through 90 degrees so that each round in turn is presented to the action in the correct alignment. The magazine is made of semi-transparent polymer, allowing the user to see at a glance how much ammunition is left in the weapon.

The manufacturers also offer a pistol, the Five-seveN, which uses the same 5.7mm ammunition as the P90. The Five-seveN is an easily concealable double-action pistol with a 20-round magazine capacity. Maximum use has been made of

The FN P90 is neither a rifle nor a sub-machine gun; it is classified as a Personal Defence Weapon, and fires a specially developed 5.7mm round with outstanding penetration. Photo: Fabrique Nationale.

The Five seveN pistol was developed to fire the same ammunition as the P90. As a result, it has unusually good penetration and knock-down for a pistol. Photo: FN.

composite materials in the frame and slide to produce an extremely lightweight pistol, weighing just 1.7lbs, with unusually good penetration and knock-down power.

Specifications	
Manufacturer:	Fabrique Nationale, Belgium
Model:	P90
Calibre:	5.7 x 28mm
Action:	Blowback, selective fully automatic
Feed:	50-round box magazine
Rate of fire:	900rpm
Sights:	Integral open sights and Ring Sight collimating optical sight with day/night graticules. Laser pointer optional
Weight:	3kg
Length:	500mm
Barrel:	250mm

ASSAULT RIFLES

The M16 A2 and variants

The ubiquitous M16 assault rifle has been the standard rifle of US forces since the Vietnam War, and in its latest versions is still used by more than thirty countries worldwide. It has been used in countless military engagements, and has proved popular with soldiers thanks to its reliability and ease of use in all environments, from arctic conditions to jungles and deserts.

The original version of the M16 was designed by Eugene Stoner to fire the 5.56mm round. It was quickly adopted by US forces and went into service in time to be widely used in Vietnam. Combat experience in that war led to various improve-

Above: A US
soldier fires the
standard issue
M16A2 assault
rifle. This rifle has
been the service
weapon of US
forces since the
Vietnam War.
Photo: US Army.

ments – notably the bolt return plunger known as 'forward assist'. Extended use of the original M16 in combat sometimes led to the bolt fouling and failing to close fully, preventing the weapon from firing. On the improved M16 A2, the infantryman can force the bolt home with a firm blow to the plunger.

The current version of the M16 A2 fires the standard NATO 5.56 x 45mm round, the military equivalent of the civilian .223. It has a detachable box magazine with a capacity of 30 rounds. It fires at a cyclic rate of between 700 and 950 rounds per minute, and has a nominal effective range of 400m.

Diemaco C7, C8 and SFW

Diemaco, of Ontario in Canada, produce a range of weapons derived from the M16 family. These are known by the designations C7, C8, etc. The C7 is a basic infantryman's weapon in 5.56 x 45mm calibre. It is gas-operated, offering single-shot, 3-round burst or full automatic fire. It is designed to be easily operated and maintained under severe military service conditions. All-user maintenance is performed without tools, and all-armourer maintenance can be performed at unit level, with a minimum of special tools and gauges. The C7 is fully compatible with cold-weather clothing, NBC equipment, night-vision sights and training and simulation systems. It has a 50cm

Left: A cutaway picture of the Diemaco C7, a rifle derived from the M16A2. This is the basic infantryman's version, with a combined carrying handle and rearsight. Photo: Diemaco.

Top: This is the Diemaco C8, a shortened version of the C7. The overall length of the weapon is 76cm, nearly 25% shorter than the C7.

Above: The Diemaco SFW (Special Forces Weapon). It has the C7's long barrel and a tele-scoping stock. Sighting systems and an M203 can be fitted. Photos: Diemaco.

barrel and fixed buttstock, and measures 1m long overall. The standard C7 has a carrying handle/rearsight. There is a 'flat top' version, the C7FT, with a standard Weaver sight rail that permits the use of a range of sights and tactical accessories.

The C8 Carbine is a lightweight, short version of the C7 family, and is intended for tank crews, drivers and other support troops who require a more compact weapon that retains the firepower of 5.56mm ammunition. The weapon is 24 per cent shorter and 20 per cent lighter than the C7, yet retains 90 per cent of the C7's striking energy and accuracy. It has a 36cm barrel and a telescoping stock, giving an overall length of 76cm with the stock retracted and 85cm extended. Most of the C8's parts are common to the C7 family, simplifying maintenance and spare parts inventory. There is also a 'flat top' version, the C8FT, with Weaver sight rail for mounting optical sights and the like.

Diemaco also produce a special version of the C7 designed for Special Forces' use. This is designated the SFW (Special Forces Weapon), and is derived from the C7FT. It has a 41cm barrel to retain the performance of the 5.56 x 45mm round, and a telescoping buttstock similar to that on the C8. A modular hand-guard system makes it possible to fit a wide range of mission-specific accessories, such as an M203 grenade launcher (see below), bipod, laser target illuminator, etc. A special high endurance long-life barrel improves the weapon's ability to stay on target and withstand the heat of sustained semi-automatic and fully automatic fire. The weapon is available in a range of camouflage options, including arctic white, desert tan and olive drab as well as standard black.

Specifications

Manufacturer:	Diemaco, Ontario, Canada
Model:	SFW
Calibre:	5.56 x 45mm
Action:	Blowback, selective fully automatic
Feed:	30-round box or 100-round drum magazine
Rate of fire:	700–900rpm
Sights:	Standard iron sights fitted. Rail-mount permits fitting of a variety of optical and electro-optical sighting systems, as required
Weight:	3.6kg without sights, magazine empty
	4.4kg combat weight (optical sight, full magazine)
Length:	80cm with stock retracted
	88cm with stock extended
Barrel:	41cm (43cm with flash suppressor)

M203 Grenade Launcher

The M203 40mm Grenade Launcher was developed to be fitted to the M16 assault rifle, and adds considerable versatility and firepower at little cost in terms of the weapon's weight and handling – although the 40mm ammunition itself is somewhat

The Canadian soldier in the foreground is equipped with the Diemaco C7 assault rifle, fitted with Diemaco's M203 grenade launcher. Photo: Diemaco.

The M203 grenade launcher is designed to be fitted to an M16 assault rifle, and fires 40mm grenades in HE (High Explosive), AT (Anti-Tank) and AP (Anti-Personnel) to ranges up to 350 yards. Photo: Diemaco.

bulky and heavy to carry in any quantity. The combination of an M16 assault rifle and M203 grenade launcher has become popular with Special Forces – it was used, for instance, by SAS patrols in the 1991 Gulf War – and has influenced recent development work on future combat weapon systems.

There are a variety of 40mm grenades available for use with the M203, including high explosive (HE), anti-tank (AT), anti-personnel (AP), smoke and illuminating. These give a maximum effective range of 350m for area targets, and 150m for point targets. Depending on the nature of ammunition used, the muzzle velocity is around 70m/sec, with a maximum range (with the rifle aimed at 45 degrees) of around 400m.

The M203 is a single-shot, sliding-barrel, breech-loading weapon, weighing approximately 1.36kg unloaded and 1.63kg loaded. It is mounted under the forestock of the M16, with its trigger positioned directly forward of the M16's magazine. The user can quickly shift his grip on the weapon, using the M16 magazine as a pistol grip to fire the M203. A quadrant sight is fitted to the M16 to allow the user to aim the M203; this uses the M16's front post sight, but does not interfere with sighting the rifle itself. It is graduated in increments of 50m from 50 to 250m.

SA80

The standard service assault rifle of the British armed forces since the late 1980s, the SA80 – or L85A1 – has received much criticism. At the time of its introduction, it was hailed as a major advance over its predecessor, the L1A1. The bullpup design made it a compact weapon, and the 4x magnification SUSAT sighting system allowed the average infantryman to achieve a much higher level of accuracy at normal battlefield ranges. The weapon also represented a move away from the old .30 calibre rifles, with their heavy recoil, to the new generation of high velocity .22 calibre rounds which were less tiring and easier to shoot accurately.

The SA80 fires the standard NATO 5.56 x 45mm round, contained in a 30-round box magazine that is interchangeable with that of other NATO weapons such as the M16. The SA80 weighs approximately 5kg and measures 77cm long. The design makes extensive use of modern plastics and stamped metal parts. It is fitted with an adjustable sling that enables the user to wear the weapon close to his body, leaving his hands free to perform other tasks.

The weapon has a gas-operated mechanism. The bolt is carried on two guide rods, and rotates as it closes, engaging in two lugs behind the breech. On firing, the mechanism first rotates the bolt to unlock it, and the bolt then travels rearward, driven by gas pressure, to eject the fired case and cock the mechanism. At the rearmost point of its travel, it reverses direction and is driven forward by spring pressure to collect a fresh round and load it into the chamber.

A number of problems were reported with early models of the SA80. In particular, the plastic protectors around the barrel were inclined to fall off on firing, and there

were reports of magazines dropping out. A higher than normal incidence of stop-pages was also reported, particularly in harsh environments such as arctic condi-tions, jungles and deserts.

Many of these criticisms were addressed in an improved version, known as the SA80-A2. The upgrade was launched in 2000. Heckler & Koch won the contract, and rebuilt components were retro-fitted to the British armed forces' 300,000 or so SA80s. The upgrade programme was completed in 2002, at a cost of around £92m. Live firing trials suggested that the main faults had been corrected, particularly the weapon's tendency to jam in adverse weather, although even then there were suggestions that the test conditions had not been realistic.

Experience in Afghanistan and Iraq appears to confirm that the weapon is now considerably more reliable, but it is still unpopular with many soldiers. The Royal Marines are said to have experienced at least three stoppages in Afghanistan. The balance of the weapon is still unwieldy, and it cannot safely be fired left-handed. The SUSAT sight, for all its advantages, is still prone to misting up in cold, damp condi-tions, rendering it unusable.

At the time of writing, there is considerable pressure for the British armed forces to scrap the SA80 and adopt a new weapon, probably the Heckler & Koch G36, currently in use with the SAS.

British forces have used the SA80 or L85A1 since the late 1980s. A much criticised weapon, it nevertheless allowed the average infantry-man to achieve a much higher standard of accuracy than its predecessor, the L1A1. Photo: UK MoD.

An upgrade programme launched in 2000 saw the British forces' 300,000 SA80s upgraded to the SA80-A2. This has improved reliability in adverse weather and sandy conditions. Photo: author's collection.

Specifications

Model:	SA80-A2 (L85A1)
Calibre:	5.56 x 45mm
Action:	Gas-operated, selective fully automatic
Feed:	30-round box magazine
Sights:	SUSAT 4x optical sight, can be removed and weapon
fitted	with a variety of optical and electro-optical sights
Weight:	3.9kg without sights, magazine empty
Length:	77cm
Barrel:	52cm
Muzzle velocity:	900m/s

Heckler & Koch G36

The G36 is a relatively new assault rifle system from Heckler & Koch in 5.56mm x 45mm calibre. The weapon is constructed almost entirely of a tough, fibre reinforced polymer material and uses a simple, self-regulating gas system. It is a high-performance, lightweight weapon that requires very little maintenance. The G36 has been adopted by the German Armed Forces (including the new NATO Rapid Reaction Force), and is also used by Britain's SAS.

Features of the G36 include a folding buttstock and a chrome-plated, cold hammer-forged barrel. There is an ambidextrous cocking lever that doubles as a forward assist lever, and can be used to chamber a round silently. Empty cases are ejected downwards, which reduces the weapon's visual signature. A removable magazine well makes it easier to clean the receiver and chamber areas. The polymer components can easily be cleaned with water-based cleaning solutions, or even water.

The G36 gas system is very resistant to fouling. In tests, it has remained reliable even after firing more than 15,000 rounds without cleaning.

The tough 30-round translucent polymer magazines lock together without a magazine clamp. They are 30 per cent lighter than metal magazines and are corrosion proof. An optional 100-round drum magazine can also be used.

The locations and functions of the G36's controls are similar to those on other Heckler & Koch weapons systems such as the MP5 series of sub-machine guns, HK53 and G3, reducing the need for training and making it easier for soldiers to switch from one weapon to another.

The Heckler & Koch G36 is a modern 5.56mm assault rifle which has been adopted by the German armed forces and is often used by the SAS. Photo: © James Marchington.

The standard G36 has a dual sighting system, comprising a 3x optical sight and an electronic red-dot sight. The G36E (Export) model has a 1.5x optical sight, with back-up open sights.

Specifications

Manufacturer:	Heckler & Koch, Germany
Model:	G36
Calibre:	5.56 x 45mm
Action:	Gas-operated, selective fully automatic
Feed:	30-round box magazine optional 100-round drum magazine
Sights:	Standard G36 has dual sighting system comprising 3x optical sight and electronic red-dot sight. Export 'E' model has 1.5x optical sight and back-up open sights
Weight:	3.6kg without magazine
Length:	76cm with buttstock folded, 1m with buttstock extended
Barrel:	48cm
Rate of fire:	750rpm

OICW (Objective Individual Combat Weapon)

The OICW is a revolutionary new rifle that is being developed by the USA to replace the current M16A2 assault rifle and M203 grenade launcher. The programme was begun in 1994, and at the time of writing is well into development and testing. The schedule is for the first units to be equipped with the new weapon in 2005, although

The revolutionary OICW is part of the US Land Warrior programme, and combines a 5.56mm rifle with a 20mm cannon, with a sophisticated aiming and fire control system. Photo: US DoD.

it is unusual for such programmes to run to schedule and this may well end up being delayed.

The OICW programme is closely tied in with the USA's Land Warrior programme, which aims to equip the individual soldier with a range of hi-tech clothing, communications, location/navigation and weapons systems to improve his effectiveness on the battlefield.

The OICW combines a 5.56mm rifle, similar to the M16, with a 20mm cannon and a sophisticated aiming and fire control system. The parameters drawn up for the new system require a 500 per cent increase in the probability of incapacitation, an effective range of up to 1,000m, and the ability to defeat targets in defilade (for example, an enemy soldier hiding behind a wall). All this is to be achieved with a substantial weight reduction vs the M16/M203 combo, and with an ergonomic design.

The rifle part of the OICW has little about it that is new. The 20mm cannon, arranged piggy-back on top of the 5.56mm receiver and barrel, is a true leap forward, however. It is designed to

Above: The Land Warrior programme will equip every soldier with high-tech clothing, communications and navigation kit, as well as the new Objective Individual Combat Weapon. Photo: US DoD.

Left: The OICW fires standard NATO 5.56mm rifle ammo, plus a 20mm cannon round. Photo: US DoD.

The OICW has a laser targeting and rangefinding system which sets the cannon shell's fuse to burst over the enemy. Photo: US DoD.

work closely with a laser targeting and rangefinding system, which not only calculates the correct aiming point but also sets a fuse in the projectile, so that it bursts at exactly the right moment for maximum effect on the target.

The soldier, then, can fire a shell to explode directly over the heads of enemy soldiers hiding behind an obstacle, or inside a room or bunker – even a kilometre away. This represents a quantum leap in the effectiveness of the individual soldier. If the contractors can deliver these results in an affordable package, then it will give the US and its allies a decisive advantage in future conflicts.

Specifications

Manufacturer:	Alliant Techsystems, Hopkins, MN, USA (Prime Contractor). Heckler & Koch, Germany and UK (5.56mm/20mm weapon). Brashear LP, Pittsburgh, PA, USA (Fire control system)
Model:	OICW (Objective Individual Combat Weapon)
Calibres:	5.56mm assault rifle and 20mm HE cannon
Action:	Selectable semi/full-automatic
Feed:	10-shot detachable box magazine (20mm HE), 30-round detachable box magazine (5.56mm)
Sights:	Red-dot night/day sighting system. Laser ranging and fuse setting system for 20mm projectiles
Weight:	12lbs
Length:	33ins overall

The Land Warrior programme sets demanding targets for the OICW, including an effective range of 1,000m and a 500% increase in hit probability. Photo: US DoD.

The Colt 1911 A1 remained a favourite sidearm of military and non-military users for decades, and its design still influences pistol manufacturers today. Photo: © James Marchington.

PISTOLS

SIG P226

The SIG-Sauer P226 is typical of the modern type of semi-automatic pistol, using the Colt/Browning short recoil mechanism. It was developed from earlier SIG-Sauer models to compete in the US Army's trials for a new combat pistol to replace the ageing Colt .45 1911 A1. It performed well in the trials, but eventually lost out on price to the Beretta 92F. However, its performance was not lost on some observers, and it has since been adopted by, among others, Britain's SAS and the FBI.

The SIG P226 has a double-action mechanism with a decocking lever allowing it to be fired either double- or single-action. When used in the double-action mode, the hammer can be safely dropped on to a loaded chamber by means of the decocking lever, so that the pistol can be carried in a safe condition but ready to fire simply by pulling the trigger. A firing pin safety mechanism locks the firing pin so that an accidental blow to the hammer will not fire the pistol – the firing pin is released only when the trigger is pulled back fully.

The mechanism is similar to the Colt/Browning short recoil action found in much older weapons such as the Colt 1911 A1 and the Browning GP35 High-Power. The locking mechanism is modified, however, so that the slide and barrel are locked by the squared-off chamber part of the barrel, which engages into the rectangular ejection port on top of the slide. The slide and barrel recoil a short distance together before a cam on the barrel engages in the frame, dropping the barrel out of engagement and arresting its travel. The slide continues rearward to eject the spent case, recock the hammer mechanism and load the next round on the return stroke, collecting the barrel on the way and pushing it back into the engaged position.

The decocking lever is located at the top of the left grip, behind and above the trigger. Immediately behind this is the slide release, which is used to strip the weapon. The ambidextrous magazine release catch is located in the grips behind the trigger guard, where it can be operated by the thumb of the firing hand, either left or right. The slide lock catch is on the left of the frame, above the trigger. There is no safety catch as such; the safety is automatic in that it locks the firing pin until the trigger is pulled fully rearward.

The model P226 has a 15-round magazine and is 9mm Parabellum calibre. Other models in the series offer different magazine capacities and calibres.

Specifications

Manufacturer:	SIG-Sauer, Switzerland/Germany
Model:	P226
Calibre:	9mm Parabellum
Action:	Short-recoil double-action semi-automatic
Feed:	15-round magazine
Sights:	Blade and notch open sights. Various add-on sighting and target illumination systems available from third-party manufacturers
Weight:	750g
Length:	196mm
Barrel:	112mm

The SIG-Sauer P226 has been adopted by several units with a counter-terrorist role, including Britain's SAS and the US FBI. Photo: SIG-Sauer.

Glock 17

The Glock 17 caused a stir when it was introduced in the early 1980s. It was produced by a company that had previously concentrated on knives and other edged tools, and could approach the business of designing a pistol from an objective angle. The result was a pistol that broke the mould. It made extensive use of polymers, had a squat, modern look with a squared-off slide and uncluttered lines. It did not appeal to everyone, but has proved itself to be a robust and dependable weapon and has been widely adopted by police forces and military users.

The Glock's basic operating system is nothing new – it uses the familiar Colt/Browning short-recoil dropping barrel design. It employs the elegant, SIG-style development of this principle, however, using a squared-off breech that locks into the ejection port.

The firing system is more radical, with no hammer as such but instead a self-cocking striker mechanism that is cocked and released as the trigger is pulled – in effect a double action only (DAO) mechanism without the external hammer. The trigger mechanism incorporates two safety systems. There is a safety spur that blocks the trigger until released by the pressure of the user's finger on the trigger blade; and the firing pin is locked until released by the movement of the trigger.

A Glock 17.
Photo: Pageant-Pix.

Controls on the Glock are deliberately kept to a minimum, in order to make the weapon simple and intuitive to use. There is no need for a manual safety catch, and no external hammer. Besides the trigger, there is a push-button magazine release

catch on the left grip, behind the trigger guard. A small slide-release catch is located in the side of the frame, just above the trigger.

The Glock 17 has a relatively large magazine capacity of 17 rounds, using a double-stack magazine. Other models in the Glock family offer different calibres and barrel lengths; there is also a compact version, the 19, and a model offering full-automatic fire, the 18.

Specifications	
Manufacturer:	Glock, Austria
Model:	17
Calibre:	9mm Parabellum
Action:	Double action only (DAO) semi-automatic
Feed:	17-round double-stack magazine
Sights:	Blade and notch open sights with white U and dot to aid aiming in poor lighting conditions. Various add-on sighting and target illumination systems available from third-party manufacturers
Weight:	650g
Length:	188mm
Barrel:	114mm

Beretta Mod 92FS

The Beretta Model 92FS was developed for the US Army's trials, and was adopted as their service pistol in 1985, with the designation M9. It is a robust and reliable weapon firing the 9mm Parabellum round with a double-action mechanism. It carries a 15-round magazine, and is recognisable by the distinctive cut-away slide design. The barrel is internally chromed to protect against corrosion and wear, and the outer surfaces are coated with Bruniton, a Teflon-like material which protects against harsh environmental conditions.

Like so many modern pistols, the 92FS uses Browning's short-recoil principle. There is a wedge-shaped locking block which locks the barrel in place when the action is closed. When the gun is fired, the block is driven downward, unlocking the barrel from the slide and stopping the barrel's rearward movement. The weapon has a double-action mechanism, and can be fired in single- or double-action mode.

The weapon's controls have been developed over many years to fall naturally to hand and operate smoothly and quickly when required. There is a combined safety/decocking lever on the rear of the slide. This also moves the trigger bar away from the sear and locks the firing pin. The magazine release is a push-button located at the rear of the trigger guard, where it can easily be operated by the thumb of the firing hand without releasing the grip.

A number of variants are available, including a compact version, a DAO version, alternative calibres, and a 93R fully-automatic model with extended magazine and folding buttstock.

Beretta Model 92FS. Photo: US DoD.

Specifications	
Manufacturer:	P. Beretta, Italy
Model:	92FS (US Army Pistol M9)
Calibre:	9mm Parabellum
Action:	Short-recoil double-action semi-automatic
Feed:	15-round magazine
Sights:	Blade and notch open sights, rearsight dovetailed to slide
Weight:	960g
Length:	217mm
Barrel:	125mm

H&K USP

The Heckler & Koch USP (Universal Self-Loading Pistol) was conceived as a 'system' rather than a single weapon. There are laser sights, a silencer and other accessories designed specifically for the weapon. It is a modern type of pistol, making use of fibre-reinforced polymers as well as steel in its design, reducing its weight considerably. It incorporates an ingenious recoil damping mechanism, making it particularly comfortable to shoot and allowing the user to fire a series of aimed shots more quickly; the recoil produces little more than a flick of the wrist, and the pistol is quickly brought back to the aim.

The USP was adopted by US Special Operations Command (SOCOM) as the Offensive Handgun Weapon System (OHWS) for US Navy Seals, US Army Special Forces and Delta Force. This is a departure from the normal approach to handguns, which are normally seen as a 'last resort' defensive weapon rather than an offensive weapon to be used in hostage rescue actions and the like, where it is difficult to achieve the necessary degree of accuracy with a pistol.

The USP's mechanism is based on the Browning system, but incorporates a special recoil damping mechanism that buffers the barrel and slide in their rearward movement, preventing the recoil forces being transmitted directly to the frame and on to the user's hand.

On firing, the barrel and slide are initially locked together, and are forced back as one by the recoil. As they travel rearward, the barrel tilts down and unlocks from the slide. At the same time, the barrel catches in a spring buffer which arrests its rearward movement and absorbs much of its recoil force. The slide continues rearward, while the buffer pushes the barrel back into its forward position. At the end of its stroke, the slide hits the buffer, compressing the buffer spring which pushes it forward again, collecting and chambering the next round. The light weight of the slide, together with the recoil damping effects of the mechanism, help to ensure long life for the various parts and reduce the need for maintenance.

The USP has a modular trigger and safety system, allowing the user to specify the configuration required. A weapon can be adapted by exchanging parts. The standard variant (V1) has a single/double-action trigger mechanism and a manual safety

The H&K USP has a recoil damping mechanism which makes it particularly comfortable to shoot, and enables rapid follow-up shots. Photo: © James Marchington.

catch/decocking lever on the left side; this can be moved to the right side (V2) for a left-handed user. The single/double action mechanism can be replaced with a double-action only (DAO) mechanism (V5-8) which decocks automatically after every shot. Variants 9 and 10 have the single/double-action trigger but no decocking mechanism.

All the variants are equipped with automatic firing pin and hammer safeties, which disengage when the trigger is pulled. This prevents the pistol discharging accidentally if dropped.

Specifications

Manufacturer:	Heckler & Koch, Germany
Model:	USP (Universal Self-loading Pistol)
Calibre:	9mm Parabellum
	also available in .40 S&W and .45 ACP
Action:	Recoil-operated semi-automatic, with redesigned
	Browning-type action
Feed:	15-round magazine (9mm)
	13 rounds .40, 12 rounds .45
Sights:	Square foresight and square U-notch rearsight, with white
	dots for rapid alignment in poor light. Laser targeting
	system optional
Weight:	720g
Length:	194mm
Barrel:	136mm

MACHINE GUNS

GPMG (FN MAG)

During World War Two, the .303 Bren and Vickers machine guns proved highly effective, and when the British Army switched to the new 7.62mm NATO round it took the logical step of adopting the 7.62mm FN MAG (Fabrique Nationale Mitrailleuse à Gaz). This weapon was introduced into British service in the late 1960s and became known as the General Purpose Machine Gun or GPMG – fondly referred to as the 'Gimpy'. It has proved highly effective, reliable and easy to use, making it a favourite support weapon of British infantry units generally and Special Forces in particular.

The GPMG uses a double pawl feed mechanism to fire 7.62mm rounds in disintegrating link at an impressive rate of 650–1,000rpm. The SAS first used the GPMG in action against the Adoo, communist-backed insurgents in Oman. The story goes that the first time the weapon was used in a firefight, it was followed by a silence in which you could almost hear the Adoo jaws dropping at the awesome firepower of this new weapon ranged against them.

This high rate of fire and destructive power, combined with the GPMG's relatively light weight (compared to other support weapons) makes it a very versatile weapon.

It can be mounted on a vehicle, used in the sustained fire role on a tripod, in the light role on its bipod, or even at a pinch fired from the hip in an assault. The GPMG can be fitted with the MaxiKite night sight, giving it full day/night capability.

The GPMG has a maximum effective range of 800m in the light role, and 1,800m in the sustained fire role. A number of well-sited GPMGs with interlocking fields of fire will create an impenetrable hail of bullets which will stop any unprotected advancing enemy force dead in its tracks.

A British soldier setting up an FN MAG General Purpose Machine-Gun. Photo: US DoD.

Specifications

Calibre:	7.62 x 51mm NATO
Length:	1,260mm
Barrel:	545mm
Weight:	10.85kg (empty, including butt and bipod)
	13.85kg (loaded)
Action:	Gas operated full auto, fed by disintegrating link
Rate of fire:	650–1,000rpm
Muzzle velocity:	840m/s
Effective range:	800m (light role)
	1,800m (sustained fire role)
Rifling:	4 grooves, RH, 1 turn in 305mm (12ins)
Sights:	Blade foresight, aperture/notch rearsight
	Optical and electro-optical sights may be fitted

Above: The SAS use the .50 cal machine gun to devastating effect, mounted on light patrol vehicles such as the Land Rover 110. It fires at a rate of 635rpm. Photo: © James Marchington.

Opposite page: A .50 cal machine-gun on its tripod mount. Photo: author's collection.

M2HB .50 HMG

The M2HB or .50 calibre Browning machine gun is a powerful weapon that can be used in the sustained fire role or mounted on an assortment of armoured and soft-skinned vehicles. The .50 cal's destructive power makes it effective against vehicles and aircraft, and a prolonged burst will soon demolish all but the most strongly reinforced positions.

The weapon is a favourite of special forces like the SAS, who have used it in various campaigns and find it effective mounted on light vehicles such as the Land-Rover 110 – despite a reputation as a temperamental weapon that jams at the most inopportune moment. Experienced operators develop an 'ear' for the rhythm of the gun firing, and can tell when a jam is about to occur.

The original design of the .50 cal dates back to World War One. The basic mechanism came from the .30 Browning M1917 machine gun, which was developed after that war into a .50 calibre weapon. This later became the M2HB (Heavy Barrel) and was adopted by the US Cavalry in 1933. It has since gone into service with many armed forces around the world.

The .50 cal has a 'short recoil' mechanism and is air cooled. It is fed with the .50 calibre (12.7 x 99mm) round via a disintegrating link belt. Rate of fire is up to 635rpm, and the weapon achieves a muzzle velocity of 916m/sec. It weighs 38.15kg, and measures 1.66m long with two-handed spade grips.

Specifications

Calibre:	.50in (12.7 x 99mm)
Length:	1,656mm
Barrel:	1,143mm
Weight:	38.15kg (empty)
Action:	Short-recoil operated full auto, fed by disintegrating link
Rate of fire:	485–635rpm
Muzzle velocity:	916m/s
Rifling:	8 grooves, RH
Sights:	Basic iron foresight/rearsight fitted. Other sighting systems may be used according to role

Minimi M249 SAW

The Belgian-made Minimi was first produced by Fabrique Nationale in 1982, and has since been adopted by many countries, including the USA where it is designated the M249 SAW (Squad Automatic Weapon). The Minimi is a 5.56mm machine gun, firing the same NATO 5.56mm round that is used in modern assault rifles such as the M16 and the SA80. It is light enough to be carried by one man and fired from the hip. With a large capacity magazine or belt feed, and firing at up to 1,000rpm, it gives a tremendous boost to the firepower of a small foot-mounted patrol.

The Minimi M249 SAW. Photo: US DoD.

The Minimi will accept ammunition from a variety of feeds without adjustment. It can take a free-hanging belt, a belt in a 200-round belt box attached to the weapon, or any NATO standard 5.56mm magazine, including the box magazine used in assault rifles such as the M16, and a variety of large capacity drum mags. A simple gate mechanism makes it impossible to inadvertently fit a belt and magazine at the same time, which might otherwise cause a stoppage.

Specifications

Calibre:	5.56 x 45mm NATO
Length:	1,040mm
Barrel:	466mm
Weight:	6.83kg (empty)
Action:	Gas operated full auto, fed by NATO standard 5.56mm box magazine or disintegrating link
Rate of fire:	700–1,000rpm (depends on feed)
Effective range:	800m
Muzzle velocity:	915m/s
Rifling:	One turn in 178mm (7ins)
Sights:	Basic iron foresight/rearsight fitted. Other sighting systems may be fitted

Mark 19 40mm Grenade Launcher

The Mark 19 is an air-cooled blowback-type machine gun that fires a variety of 40mm grenades. These include high explosive, anti-personnel and armour-piercing. It can be used on a tripod set on the ground, or mounted on a vehicle such as a Land Rover 110. With an effective range of 1,600 metres, firing HE and AP ammunition, it provides powerful support in attack or defence. The Mark 19, mounted on Land Rover 110s, was used to great effect by SAS patrols behind enemy lines during the 1991 Gulf War.

The current version is the Mark 19 Mod 3, which is considerably more reliable than the early models used by US forces in Vietnam. It is fed with belted rounds held in a box attached to the weapon.

Specifications

Calibre:	40mm
Length:	1,028mm
Weight:	34kg (empty)
Action:	Blowback type full auto, fed by belted ammo contained in box
Rate of fire:	325–375rpm
Effective range:	1,600m
Muzzle velocity:	240m/s
Mounts:	Turret, pedestal or tripod

Right and below:
The Mark 19 is a
full-auto 40mm
weapon, firing
high-explosive,
armour piercing
and anti-person-
nel ammunition. It
has a range of
1,600m and can
be vehicle-
mounted. Photos:
USMC and DoD.

ANTI-TANK WEAPONS

M72 66mm LAW

The M72 66mm LAW (Light Anti-tank Weapon) is basically a one-shot high explosive missile contained in its own launcher tube. Once it is fired, the tube is no further use and is discarded. The weapon has a range of 300m, and can penetrate up to 300mm of armour, yet is relatively small and easy to carry. In the Falklands War, each Royal Marine carried a 'Sixty-six' strapped to the top of his bergen, and the weapons proved

The M72 66mm LAW. Photo: US DoD.

highly effective at 'bunker busting'. It had previously seen combat in Vietnam, where US Marines had used it effectively against North Vietnamese armour.

The M72 measures around 66.5cm long (closed) and weighs under 3kg. To fire, the tube – which is actually two tubes one inside the other – is extended to approximately 90cm. The sights are released and flip up into position. The soldier then releases the safety catch, takes aim and presses the trigger. The weapon is recoilless; on firing, gas pressure propels the rocket from the tube, and fins spring out to stabilise the projectile.

The rocket itself has a high-explosive warhead; there are a number of variants with different levels of performance against armour, but they are generally capable of penetrating at least 30mm of armour, as well as reinforced concrete and field fortifications.

The M72 is currently being phased out by the British Army in favour of the LAW 80, which offers better performance against armour but is significantly heavier and bulkier to carry. There are considerable stocks in place, however, and the M72's good performance to weight ratio will ensure its popularity with Special Forces for some years to come.

Specifications

Calibre:	66mm
Length:	665mm closed
	899mm open
Weight:	3.45kg
Action:	Single shot rocket launched from disposable tube
Effective range:	Max. 300m
Max. velocity:	200m/s
Warhead:	Point initiating base detonating shaped charge, giving penetration of up to 350mm armour

---

LAW 80

Like the M72, the LAW 80 is a one-shot disposable shoulder-fired anti-tank weapon. It is considerably more powerful than the M72, and can engage heavily armoured targets out to 500m – defeating up to 700mm of armour plate. However, the cost is a much heavier, bulkier package that cannot conveniently be carried by a man on patrol with all his other equipment. A single LAW 80 weighs 9kg and measures 1m. It comes with bulky end protector caps which give it a characteristic dumbell-like appearance.

The LAW 80 has a built-in spotting rifle that fires a special sighting round which produces a distinctive flash and puff of smoke. When the round hits the target, the soldier knows that the main projectile is properly aimed. The projectile itself has an impact sensor that is not activated by scrub or foliage. On striking a hard target, an electrical fuse initiates the charge at its base, producing the jet of hot gas and molten metal necessary to penetrate armour plate.

Specifications

Calibre:	94mm
Length:	1,000mm closed
	1,500mm open
Weight:	9kg
Action:	Single shot rocket launched from disposable tube
Effective range:	Max. 500m.
Warhead:	Point initiating base detonating shaped charge, giving penetration of up to 700mm armour

Milan

Milan is a wire-guided anti-tank missile system which has the potential to be considerably more accurate than the 'fire and forget' types such as the LAW 80. The firer fixes the target in the sight, and must keep it there (for up to twelve seconds) while the missile flies down-range. The SACLOS (Semi Automatic Command to Line Of Sight) guidance system watches a Xenon lamp in the tail of the missile, and feeds corrections down the unravelling wires to keep it on track. The warhead has an extended probe which carries a small charge to detonate reactive armour, so the main charge can attack the armour beneath.

The firing post can be fitted on a ground tripod or mounted on a vehicle. It is generally fitted with an infra-red sight known as MIRA, which is effective in all battle-field conditions, enabling Milan to engage targets in darkness or when they are camouflaged or obscured by smoke. SAS patrols in Iraq during the 1991 Gulf War had a number of Milan firing posts mounted on Land Rovers, and found the sights

Soldiers of an Egyptian Ranger battalion with a Milan anti-tank weapon system. The firing post consists of a sighting system and a guidance assembly mounted on a tripod. The munition consists of the missile in a waterproof launch tube: two are strapped to the side of the vehicle. Photo: US DoD.

useful for spotting enemy vehicles even when they had no intention of engaging them.

Milan has been improved and upgraded during its service life. The current version has a maximum range of 2,000m, and will penetrate 350mm of armour. Milan is also highly effective against fixed positions and soft-skinned vehicles. It is due to be replaced in service by the similar Trigat, in which the missile 'rides' a laser beam rather than being controlled by wires. However, Milan will remain in service for some years to come, and in many ways is better suited to Special Forces operations.

Specifications

Missile:	Length 918mm, diameter 125mm, weight 6.73kg
Warhead:	Double shaped charge, explosive content 1.79kg
Penetration:	352mm armour
Range:	Max. 2,000m
	Min. 400m
Max. speed:	720kph
Time to max. range:	12.5sec.
Firing post:	Length 900mm, height 650mm, width 420mm, weight 16.4kg
Rate of fire:	3–4 rounds/min.

MORTARS

L9A1 51mm Light Mortar

The L9A1 Light Mortar is a small, handy and effective platoon support weapon which can easily be carried and fired by one man. It has a range of around 750m, and can fire a variety of ammunition including high explosive, illuminating and smoke. It was developed from the 1930s 2in mortar, and follows the same basic design – a simple steel tube with a belled muzzle at one end and a breech-piece closing the other end, attached to a rectangular 'spade'.

There is a sling to allow it to be carried slung across the soldier's back, and a sighting system is fixed to the tube. This uses a spirit level type bubble to indicate the correct inclination of the tube for the range set on the sight.

51mm mortar ammunition weighs approximately 0.9kg, and can be fired at a rate of around 8 rounds per minute. The mortar has a short range insert which can be slipped into the tube to reduce the effect of the propelling charge – making it possible to engage targets at close range with good accuracy.

Specifications

Mortar:	Barrel length 700mm, weight 6.275kg
Bomb:	HE 920g. Illuminating 800g. Smoke 900g
Range:	750m Rate of fire: 8 rounds/min.

L16 81mm Mortar

The L16 81mm Mortar is a battalion level support weapon which provides accurate fire out to a maximum range of more than 5.5km. It entered service with the British Army in the 1960s and has seen action in Borneo, Aden and the Falklands. The mortar breaks down into man-packable loads – baseplate (11.6kg), barrel (12.7kg), mounting (12.3kg) and sight unit (1.25kg) – but is more commonly carried in a 4x4

An 81mm Mortar being fired. Note the mortar bomb in flight. Photo: US DoD.

The 81mm mortar has been in service with the British Army since the 1960s, and proved highly effective in the Falklands. It has a maximum range of just over 5.5km with high-explosive ammunition. Photo: USMC.

vehicle. It can also be mounted in an APC, firing from the open roof hatches. This enables the mortars to keep pace with a mechanised advance and move quickly around the battlefield.

The L16 has been used to great effect by the SAS and other Special Forces, in both attack and defence. It proved very effective in the Falklands War where it was used in support of the Parachute Regiment's assault on Wireless Ridge.

The L16 has a maximum range of 5,560m with HE ammunition, and can also fire smoke, illuminating or white phosphorus rounds. With a well-drilled crew, a rate of fire of 15 rounds per minute can be sustained. It fires a 4.2kg high-explosive bomb, with a cast-iron casing designed to break into fragments of the optimum size. The propelling charge is clipped to the tail, using up to six charges to achieve the desired range. A plastic 'skirt' or obturating ring on the bomb allows air to escape as it drops down the barrel, but expands to fill the bore when the propelling charge fires. This helps to improve the weapon's accuracy and range.

Specifications

Calibre:	81mm
Barrel length:	1,280mm
Barrel weight:	12.7kg
Baseplate diameter:	546mm
Baseplate weight:	11.6kg
Sight unit:	C2 (common to GPMG in sustained fire role)
Sight unit weight:	1.25kg
Mounting length:	1,143mm
Mounting weight:	12.3kg
Traverse:	100mils L and R at 800mils elevation
Elevation:	Min. 800mils (45°)
	Max. 1,422mils (80°)
Range:	Max. 5,600m
	Min. 100m
Rate of fire:	15 rounds/min sustained

SHOULDER-FIRED ANTI-AIRCRAFT MISSILES

FIM-92 Stinger

The FIM-92 Stinger is a man-portable shoulder-fired anti-aircraft missile. Although somewhat dated – it entered US service in 1981 – it is still highly effective against low-flying aircraft at ranges up to 5km. The Stinger was used successfully by the SAS in the Falklands, to shoot down an Argentine Pucara attack aircraft near Port San Carlos on 21 May 1982.

Just a couple of years later the US began shipping thousands of Stingers to the Mujahadeen who were fighting the occupying Soviet Union forces in Afghanistan. Even in relatively untrained hands, the Stingers were credited with shooting down 269 Soviet aircraft, including MiG-17s, -21s and -23s, Su-22s and -25s, and Mi-17s and -24s. Knowing that their enemies possessed Stingers forced the Soviets to rethink their tactics, and significantly reduced the advantage of their air power. Indeed the Stinger is often credited as being the weapon that ultimately forced the Soviets to

The FIM-92 Stinger. Photo: US DoD.

The US supplied Stinger anti-aircraft missiles to the Mujahideen fighting Soviet forces in Afghanistan, not knowing that their own weapons would be turned against them sixteen years later. Photo: US Navy

concede defeat and withdraw from Afghanistan. Ironically, the Americans later came to fear their own Stingers being used against them by Taliban and al Qaeda forces in the post-11 September 2001 operations in Afghanistan.

The missile comes prepacked in a launch tube, and is clipped onto a launcher assembly which contains the firing mechanism. The missile is infra-red-seeking, and delivers a HE/frag warhead with impact fuse. If the missile misses its intended target, it will self-destruct after twenty seconds of flight, or about 8km. Stinger has an inbuilt IFF (Identification Friend or Foe) system which interrogates the transponder carried by friendly aircraft, and gives a warning if the aircraft is friendly.

Firing is quick and simple. Once the missile tube and launcher assembly are fitted together, the operator simply unfolds the antenna, removes the front cap and takes aim, squeezing the trigger to its first position. If the IFF does not recognise the target as friendly, the firing unit will lock on to the heat of the target aircraft's engines. When the system is locked-on and ready, there is an audible signal. Pressing the trigger to its second position will fire the ejector motor to eject the missile from its launch tube. After a few metres of flight, the main propulsion motor fires, and the missile is on its way at up to Mach 2.2, guided by its inbuilt IR-seeking guidance system. The missile is extremely agile, matching a pilot's evasive manoeuvres of up to 8G, and delivers a 3kg HE/fragmentation warhead

Specifications	
Weight:	Launcher 15.7kg, missile 10.1kg
Missile length:	1.52m
Missile diameter:	70mm
Propulsion:	Solid fuel ejector and main propulsion motors
Max. speed:	Mach 2.2
Effective range:	4,500m
Warhead:	3kg HE/fragmentation with contact fuse
Guidance:	Passive IR (with UV homing in later models)

The Stinger can be fired quickly from the shoulder. The solid fuel motor pushes it to Mach 2.2, the IR-seeking guidance system following the target through manoeuvres of up to 8G. Photo: author's collection.

GRENADES AND MINES

M18A1 Claymore

The Claymore is a devastatingly effective anti-personnel mine that is an established favourite with Special Forces both for defensive use and in setting ambushes. It is regularly used by SAS patrols to create a defensive perimeter around an LUP. The Claymore is a tremendous force multiplier, and is small and light, so that each man in a patrol can carry several Claymores along with his regular kit, weapon and ammo.

The story of the Claymore goes back to the Korean War of 1950–3, when the US Army needed a means of stopping the massed 'human wave' attacks employed by the enemy. The early Claymore was developed as a modern equivalent of the nineteenth-century grape shot – a giant shotgun blast of projectiles that will cut a swath through a mass of attacking troops. It was named after the huge Scottish broadsword, famed for its ability to mow down multiple enemies when swung two-handed.

The mine is basically a slab of plastic explosive, covered with 800 ball bearings, all enclosed in a hard plastic casing. The mine can be quickly deployed, using the fold-out legs to set it in the correct position – following the clear instruction 'Front Toward Enemy' stamped in large letters on the plastic case. It is detonated electrically via a command wire, blasting the ball bearings across a 60° arc, with an effective

During a training exercise a member of the 822nd Security Forces Squadron, USAF, checks a M18A1 Claymore Mine to see if it is properly aligned. US DoD.

range of more than 100m. The mine can also set up with an improvised trigger to be operated by a tripwire in an ambush.

Specifications

Weight:	1.58kg
Dimensions:	216mm(l) x 35mm(w) x 83mm(h)
Main charge:	682g C4 PE
Initiator:	M4 electrical blasting cap
Firing cable:	30m
Firing device:	M57 double impulse hand-held generator ('clacker')
Projectiles:	800 steel balls
Range:	100m lethal, 250m dangerous
Spread:	60º arc

Grenade L2A2

The L2 is based on the US M61, which in turn has been copied by South Africa with the M26, the Portuguese M312, and the Israeli M26A2. All these grenades have a thin sheet steel wall enclosing a notched steel coil and explosive core. When the grenade explodes it shatters the coil into small fragments which travel at high velocity and can

The grenade is widely used by infantry around the world. Many designs are based on the US M61, which has a lethal radius of 15m or more on hard ground. Photo: USMC.

The L2A2 uses the well known pin-and-lever type fuse. When the pin is pulled and the grenade thrown, the fuse is initiated. The main charge detonates after a delay of 4–5 seconds. Photo: author's collection.

cause casualties at up to 15m, although on hard, open, flat ground this can increase up to 150m. The L2 was first used in action during the Falklands in 1982. However, the soft ground absorbed much of its blast and many of the fragments. There were similar problems in the Gulf in 1991. This type of grenade is more effective when used on hard surfaces, such as concrete bunkers and in FIBUA/MOUT operations.

Specifications

Size:	106mm(h) x 64mm(diam)
Weight:	395g
Explosive filling:	170g RDX/TNT 55/44
Fuse:	L25A6
Delay:	4.3 sec.
Lethal radius:	15–150m